D0428722

COMMON
GROUND

COMMON
GROUND

LESSONS AND LEGENDS FROM THE WORLD'S GREAT FAITHS

TODD OUTCALT

Skyhorse Publishing

Copyright © 2015 by Todd Outcalt

All Rights Reserved. No part of this book may be reproduced in any manner without the express written consent of the publisher, except in the case of brief excerpts in critical reviews or articles. All inquiries should be addressed to Skyhorse Publishing, 307 West 36th Street, 11th Floor, New York, NY 10018.

Skyhorse Publishing books may be purchased in bulk at special discounts for sales promotion, corporate gifts, fund-raising, or educational purposes. Special editions can also be created to specifications. For details, contact the Special Sales Department, Skyhorse Publishing, 307 West 36th Street, 11th Floor, New York, NY 10018 or info@skyhorsepublishing.com.

Skyhorse® and Skyhorse Publishing® are registered trademarks of Skyhorse Publishing, Inc.®, a Delaware corporation.

www.skyhorsepublishing.com

10 9 8 7 6 5 4 3 2 1

Library of Congress Cataloging-in-Publication Data is available on file.

Print ISBN: 978-1-63220-552-0
Ebook ISBN: 978-1-63220-969-6

Printed in the United States of America

Dedication

To the Parents

Ed & Pauline Outcalt
Bill & Marilyn Osburn

"Honor your father and your mother"
is written among the most important laws of righteousness
—Aeschylus, 450 BCE

TABLE OF CONTENTS

The Fable

A man who wrote fables was passing through a secluded forest when he met Fortune. The Fabulist attempted to flee, but Fortune pursued until he captured the Fabulist.

"Why did you try to run away?" asked Fortune. "And why do you regard me with so much animosity?"

"Well," answered the Fabulist, "I don't know what you are."

"I will tell you what I am," said Fortune. "I am wealth. I am respectability. I am beautiful homes. I am a yacht and a clean shirt each day. I am leisure and I am travel. I am fine wine and a shiny hat and a warm coat. I am enough to eat."

"Very well," said the Fabulist in a whisper. "But for goodness' sake speak softer."

"Why?" asked Fortune.

"So as not to wake me," replied the Fabulist.

Preface

T his book was written during troubled times. Wars, violence, eco-
logical disasters, hunger, the Ebola crisis, and political upheavals: All of
these and more dominated the news. But perhaps it has always been so.

And yet . . . one might think that shouting and name calling has
become the preferred method of conversation—while listening (and
hearing) is disregarded. People of differing philosophies and religions
now seem to regard each other as mortal enemies instead of living by
those peaceable precepts that could build a harmonious society. Even
the greatest teachings of the past seem to be cast aside in exchange
for hateful rhetoric or morphed into philosophies that prefer death
to life.

My hope with *Common Ground* is that people from all walks of life,
from divergent faiths and differing perspectives, can discover beauty
and pleasure in what they do not yet know, but might learn from the
great teachers and sages of the past. Not all faiths and philosophies are
the same, of course—but in fact, each is unique and should be honored
as separate and solitary by rights and personal choice.

Nevertheless, one can discover common truths within the
diversity—wonderful and beautiful parables, teachings, stories, mor-
als, and mysteries—that can be bridges to understanding and peace.
One learns when one encounters the new idea, the different idea. And
through learning, through openness, one begins to appreciate the vast

trove of teaching literature that exists, and which can eventually create a common ground with others.

A book can be a bridge, too. And this one celebrates the one joy that can be known through a deeper understanding of the many.

Introduction

*And so, in all interactions, the superior person carefully considers
the beginning.*

—I Ching

*No one begins building a tower without first considering whether
he can complete it.*

—Jesus

*T*here are many ways people can encounter truth—through
wisdom, example, prayer, story. But much truth is conveyed through
metaphor—those images that produce a surplus of meaning and cause
one to ponder the deeper layers beneath. Metaphors stand at the center
of many teaching stories—both religious and moral and humorous—
and serve as an invitation to place oneself inside the meaning. As such,
metaphors are rarely transparent and more commonly produce questions than answers. This is their intent.

Superior metaphors are also able to cross time and culture. They
speak to the human condition and to truth regardless of place or cir-
cumstance. These metaphors are ubiquitous, universal, common.

Take the metaphor of a tree.

This image has been used in all cultures, times, and places to address
deeper truths, and the tree frequently stands at the center of a revelation
or teaching.

Consider, for example, the first chapters of Genesis, where the tree of life and the tree of good and evil appear. The tree is many things: a source of life, an invitation, a temptation, a symbol of that which is lost. And later, in Exodus, the burning bush of Moses hearkens back to these earlier themes of life, invitation, human weakness, and the call of God. Jesus used the metaphor of the tree in numerous parables: a tiny mustard seed that grows into a giant, sheltering bush; a farmer who determines the health of a tree by observing its fruit; vines that are pruned so that they can produce abundant fruit; seeds that fall on various types of soils. And at the end of the Christian scriptures, the book of Revelation contains an image of the tree of paradise, its branches arching and leaves providing healing for the nations.

The Buddha also used the metaphor of the tree to speak of the importance of roots, of fruitfulness, of joy. So did Confucius. And there are thousands of Native American stories that speak of the whispering pines and the towering strength of the sycamore through which the Great Spirit speaks.

St. Francis, who lived in the thirteenth century, sang praises to the sun, moon, and stars—but also reveled in the metaphor of the tree:

Dear mother earth, who day by day unfoldest blessings on our way,
The flowers and fruits that in thee grow, let them God's glory also show.

In this collection, one will discover marvelous fruits that have been harvested from many voices. This tree is large, and varied, but the reader will certainly find ample shade and encouragement through the stories, tales, and teachings represented in this amazing tree of wisdom.

One doesn't have to bite into every fruit, of course. These teachings will be sweeter to some than to others, not all will taste the same. But that is also the beauty of variety. Metaphors have the power to change flavors and a metaphor's impact can be much stronger in certain seasons of life. Even if one is not familiar with a certain fruit, it can be fun to bite into a new variety.

My hope is that *Common Ground* will contain something for everyone—and that every reader will be able to enjoy some new or exotic fruit every time these pages are opened. Moreover, I trust that readers will appreciate the deep roots and the over-arching branches of truth that these stories contain.

Of course, every reader will have favorites—but may also gather some low-hanging fruit that may have previously been overlooked. One doesn't have to hate one fruit in order to enjoy another.

Centuries ago, Aesop spoke of this truth in his fable about a hungry fox:

A hungry fox noticed some delicious-looking grapes hanging on the vine. But as he attempted to eat the fruit he discovered that the clusters were beyond his reach. No matter how fast he ran and leaped, he could not attain even a single grape. Walking away from the vine the fox said, "The fruit was no good anyway. I don't need these sour grapes."

My hope is that everyone will be able to enjoy this fruit—but if there are metaphors that seem beyond our reach, that we may not despair over or disparage in the teaching. The tree is large. And it has deep roots in common ground.

Chapter One

Sage Wisdom

Can you let your body become supple as a newborn child's?
Can you cleanse your inner vision until you see nothing but the
light?
—Tao Te Ching

Happy are those who find wisdom,
and those who get understanding.
—Proverbs 3:13 (Hebrew Bible)

W hen we hear the phrase "sage wisdom" we commonly think of stories and insights that are helpful in daily life. Stories about wise men, authoritative women, and provocative visionaries come to mind. Sage wisdom can be inspiring, but not always because the insights originate from perfect people. Rather, much wisdom is born of human struggle and failure. We not only learn from saints, but from sinners, too.

Wisdom comes in many forms. Stories, sayings, blessings, prayers— all of these can be sources of insight. But wisdom can also be found in humor, in saga, in drama, and in metaphor. Sometimes, when we hear a fresh word from a familiar source, we are at once astounded and confused. Or we may return time and again to those parables and quotations that offer us hope or encouragement.

In the past century many ancient documents have been discovered that continue to confound and excite by their possibilities. The Dead Sea Scrolls, the Nag Hammadi library, the Jesus Sutras (China), and even newly discovered stories by more modern sages such as Mark Twain and Shirley Jackson seem to offer new wine from old wineskins. It is not just the discoveries themselves that inspire us, but more accurately the excitement of hearing a distant voice in a fresh way.

When we hear Jesus saying in the gospel of Thomas, for example, "Be passersby," our imaginations may take flight by asking, "What did Jesus mean by this?" Or when we hear the Buddha saying, "I am awake," we are at once perplexed and inspired by these familiar, and yet always contemporary, words. This is the power of ancient wisdom, as these words have crossed continents and cultures and are still producing conversation in our time.

But we dare not think that all wisdom originates from a religious mindset. Some wisdom—such as Aesop's fables for instance—has a didactic quality that endures the test of time. These sources demonstrate that people have long possessed a desire for learning, for growing, and for discovering an ethical center from which to live a meaningful life. The sage, then, can be someone who makes us think, who challenges our perceptions, or who adds a new element into the mix of the tried and true. Sometimes our ideas need to be examined more closely or we may need to question our foundations. The sage can be someone who upsets or encourages us. Sages can confound or confirm. Sages can be equal parts troubling and comforting.

The wisdom we find in these teachings—these parables, legends, and tales—can be matched only by the size of our imaginations. Sometimes the saints will inspire us through their example. Or we may discover ourselves in the far country of doubt, beset by worry, only to return to the wisdom of the ages.

Centuries ago, when an editor began collecting the Hebrew proverbs, the book began with this invitation:

The Proverbs [are] . . . to know wisdom and instruction;
To perceive words of understanding;
To receive the instruction of wisdom, justice, judgment, and equity;
To give subtlety to the simple, to the young knowledge and discretion.
A wise man will hear and will increase learning;
And a man of understanding shall attain to wise counsels:
To understand a proverb and the interpretation:
The words of the wise and their dark sayings.
—Proverbs 1:1-6

Once, some students asked C. S. Lewis—the noted Oxford don who taught Medieval literature and also wrote many well-known fantasy works such as *The Chronicles of Narnia*—if writing fantastic stories might compel some people to forsake reality and begin to live in a fantasy world. Lewis replied that, "Far from dulling or emptying the actual world, stories provide a new dimension of depth. The one who listens to stories does not despise real woods because he has read of enchanted woods. The reading makes all real woods a little enchanted."[1]

Through the ages, many wise sages and teachers have embraced this same philosophy—especially in regard to using legendary material to guide and inspire. Great stories influence and heighten our awareness of reality. A wise story can help us make better decisions and can awaken our senses.

Likewise, just as many great teachers have offered their own stories, there have been many more which have emerged about the teachers themselves. Often, it is impossible to tell which came first—the story attributed *to* the teacher, or the story told *about* the teacher.

---

[1] From C. S. Lewis, *Of Other Worlds: Essays and Stories* (New York, Harcourt Brace, 1966), p. 29–30

Wisdom, of course, comes in many forms. Sometimes the lessons come neatly packaged in straightforward prose: "If you find your mind tempted and entangled in greed, you must suppress and control the temptation," the Buddha told his followers. And at other times, the lessons are shown through legendary stories about the teacher (as in this story detailing how the Buddha came to control his own greed):

One day Siddhartha, the Prince, visited a hermit and watched the ascetic's practices. The Prince was so moved by the simplicity of the hermit that he himself decided to live a life free of greed. Siddhartha lived in the forest for six years, and afterwards received nothing but a bowl of milk from a young maiden who lived nearby.

Nearly every religion and culture has a wisdom tradition attached to it. Sometimes these traditions emerge as a counter-movement against the institutionalism of the faith, and at other times might represent the best and the brightest voices speaking for the faith. Sufism, for example, emerged as the wisdom movement of Islam during the twelfth century, and over time, developed into several schools of thought. The various monastic orders of the church would be of similar intent, as would the Desert Fathers tradition in Egypt. Hassidic beliefs would constitute some of the wisdom traditions of Judaism.

But there are other sources of wisdom as well. Often, as the legends in this chapter reveal, we can see how stories about saints and sages have emerged to offer new understandings of life—as people found themselves in ever-changing circumstances and new predicaments. Quite often, people appealed back to the sages of old to make sense of the difficulties they were experiencing. And so the work and words of Moses or Elijah, of Jesus or Mohammad, were given new life through new story.

Perhaps the legends here can help us to discover a greater appreciation for life, or for others, or even for our particular moment in time. Wisdom never dies. But it does change and adapt. By allowing these legends to take hold within us, we can learn to face our own challenges and difficulties with confidence and understanding.

There is enough sage wisdom in the following to last a lifetime and to increase our own learning. One never has enough knowledge. In the following we will discover enough common ground to unite us with both ancient ideas and contemporary discussions. Let the wise understand. And let the learner learn.

Feathers in the Wind (Jewish)

A man once sought the advice of the famous rabbi, Hillel. "Rabbi," he said, "I have a question about the commandments."

"And what is that?" asked Hillel.

"I understand why we are commanded not to kill. I understand why there is a commandment against stealing. But I do not understand why God has given a commandment against slandering the neighbor."

"The answer is easy enough," Hillel said. "But first, I must ask you to gather a sack of feathers and place a feather on the doorstep of every house in the village. When you have completed this task, return and I will give you an answer."

The man did as he was told, and returned the next day. "I've completed the task," he said. "I've placed a feather on every doorstep. Now . . . give me the answer."

"Oh, yes," said Hillel, "about that. Now I must ask you to go back and retrieve each of the feathers."

"What? But that is impossible! The wind will have carried all of the feathers away."

"Yes," answered Hillel, "and so it is with the lies we tell about our neighbors. They can never be retrieved. They are like feathers in the wind."

*Who has not experienced the pain of knowing that a friend has gossiped about a personal situation or secret? And who has not experienced the temptation to repeat damaging hearsay or unfounded rumor? Although it has often been said that words cannot harm us, on the contrary, words are quite powerful, and can hurt just as much as, or more than, a physical blow.

The wisdom of truth-telling goes far beyond the information itself. When we tell the truth, or when we guard the secrets of others, people learn to trust us. The ability to keep a secret and avoid the temptation to gossip is a mark of integrity that other people will look for in good friends and colleagues. Often, a betrayal of personal information can lead to the downfall of a friendship.

This legend of Hillel demonstrates one of the famous rabbi's most familiar traits: knowing how to use words wisely, and, just as importantly, when to remain silent.

The Miser and His Treasure Gotthold Lessing

A miser had spent the better part of his life accumulating a great treasure, which he kept hidden in the garden behind his house. In his heart, he fancied that he was the richest man in the world, and he loved to inform people of this fact whenever he met them.

One night a thief dug up the miser's treasure. In its place the thief deposited a large stone. The next morning, when the miser discovered that his treasure was gone, he was heartbroken. His neighbors came to console him, but he kept crying, "O wretched man that I am! What will I do?"

One of the neighbors pointed out that he never used any of his money anyway. "Why don't you pretend that the rock is the treasure, seeing as how it is the same and will simply remain buried in your yard? That way, you can go on enjoying your life."

But the miser replied, "Oh, but how can I enjoy life knowing that there is someone richer than I?"

*Sometimes wisdom eludes us at the point of our vices. Wealth is not true wealth unless it is of benefit to ourselves and others. The point of having enough is knowing when we *have* enough. The mind is indeed a powerful tool. That is why many of the poor regard themselves as rich, and many of the rich live in utter misery. Perception is reality. And when it comes to wealth, it is best used to bless others than to be buried inside self-absorption.

The Distinguished Stranger Robert Louis Stevenson

Once upon a time there came to this earth a visitor from a neighbouring planet. And he was met at the place of his descent by a great philosopher, who was to show him everything.

First of all they came through a wood, and the stranger looked upon the trees. "Whom have we here?" said he.

"These are only vegetables," said the philosopher. "They are alive, but not at all interesting."

"I don't know about that," said the stranger. "They seem to have very good manners. Do they never speak?"

"They lack the gift," said the philosopher.

"Yet I think I hear them sing," said the other.

"That is only the wind among the leaves," said the philosopher. "I will explain to you the theory of winds: it is very interesting."

"Well," said the stranger, "I wish I knew what they are thinking."

"They cannot think," said the philosopher.

"I don't know about that," returned the stranger: and then, laying his hand upon a trunk: "I like these people," said he.

"They are not people at all," said the philosopher. "Come along."

Next they came through a meadow where there were cows. "These are very dirty people," said the stranger.

"They are not people at all," said the philosopher; and he explained what a cow is in scientific words which I have forgotten.

"That is all one to me," said the stranger. "But why do they never look up?"

"Because they are graminivorous," said the philosopher; "and to live upon grass, which is not highly nutritious, requires so close an attention to business that they have no time to think, or speak, or look at the scenery, or keep themselves clean."

"Well," said the stranger, "that is one way to live, no doubt. But I prefer the people with the green heads."

Next they came into a city, and the streets were full of men and women. "These are very odd people," said the stranger.

"They are the people of the greatest nation in the world," said the philosopher.

"Are they indeed?" said the stranger. "They scarcely look so."

*Stevenson's fables, while often shot through with religious overtones and criticism of contemporary mores, also possessed a certain playfulness. In this *other-worldly* parable, Stevenson takes on the whole of humanity by asking some basic questions such as: "What makes a people great?" "What makes a nation great?" "How do we explain ourselves or justify our own existence before others?"

Lord Krishna's Request (Hindu)

Lord Krishna summoned two kings in order to test their wisdom. To the first king he offered this challenge: "Travel throughout the world, search high and low, and find for me one truly good man."

The first king roamed the earth, talked to many people, and some time later returned to Krishna with his findings. "I have done as you requested," the king said. "I traveled the earth, but was unable to find one good man among so many. They are all selfish and wicked. Not a single one who has a genuine heart of good."

Krishna then called for the second king. To him he offered this challenge: "Travel throughout the world, search high and low, and find for me one truly wicked man."

This king departed into the world, talked to many people, and some time later returned to Krishna. "I have done as you requested," the king said. "I traveled the earth, but was unable to find one truly wicked man. Many are misguided, many walk in darkness, some are full of failure, but as for a truly wicked man, there is not one to be found. There is some good in all, despite their weaknesses."

*Humanity is a mixed bag—as is each person. All have strengths and weaknesses, successes and failures, gifts and sins. Striving to see the best in others is a mark of wisdom.

Reminiscent in this Krishna legend is the affirmation that something of the divine exists in all people. If all are created in God's image and proclaimed as good, then surely there is some good to be found in everyone. There may also be failure and wickedness, but the highest principle prevails.

We are changed when we look for the good in others.

Progress (Taoist)

One day Yen Hui told Confucius, "I have made progress."

Confucius said, "Tell me what you mean."

Yen Hui said, "I think no longer about people and have no responsibility."

Confucius answered, "This is good, but it is not enough."

Some days later, Yen Hui approached Confucius again and said, "I have made progress."

Confucius said, "Tell me what you mean."

Yen Hui answered, "I no longer give any thought to ritual or music."

"This is good, but it is not enough," said Confucius.

Still later, Yen Hui approached Confucius and said, "I have made progress."

Confucius said, "Tell me what you mean."

Yen Hui answered, "I sit in forgetfulness."

Confucius was surprised and said, "Tell me what you mean by 'sitting in forgetfulness.'"

Yen Hui said, "I give no mind to my body and do not rely upon my intellect; I have forgotten about my physical self, have left all understanding behind, and have become one with the Universe. This is what I mean by sitting in forgetfulness."

When Confucius heard this he said, "When everything is the same, there are no preferences; when everything is in a state of flux, there is no constant. Can it be that you have obtained such wisdom? If so, I would follow you."

*In Taoism, one encounters the concept of wei wu wei, which means, "doing not doing." The idea has nothing to do with passivity, but rather practicing right living and awareness to the point where one's actions flow from the center of being—much like an athlete might master certain movements to the point where they become unconscious, or a painter might master the stroke of a brush without having to think about it. In Taoism, a person becomes one with the universe when he or she masters "doing not doing."

In other faiths, in other philosophies, these practices might be considered disciplines—those actions and thoughts and processes that one carries out without thinking about them.

This legend of Confucius provides a glimpse of the type of understanding one is expected to attain when one reaches this state of wisdom. You let go of the self in order to become a greater self. You release desire and attachments in order to live in present love and harmony. The goal is to become Tao—the Truth—the Life.

The Two Matches (Stevenson)

One day there was a traveler in the woods in California, in the dry season, when the Trades were blowing strong. He had ridden a long way, and he was tired and hungry, and dismounted from his horse to smoke a pipe. But when he felt in his pocket he found but two matches. He struck the first, and it would not light.

"Here is a pretty state of things!" said the traveler. "Dying for a smoke; only one match left; and that certain to miss fire! Was there ever a creature so unfortunate? And yet," thought the traveler, "suppose I light this match, and smoke my pipe, and shake out the dottle here in the grass—the grass might catch on fire, for it is dry like tinder; and while I snatch out the flames in front, they might evade and run behind me, and seize upon yon bush of poison oak; before I could reach it, that would have blazed up; over the bush I see a pine tree hung with moss, that too would fly in fire upon the instant to its topmost bough; and the flame of that long torch—how would the trade wind take and brandish that through the inflammable forest! I hear this dell roar in a moment with the joint voice of wind and fire, I see myself gallop for my soul, and the flying conflagration chase and outflank me through the hills; I see this pleasant forest burn for days, and the cattle roasted, and the springs dried up, and the farmer ruined, and his children cast upon the world. What a world hangs upon this moment."

With that he struck the match, and it missed fire.

"Thank God!" said the traveler, and put his pipe in his pocket.

★As Jesus said, "Let today's worries be sufficient for today." Indeed, there are enough stresses in life without creating imaginary ones. But that is where most of our worries reside—in the mind. This parable points out the futility—and pointlessness—of attempting to create "what if." In the moment when we allow worries to overtake us, we often miss the opportunities available to us. And what is more, we can also fail to accomplish what we could easily achieve.

The Meaning of Work (Desert Fathers)

Young John came to the leader of the community and said, "I wish to be free from work so that I can worship God without distraction."

After saying this, he removed his vestments and retreated into the desert.

A week later, however, weary and worn, Young John returned to the community and knocked on the teacher's door. From inside he heard a voice, "Who is it?" "It is John," he said.

The teacher said, "That cannot be. John has grown so holy, he has become an angel. He is no longer among the community anymore."

"But it is me!" John shouted.

The teacher, however, did not open the door until the next morning. When he did answer the door, he told John, "If you are a human being, you must work in order to live."

John answered, "Forgive me, teacher, for I was wrong."

★

Is true forgiveness possible? Surely it is, when one is able to embrace hospitality and see beyond the past. Many of the legends associated with the Desert Fathers—fourth-century monastic Christian ascetics—are stories of community and forgiveness.

But this little parable is also about the nature of worship and study. One who leaves behind community for the purpose of knowing nothing but God may quickly discover that God will not provide everything. People need each other. And most commonly we experience God through human contact and in our capacity to contribute to the common good.

Being spiritual is not so much a quest for the extreme as it is a search for the God who is present in the proximity of others and in daily life. Joy is everywhere. One can journey a thousand miles to see a flower, but miss the bloom growing at one's feet. Likewise, one can find God in holy places without leaving home. The only sanctuary one needs is the heart.

Flower Garden (Sufi) One day Mulla Nasrudin planted a flower garden. He prepared the soil and waited patiently for the beautiful flowers to grow. But when they spouted and bloomed, he was surprised to see that the garden was not only filled with beautiful flowers, but also dandelions. Seeking advice from many experienced gardeners far and wide, he tried every way possible to rid his garden of the nasty weeds. As a last effort, he traveled all the way to the capital to seek the advice of the shaykh's master gardener. This wise old man gave many tidbits of advice, but Mulla Nasrudin had tried them all. They sat together for a long time without saying a word. Finally the old man told Mulla, "Well, then I suggest you learn to love them."

★Sufism, the mystical tradition of Islam, offers many wonderful legends about love and life featuring the charming Mulla Nasrudin. As this parable demonstrates, there are many aspects of life that cannot be changed.

Perhaps the most frustrating are the people we would like to change, but cannot. With people, we must learn to overlook their unlovable qualities if we are to see their true beauty. Life is filled with diversity and it is evident that every individual is unique. Learning to accept what we cannot change, and learning to appreciate the best in others, is the first step on the road to loving well.

This legend uses the image of a garden as a metaphor for life. And in life, our experiences with others are always a mixture of frustration and blessing. There are those who are lovely and lovable . . . and there are those who need to be loved, despite their flaws.

Journey to the Beloved (Islamic) Centuries ago, in the city of Mecca, there lived a pious Sufi by the name of San'an. This man had devoted himself to teaching and to serving God and others. Because he lived in the sanctuary of God, he often guided others in their spiritual quest, and at night, he prayed with such power and devotion that God often revealed to him the mysteries of the universe.

One night, San'an had a dream in which he saw himself in the Byzantium empire, bowing to an idol. Awaking in distress, San'an feared that the dream might be a warning from God about some future event, but he quickly dismissed it. However, when the dream returned to him night after night, he decided he would have to travel to Byzantium to find the key to understanding what God was trying to tell him.

One morning San'an set out on the long journey with his disciples. He warned them that the trip would be long and arduous, but none desired to stay behind in Mecca, except one. Refusing to complain about the hardship, four of San'an's disciples accompanied their teacher into the foreign land.

No sooner had they arrived at the outskirts of the city of Rum when San'an heard a beautiful voice coming from inside a church. The voice was so touching and compelling that San'an found himself drawn to a nearby window.

When he looked inside the church, he saw a young Christian woman sitting near the window, combing her long, silky hair and singing a song filled with such sadness and haunting that San'an found it impossible to look away from her beauty. His heart began to beat faster, his palms began to sweat, and in a few moments he realized that he was deeply in love with the young maiden.

When the young woman left the church, San'an sat down outside and began to weep. He prayed to God, "O Lord, what am I to make of this? How can I quench this fire that is burning in my soul for this lovely girl?" San'an prayed this prayer over and over, each time becoming more intoxicated by love. After some time, he lost all memory of where he had come from and what he was doing in the foreign land. All he could think about was the young woman.

When his disciples returned, they found their teacher sitting outside the church, weeping in misery. They asked him what was wrong, but San'an was unable to express what was in his heart. Some of his disciples realized that he was intoxicated by love, and suggested that he was merely going through a phase, and that it would soon pass. Others tried to comfort the teacher by weeping along with him. But all of this was to no avail.

That night, San'an stood watch outside the church, realizing he had fallen in love with a Christian. His only desire was to again see the young woman, and he could envision only the blue of her eyes and hear the enchanting melody of her song. He clawed in the dirt, rolled in the dust, and beat his chest, attempting to free himself of the great love that had overtaken him, but the night was so long, and each time it seemed her memory would pass from him, it would return with even more fervor than before.

When a second night passed in this manner, San'an's disciples gathered around him and tried to coax him out of his misery. "Why don't you forget about this girl?" one suggested. "Just put her out of your mind and then we can forget this nonsense and go home."

Another disciple said, "If you will only repent of your sin, I know God will forgive you and heal you of this passion. The Lord will be faithful to restore you to your position as teacher of us all."

Still another disciple said, "Don't you realize you are our light? You know the way to God. Surely God will help you if you will but call out to the Lord."

But to each of these arguments and assaults, San'an gave a ready answer. "Don't talk to me about love," he said. "You know nothing of it until you know it is an all-consuming fire. As for repenting, I repent of the years I was a teacher, and nothing more. And as for prayer, I can only pray for her, that I might see her again."

"What are you saying?" one disciple asked. "Are you not sorry of this love that has driven you completely out of your mind?"

"I am sorry for only one thing," answered San'an. "That I did not fall in love sooner."

"But don't you care what others think?" asked the disciple. "Don't you think people will gossip about this pious teacher who has gone astray?"

"Why should I care what others think now? I have a new life. I am free of the past."

"Don't you care about us, your friends?" asked another disciple.

"All I care about is my beloved," San'an answered. "No one else can bring me happiness."

"Come with us," suggested another. "Let's go back to Mecca right now and we will help you find yourself again."

"My only Mecca is this church, and it's Ka'ba is the girl." "But won't you consider paradise? You are getting on in years, and it may not be long before you will go to heaven. Will you give up your hope of eternity for this foolishness?"

"What greater heaven could I ask for," answered San'an, "than the love of this girl?"

"Have you no shame?" the disciples asked. "All your life God has been your sole reason for existence. Would you betray God now?"

"But how can I escape this trap that God has led me into?" San'an replied.

"For God's sake, come back to Mecca with us. Don't betray your students!" the disciples shouted. But when they realized their teacher would not change his mind, they went away to a place nearby and waited to see what would become of their teacher.

Days passed, and San'an imagined himself with the girl every waking moment and also in his dreams. He gave her a name—calling her Sunshine. And he began to compose poetry and music in her honor.

Consumed with love, San'an slept outside the church in the open air among dogs. When others tossed scraps of food to the animals, he ate of these. He had grown haggard-looking and thin, but he noticed nothing of himself and his surrounding. He was only aware of the young woman who came each day to the church.

One day, out of sheer curiosity, the maiden happened to speak to San'an. She asked him, "Why do I see you wallowing in the dirt each day outside the church? Don't you have a family or a place to stay?"

San'an was so enraptured by the woman's voice and her attention that he answered quickly, "I have no place to go. My only thoughts are of you. And I will stay here until I win your love."

Sunshine laughed in San'an's face. "What a foolish old man you are! Don't you realize you are old enough to be my grandfather? From the looks of you, you are ready for the grave. A young, beautiful girl like me should have a young, handsome man at my side."

Using his wisdom, San'an answered, "True love knows no age. And love sees beyond the flesh. I will remain your devoted servant and do whatever you ask."

San'an's eloquence and sincerity were captivating. Gradually Sunshine began to see something promising in the old man when she came to the church each day. Eventually she told him, "If your love for me is true, then you must first renounce your faith and convert to Christianity. You must burn your Koran and abandon the rituals required of your faith. Finally, I ask that you drink wine and renounce your leadership."

San'an looked at the young woman and answered calmly, "Love presents many challenges, which a person must face. Sometimes the tests are cruel, but the end is sweetness and joy. One who truly loves knows no faith, for love itself becomes the only belief. One who truly loves knows no leadership nor position, for there is no status of existence higher than that of love."

Now, when the Byzantine monks heard of this famous Sufi teacher who had agreed to abandon his faith, they celebrated. They arranged several rituals in which San'an was asked to renounce his faith. He tossed the Koran into the fire, tore off his Sufi robes, and donned the clothing of a monk. Then he drank wine and bowed in submission to Sunshine. San'an celebrated with the monks, saying, "I have become nothing for the sake of love. I know nothing but love. I am disgraced by love. There is no one who can see what I see through the eyes of love."

Now, while the Christians were celebrating inside the church, San'an's disciples were lamenting outside the church. They wept and wailed, calling out to their teacher to return to them, to travel back to

Mecca and take up his life as a Sufi master once again. But their cries
fell upon deafness.

The following day, when San'an asked Sunshine what he could
do for her, she replied, "I want everything you have. You must buy me
jewels, and lavish me with gold and silver. If you can't do this, old man,
then don't waste my time and get out of my sight."

San'an reminded her that he had no worldly possessions. He had
forsaken all to win her love. All that remained was his heart, and his love
had all ready been given in full. If only he could have her completely in
return, that was his only desire.

"So," Sunshine answered, "it is marriage you seek. Well, here are my
terms. You must tend my pigs for a year. Afterwards, if you have done an
adequate job, I will agree to become your wife."

San'an was so overwhelmed with the promise of her hand, that he
gladly took up full-time residence in Sunshine's pigsty. He tended and
cared for the animals he had once loathed.

When the disciples discovered their teacher among the swine, they
were embarrassed to be called his followers. "What do you want us to
do now?" they asked. "Is this a sign you are trying to give us? Are you
telling us that you would like for us to convert? You know, we will follow your leadership and will do whatever you ask of us."

"Go home," San'an said. "I want nothing to do with you any more."

"What should we tell others when they ask of you?"

"Tell them the truth," San'an replied. "Tell them I know nothing
but love. Now leave me be, and allow me to tend to these pigs, that I
might win my beloved's heart."

In deep sorrow, the disciples returned to Mecca, but took great
care to seclude themselves so that others would not ask them questions about San'an. There was, however, the one disciple who did not
make the journey abroad. This disciple had stayed behind, and when
the other four returned, he was curious to know what had happened
to the great Sufi teacher.

Unable to restrain themselves any longer, the four disciples broke down and told their friend everything that had happened.

When they finished, the fifth disciple cried out in anguish, "What have you done? What kind of disciples are you? If you made a vow to follow your master, you should have kept your promise. If your master burned his Koran, you should have done the same. If he renounced the faith, you should have followed. If he tore off his robes and lived in a pigsty, you should have been there alongside him. By what authority did you tell your master to deny his love and abandon his feelings?"

Cut to the heart by the fifth disciple's words, the other four realized they had made a mistake. For forty days they grieved and entered into a time of prayer and fasting. The other disciple joined them as he was filled with selfless love for his master.

On the fortieth day, the fifth disciple had a vision in which he saw a thick cloud of dust hovering between his master and God. When the dust suddenly dispersed, the disciple saw San'an embraced by the Light. And there was a voice which said, "One must be burned in the fire of love to be worthy of seeing the Eternal Beloved. Name, religion, and position have no value in the creed of love. Before one can see the Truth, the dust of existence must be cleansed from the soul. Only then can one see the reflection of the true Beloved, which is the greatest longing."

The disciple ran to tell the others of this revelation, and together they left immediately to seek their teacher again. When they arrived in the city of Rum, they discovered San'an with his forehead pressed to the ground in submission to God. He had passed beyond mosque and church, beyond Islam and Christianity, desiring no position or worldly attachment, and was at last united with his Beloved God.

When the disciples looked into San'an's eyes, they recognized all of this, and saw that he had discovered the secret joy known only to the lover and the Beloved. They gathered around their master, San'an blessed them, and together they set out for Mecca.

Not long after they departed, however, the woman San'an had named Sunshine had a powerful and vivid dream. In her dream, she saw the Lord in brightness as the sun. She fell to the ground and prayed, "O Lord, how ignorant I have been. How foolish of me not to have seen you before. I am lost, for I have not known you. Please show me the path that leads to your joy, for I have beheld your beauty, and I desire only you. I cannot rest until I find my rest in you."

God soon spoke to her saying, "Go to Mecca and search for the old man who once tended your pigs. He will show you the way."

Leaving immediately for Mecca, Sunshine ran ahead without shoes or provisions. She crossed the sands without food or water, and her only desire was to find the way to her Beloved God. Along the way, her tears wet the sand, and when she arrived in Mecca many days later, she began to cry out for the old man.

Now, it happened that San'an heard her cries. He sent his disciples to bring the young woman to him.

They found her wandering the streets of Mecca, calling out for San'an, and they brought her to their master.

As soon as the young woman laid eyes upon San'an, she threw herself at his feet and begged, "Great master, I am burning with love. I long to see my Beloved, but there is nothing but darkness. Help me to see the Lord, for I want nothing but my Beloved God."

San'an placed his hands gently upon the woman and gazed into her eyes. He could see that she longed for nothing but God. All at once, she cried out in a loud voice, "O my Love, I can bear this separation no more." Upon saying this, Sunshine abandoned all desire, her body slumped, and her soul was united at last with God.

San'an stood still for a long time, and his disciples feared that he may have gone mad again, seeing the young woman. But eventually the master lifted his head, looked far off into the desert, and said, "How blessed are those who complete the journey of life and are united with the Beloved. They are truly free, for they live in union with God forever."

After sighing, he added, "And sad is the life of those who must lead others to God, for they must abandon this union for now, and be bound for the sake of God's pleasure and will."

★This is among the most powerful of all Sufi legends. Attributed to a wealthy Sufi master named Attar, who was born around 1136 in Persia, this moving legend may also serve as a testimony to the poet's life. According to tradition, Attar was captured by a Mongol during the invasion of Genghis Khan around 1230. Filled with selfless love for his captor, he advised the Mongol warrior not to sell him for a thousand pieces of silver, after it was offered as a bounty for his release. Attar told his captor, "Do not accept such an offer, for it is not yet the right price."

Later, when someone offered the Mongol warrior a sack of straw for Attar's release, the Sufi master said, "Sell me now, for this is all I am worth." Upon hearing this, the Mongol warrior grew enraged and cut off Attar's head.

As this legend teaches, love is the true aim of all faith and believing. Religious labels, creeds, positions, and movements are but outward manifestations of the true desire, which is to be united with God.

Reminiscent of St. Augustine's remark, "We are restless until we find our rest in God," the parable also possesses interesting facets that are very similar to Jesus's parable of the prodigal son, and to Buddha's parable of the forgetful son who returns home to seek the father. There is no doubt that this is among the greatest legends of Islam, and is a story demonstrating the heart of the faith—which is complete submission. Those who want to understand Islamic faith would do well to study this parable in its full depth.

As a final thought on this story, consider this parable attributed to the Sufi master Attar, who first worked as a pharmacist:

One day a seeker of God came into Attar's pharmacy to ask for medicine. But the young man was so overwhelmed by the opulence and order of Attar's shop, that he stood speechless for a long time, staring at Attar.

When Attar asked the seeker why he was staring at him, the young man said, "I was just wondering how you plan to die when you have to leave all of this wealth behind?"

Insulted by this remark, Attar replied. "I will die just as you will."

"Ah," replied the seeker, "but there is a difference. I have nothing to worry about. All I have is a shirt on my back and this bowl to beg with. Now do you still maintain that you will die as I will?"

"Of course," answered Attar.

Hearing this, the young man uttered the name of God, lay down, and placed his head on his begging bowl, and died in the doorway.

Tradition has it that Attar was so moved by this demonstration that he left behind his wealth and took up the life of a Sufi. His only desire was to know God. And his parables demonstrate the life-transforming power of love.

Muhammed and the Cat (Islamic) Muhammed was teaching in the desert, reciting from the Koran to a group of spell-bound listeners. As he was speaking, a sick cat meandered into the camp, sidled up next to Muhammed, and went to sleep on the hem of his exquisite robe.

Now Muhammed was unaware of this cat even though he continued to speak for the remainder of the day. All day the cat slept on the hem of his robe, finding warmth and healing in the shadow of the prophet.

When the day came to an end, everyone returned to their tents for the evening. But the prophet, seeing the cat asleep on his robe, took a sharp knife and cut off the hem of his robe where the cat was sleeping. In this way the prophet destroyed the most beautiful of garments, but left the cat undisturbed in its slumber.

*Does love have boundaries? Perhaps not. There may be moments in life when we are called upon to extend love in ways we never imagined. Sometimes sacrifices are required. Sometimes we must trade one priority for another. A heartfelt compassion can move a person to strange acts of kindness.

One truth about love which has withstood the test of time: Love is the greatest power.

The Sick Kite (Aesop) A kite, which had been ill for a very long time, came to its mother and said, "Don't cry, mother . . . but go to the gods and pray that I might recover from this dreadful disease." But the mother kite said, "But, child, which of the gods can I pray to, for you have robbed all of their altars."

In its origins, the Hippocratic oath offered in part (ἐπὶ δηλήσει δὲ καὶ ἀδικίη εἴρξειν): "abstain from doing harm." This has come down in the modern idiom to mean: "First, do no harm." Aesop's teaching echoed these sentiments, which are often lacking in human practice, particularly when it comes to relationships. If we desire to receive good from others, then it only stands to reason that we would first practice goodness in our relationships. The rabbi Hillel noted this as: "Whatever you would not desire to have done to you, do not to do this to a neighbor." Jesus expressed this Golden Rule as: "Do unto others as you would have them do unto you."

The Aesop teaching isn't a unique philosophy, but common sense. And yet how often common sense eludes us. We often create our own outcomes. And when we do, we have no room for complaining. If we desire to receive generosity, we should be generous. If we desire love, we need to love. If friendship . . . then be a friend.

Common sense? Yes. But still a profound truth for the ages.

Two Forms of Knowledge (Upanishads) There was a wealthy landowner named Saunaka who asked the sage, Anigras, about knowledge: "How does a person come to know the world?"

Anigras told him: "There are two forms of knowledge—the higher and the lower. The lower forms of knowledge consist of the disciplines such as science, grammar, astronomy, and mathematics. But the higher form of knowledge is that by which people understand the eternal. The eternal is what cannot be seen, what cannot be understood, and is not attached to the senses. The eternal is all-pervading, yet present everywhere—unchangeable, and only the wise perceive it."

★The Upanishads were written during a time of great social and religious upheaval. In addition to describing those rituals and concepts adopted by Buddhism and Jainism, the Upanishads are the vedic scriptures of the Hindu faith.

Here, in this scripture, we see that understanding is more than knowledge—and this of two types. A person can understand the world and yet not understand the eternal things. This learning comes not so much from the head as from the heart of human experience and the disciplines of practice.

Mercury and the Woodsman (Aesop)A woodsman was felling a tree on the banks of a river when his axe fell into the water. Lamenting his loss, he sat down on the banks of the river to weep. But the god Mercury, whose river it was, noticed the man's distress and came to assist him. When the woodsman told his tale of woe to the god, Mercury at once dove to the bottom of the river and brought up a golden axe. "Is this your axe?" asked Mercury. The woodsman denied that it was. So again, Mercury dove to the bottom and this time brought up a silver axe. "Is this the axe you lost?" asked Mercury. "No," the woodsman replied. A third time Mercury dove to the bottom and brought up a third axe—plain and wooden. "Is this your axe?" asked the god. The woodsman affirmed that it belonged to him. So impressed was Mercury with the woodsman's honesty that he gave the other two axes to the woodsman as reward.

Later that day, when the woodsman related this story to a friend, the friend decided that he would try the same ploy on Mercury. He walked to the river and dropped his axe in the water, then sat on the bank to lament his loss. When Mercury appeared he dove to the bottom of the river and at once brought up the golden axe. "Is this your axe?" he asked the fellow. The man replied, "Indeed it is."

But Mercury, knowing the man's heart, replied, "But indeed it is not. And because you have lied to the gods and to yourself even what you have will be taken from you." And with that word, Mercury departed, leaving the man standing on the bank with his own axe at the bottom of the river.

*Many of Aesop's fables relate lessons in morality through the attributes of animals and nature. But here we see the very human condition of greed splayed open in a human situation. Practical, yes . . . but the implications of dishonesty go far beyond the material things. As this fable reveals, dishonesty is first and foremost a loss of integrity which strikes at the heart of the self, and ultimately can leave a person poorer in the outcome.

On the other hand, honesty is one of the highest and most honored attributes, as honesty is integrity personified, and as such offers one a rich surplus of both material and spiritual blessings. Honesty is what enables a person to live in harmony with the universe and oneself. Those who seek shortcuts to wealth, or through dishonest means, eventually discover that the true wealth is elusive—and that they are exposed by their true self-interests.

A Light for the Blind (Jewish) Rabbi Yose said, "I have always been confused by the verse: 'You will grope at high noon just as the blind grope in the darkness' (Deuteronomy 28:29). I have wondered . . . what is the difference between light and darkness to a blind man? The answer came one evening as I was walking down the road in total darkness.

There I met a blind man who was carrying a torch. I said to him, "But you are blind . . . so why are you carrying a torch?" The man said to me, "I carry the torch so people will see me and will thereby help me from stepping into holes, thorns, or snares."

*There is more than one way to be a light to others. We can hold a light, but we can also be a light. We can point to light, but we can also walk in it. Sometimes the offer of helpfulness is paramount to helping—and there are frequently occasions when we may be the light bearer for someone else who is doing the hardest work.

Tongues (Jewish) Rabbi [Judah] cooked a meal for his disciples and served up beef tongues—some of which were tender and others tough. He noticed right away that his disciples were selecting only the tender tongues and were leaving the tough tongues on the serving plate. The rabbi said to them, "Take note of what you are doing. It should be like this in your lives. Do not have a tough tongue, but let your tongues be tender and gentle toward one another."

*As we become adults we acquaint object lessons with childhood, and yet our lives are saturated with metaphors and innuendoes every day. Often, we fail to grasp these deeper concepts and adopt them into our outlook. Here is a lesson on speaking that—in this age of rapid and (often) thoughtless communication—provides an ample amount of wisdom. We dare not be overly-critical. But perhaps we should always reserve our harshest criticisms for ourselves.

The Grateful Lion (Gesta Romanorum) There was a knight who devoted much of his time to hunting wild beasts. One day, as he was riding on his steed through the forest, he happened upon a lame lion. Dismounting from his horse, the knight approached the lion and removed a large thorn from its paw. The knight also applied a healing balm, and wrapped the lion's paw so that it could heal.

Some days after this, the king of the land was also hunting in these same woods. He came upon the lion, captured it, and held it in a cage for many years.

Now, it also happened that the knight fell out of favor with the king, and the knight had to flee into a far land. The king sent envoys to capture the errant knight, and after many years, eventually the knight was brought before the king to be sentenced. The king said, "Because you have disobeyed your king, I hereby sentence you to be cast into a lion's den."

At this word, the knight was taken to the lion's den and he was given over to death. But when the king returned the next morning, the knight was still alive. The king had the knight brought before him in the palace and asked, "How is it that you have been spared from the mouth of the lion?"

The knight said, "Your majesty, many years ago I met this lion in the woods. I removed a large thorn from its paw and healed its wound. It has shown mercy upon me by sparing my life."

When the king heard this he said, "Just as the lion has spared you, so shall I. Go, be restored to your duties, and serve me faithfully from here on." The knight did so, and he lived the remaining years of his life in peace with the king.

*The Gesta Romanorum is a collection of tales that frequently touch upon Christian themes. From sources unknown, the Romanorum has a Latin feel and also contains some beautiful stories—such as this one about the knight and the lion—that have been adapted into children's books and morality plays.

Friendship, indeed, is a powerful force. But so is memory. And when the two are united they create mercy. Salvation as such is not just a heavenly theme, but in its origins redemption was wholly fastened to this earth and had to do with changed direction, being "bought back" from certain death, or a change in the social structure that moved people from slavery to freedom.

Doing good is reward enough—but one never knows how salvation may return and take up residence outside one's front door.

Rich Man, Poor Man (African) There once lived a rich man and a poor man who were the best of friends. The rich man always supported the poor man through his difficulties, and in return the poor man provided an exchange of labor in the fields or helping out in the rich man's house.

In time, however, a great famine swept over the land and both rich and poor were living in misery and hardship. The poor man was struggling for the basic necessities of life and the rich man, as he watched his wealth decline, grew desperate to hang onto his money. The poor man suffered for want of food, but the rich man grew despondent and selfish in his attitudes toward the poor man.

Eventually the poor man had to watch his children die of starvation, and his wife was dying, too. But in his desperation, the poor man set off one day to look for food in the garbage dump. He found nothing, but on his way home a kindly woman took pity on him and gave him a handful of corn. The poor man returned home with the corn and began to make a large pot of watery corn soup. But because he had no meat or seasoning to add to the broth, the soup was bland and it had no pleasing aroma.

But the poor man had an idea. He made his way to the rich man's house, wondering if the rich man might have some seasoning. Sure enough, when the poor man peered inside the rich man's house, he noticed a delicious meal of chicken and gravy on the table. The aroma of the meal wafted through the windows. Returning to his home the poor man poured a bowl of the bland soup, and then hastened back to the rich man's house where, as he sat down with his meal in hand, ate the bland corn soup while taking in the delicious aroma of the chicken in the rich man's house.

A few days after this, the rich man and the poor man met in the street and the poor man said, "I came to your house a few days ago carrying a bowl of watery soup. I sat outside your house and enjoyed the aroma of your meal while eating my brothy soup."

"Aha," said the rich man, "so you are the culprit who stole my aroma. I wondered why that meal tasted so bland. I'm sorry, old friend, but I'm going to sue you for stealing my flavor, and we will let the judge decide your fate."

That afternoon the poor man had to appear in court and the judge ordered the poor man to give the rich man a goat to make up for stealing the rich man's flavor. Heavy-hearted, the poor man began his journey home, realizing that he didn't have even a single grain to give to the rich man, much less a goat.

But on his way home he met a wise old man who asked him why he was so downcast. The poor man told the wise man his story and the wise man said, "I have a goat I will give you. But when you take the goat before the judge to give it to your rich friend, allow me to be there to help plead your case."

Bewildered by this turn of events the poor man did receive the goat, and when the time came for him to appear once again before the judge, the poor man was relieved to find the wise man standing next to him in the courtroom.

"Have you brought the goat in payment to the rich man?" the judge asked.

"I have brought it," the poor man said.

But the wise old man asked the judge if he might make a point before the sentence was carried out.

"Very well," said the judge. "You may speak as you wish."

The old man said, "A man who has stolen should only be asked to pay back that which he has stolen, isn't this so?"

The judge agreed.

"Well, in this case, the poor man is accused of stealing the aroma of the rich man's food, so he should only pay back the aroma of the food to the rich man."

"That seems logical," the judge admitted.

"Then here is what should be done," the wise man said. "Let the rich man not have the goat until he agrees to a fair exchange. The rich man should beat the goat with his staff until it bleats, and then he should take the bleating as payment for the aroma of his food. Surely this is a fair exchange."

The judge agreed with this verdict.

And so it was that the poor man was saved from an unfair sentence and was released. But the rich man was made to look like a fool and was exposed as a selfish individual before the entire village. The poor man returned to his home with his head held high. The rich man slipped away silently out of the courtroom.

The people in the village praised the poor man for his victory. But whenever they saw the rich man they said to themselves, "Whoever rides a horse of greed at full speed will eventually have to dismount in shame."

★This African morality tale is a humorous take on poverty and greed. As the story points out, neither extreme is preferred, but there is a moral obligation of the wealthy to be generous and helpful toward those less fortunate. As in many cultures, African stories often poke fun at the extravagances of wealth while offering a backdrop of African life that does not hide the harsher realities of life.

One does not want to appear foolish and wealthy at the same time—and wisdom does not always reside among the most educated or privileged segment of society. Wisdom often comes from living the harsher realities. Life experiences count for much—and it is often the case that we learn more through struggle than through success.

The Archer and the Nightingale (Gesta Romanorum)An archer caught a nightingale and was about to kill it when the bird spoke. Astonished by this gift of speech, the archer listened as the bird said, "What good would it do to kill me? I cannot satisfy your appetite. But if you release me I will give you three bits of wisdom from which you may derive great benefit if you follow them."

Thinking that the bird would be more beneficial in this way, the archer promised to release the bird if it would dispense these bits of wisdom. So the nightingale said, "The first rule is: Never attempt something that is impossible. The second is: Do not lament a loss that is not recoverable. And third: Do not believe what is incredible. Keep these three and you will benefit greatly."

After the bird had spoken, the archer kept his promise and released the nightingale. It immediately flew to the top branch of a tree and said, "You are such a silly fellow. You didn't know it, but inside of me there is a large pearl. You could have been rich."

Sensing that he had been tricked, the archer shot an arrow toward the nightingale, but missed. Then he said, "Listen, why don't you come down from that tree? I'll take you home with me and show you every comfort. I'll feed you, and you can fly around as you like."

But the nightingale said, "Now I know you are a fool, as you haven't regarded the second counsel and I gave you: Do not lament a loss that is not recoverable!"

The archer shot another arrow, but missed, and the nightingale said, "Indeed you are a fool and will remain one. For you continue to believe the unbelievable, that inside of me is a giant pearl. Do you really think that I could fly like this with a pearl inside of me?" And with that word the nightingale flew away, never to be seen again.

★As the old maxim says, "Don't believe everything you hear." In this age of Internet sensation, wild rumor and news that is little more than celebrity profile, one must look beyond the sensational and the rumor to find truth. It is best to weigh all information before reaching a judgment, and often the first word is not the most accurate word. Truth is always deeper than meets the eye . . . or the ear.

The Pears (Tolstoy) One day a master sent his servant to the market saying, "Bring back a basket of the best pears." The servant made the journey and said to the merchant, "Give me your best pears."

The merchant placed a pear in the servant's hand, but the servant said, "No, I want only the best pears."

"Well," the merchant said, "taste it. See if this isn't the best pear you ever tasted."

The servant bit into the pear, found it delicious, but then said, "Yes, but how can I know that *all of your pears* are this good?"

The merchant filled the basket with pears and the servant took a bite out of each one to ensure its quality. But when he returned home with the pears the master was not happy and dismissed him.

★A delicious story with some wit attached to it. As with many Tolstoy parables, we often have to consider the deeper meanings. What is this parable about? A lack of faith or confidence (in one's judgment? In God?). Is it meant to point out the deficiencies of doing a job halfway, or in the wrong way? Or is this parable a commentary on the mores of society and the insatiable appetite to consume only the best of everything?

The Load (Tolstoy) After the war, there were two peasants who went out to search for treasure. One was stupid and the other wise. They walked together into the burned portion of the city and found there some bundles of wool that could be useful. Both of the peasants loaded a bundle of wool on their backs and began the return home with their find.

On the return, however, the men came upon some bundles of cloth that could be useful. The wise peasant unloaded the wool from his back and picked up the cloth instead. The foolish peasant said, "But why should I unload a perfectly good bundle of wool that is already loaded on my back?"

A bit further up the road they came upon some good clothing. The wise peasant unloaded his cloth bundle and loaded the clothing instead.

But the foolish peasant said, "I have come this far with the wool, and why unload it when it is already on my back?"

Still further up the road they found some silver plates. The wise peasant unloaded the bundles of clothing he was carrying and picked up all of the silver he could carry. The foolish peasant said, "The wool is already loaded on my back, why take the trouble to unload it?"

And finally they stumbled upon some gold along the outskirts of the city. The wise peasant unloaded the silver, picked up the gold, and loaded it on his back. The foolish peasant continued to say, "But the wool is already bundled on my back and I've come this far with it."

As the two men neared their home, it began to rain. The rain soaked the wool bundle and made it useless. But the man with the gold returned to his home and became very wealthy.

★This is a parable principally about life. Life is a journey filled with many choices. Along the way we will experience triumph and success, as well as tragedy and sadness. But one of the most important questions is: What will we choose to carry with us? These distinctions are not always easy to ascertain. Sometimes we choose to carry burdens—which is baggage that weighs us down and holds us back. But sometimes we need the ballast of the past to give us a foundation or keep us from making mistakes (which we are prone to repeat).

So often, we fall into the trap of making excuses. These can range from an inability or unwillingness to take personal responsibility to focusing on our difficulties rather than our opportunities. Life offers both.

What the parable illustrates is this dichotomy.

In order to obtain high goals in life—whether education, family stability, love, or even wealth—sacrifices must be made. Often, one blessing must be exchanged for another—or at least we need to be willing to leave behind our ease and exchange it for uncertainty. Complacency is at the heart of this parable, and this approach is one of the most insidious of attitudes. Or, as the classic Christian theology would call it: sloth.

As we think about the greatest achievements in our lives we discover that all of these successes were born of hard work, sacrifice, and an ability to embrace the unknown. Chance has little to do with our successes.

Awake (Buddhist)Soon after the Buddha received enlightenment he was sitting by the road in perfect peace, his face radiant with contentment. A man stopped to ask him, "What are you, my friend? Are you an angel or a god?"

"No," replied the Buddha.

"Well then, are you a wizard?"

"No."

"Are you a man?"

"No."

"Well then, what are you?"

The Buddha replied, "I am awake."

★This Buddhist teaching is a mainstay in classical forms as well as Zen— and it awakens our sense of the interior. Jesus talked about "an abundant life," the teachings of Chuang Tzu noted that discernment is the path of wisdom, and in classical Jewish teaching (both law and prophets) there is the urging to focus on life, which is a recognition of the divine in all things. To be "awake" is to be fully cognizant of oneself ("know thyself") and also of others.

Martin Buber, a Jewish teacher, once spoke of this awareness as "I/ Thou." When we are aware of our own feelings, our histories, and why we think and act as we do, then we can also be aware of others and their needs . . . in this dichotomy we discover that we are fully alive. Focusing too much on ourselves—even our own self-improvement—is a recipe for arrogance and pride, even self-absorption. But true spiritual growth is outward focused as well as inward. All religions teach these truths, and it is a fine line we walk between helping ourselves and helping others. When we discover the balance, however, then we become fully awake.

Soul Food (Diogenes—Greek Philosopher)It is obvious that humans and animals live on air, by breathing. Air is body and soul. In my opinion, then, what we call intelligence is air, and by it all things are directed, it has power over all things. This substance is what I hold to be God.

Breath (Ecclesiastes—Hebrew Bible)For the fate of humans and animals is the same. As one dies, so dies the other. They all have the same breath, and humans have no advantage over the animals, for all is vanity. All go to one place, for all are from the dust, and all turn to dust again. Who knows whether the human spirit goes upward and the spirit of animals descends to the earth?

*In the Hebrew Bible there is much word play. These double-and-triple meaning words and phrases—even for the name of God—are sometimes puns, and sometimes they point to the inexpressible mystery. When God is called "I Am," this simple Hebrew verb denotes a great mystery that cannot be simply expressed. (The intent seems to be that God is not our commodity to control and broker.) And in the creation of the first man we see in the Hebrew word "Adam" a play on words, which has the double-meaning of "earth" or "earth-creature."

Here, in both the quote from Diogenes and the book of Ecclesiastes (3:19-21) we visit a double meaning for the word spirit (*ruah* in Hebrew and *psyche* in Greek). Both words have a surplus of meaning that cannot be easily conveyed.

In essence, spirit is both wind and substance. Spirit is felt but not seen. And when it comes to life itself, the ancients noted that all living things (flesh) had this breath, this wind, this air, inside of them. When the air departs, we call this death. And there was always the question, where does the wind go? What happens to the spirit?

It is still a fascinating question. What do you think? Do all dogs go to heaven?

Spirit (Jesus) What is born of the flesh is flesh, and what is born of the spirit is spirit. Do not be astonished that I said to you, "You must be born from above." The wind blows as it chooses, and you hear the sound of it, but you do not know where it comes from or where it goes. So is everyone who is born of the Spirit. (John 3:6–8)

The Wind (Buddhist) Two monks were engaged in an argument about a flag moving in the breeze. One monk said, "The flag moves." The other monk replied, "No, it is the wind that moves." They continued like this for some time, but could not agree.

Eventually one of the elder monks intervened and said, "Gentlemen, it is not the flag that moves. It is not the wind. It is your mind that moves."

*What is spirit and how does it move? What moves us? When we recognize a higher power we are open to change, to movement. Spirit is not principally an inner discipline—something we possess or that possesses us—but is the power that moves our hands and feet into action. Spirit molds and melds. Spirit is life.

As the previous two narratives illustrate, there is a life force that not only gives life, but also empowers us along the way. Likewise, Spirit is that divine wind that blows through the human heart and creates all things new and fresh. When minds and hearts are changed, the Spirit is at work.

Spirit is a verb.

The Rabbis' Debate (Talmud)

Once Rabbi Yohanan ben Zakkai asked of his five disciples: "What is the most desirable thing to strive for in life?"
Rabbi Eliezer answered: "A good eye."
Rabbi Joshua answered: "A good friend."

Rabbi Yose answered: "A good neighbor."

Rabbi Simeon answered: "Wisdom to foretell the future."

Rabbi Eliazer answered: "A good heart."

Rabbi Yohanan then said to this disciples, "Eliazar's words please me the most, for his thoughts include all the rest."

On another occasion Rabbi Yohanan asked, "What is the one thing that a man should avoid most in life?"

Rabbi Eliezer answered: "An evil eye."

Rabbi Joshua answered: "An evil friend."

Rabbi Yose answered: "A bad neighbor."

Rabbi Simeon answered: "One who borrows money and doesn't return it."

Rabbi Eleazar answered: "A bad heart."

Rabbi Yohanon then said, "The words of Eleazar please me the most, for this thoughts include all the others."

True Goodness (Jesus)

For out of the heart come all manner of evil (Matthew 15:18).

Why do you call me good? For there is no one good but God alone (Matthew 19:17)

★What makes a person "bad" or "good" has always been a matter of debate. For some "good" is that which we strive for—and as such good is a moralistic achievement, the manner in which others perceive us. For others, good is an absolute—like Plato's perfect plain. And still for others "good" is that which is reserved for God alone. Good is perfection—an unobtainable end—and one is "good" only in faith or spirit.

But regardless of the differences, people have a desire to strive for good—and we often see this spirit flowing out in times of disaster. These tragic times remind us that people do have the capacity to at least do good, to help a neighbor, and for a little while, possess a willingness to focus on the good of another. There is still much good in the world—and if we look closely enough, we can find it.

The Rabbi's Dream (Jewish) A rabbi fell asleep and dreamed he had entered Paradise. There, much to his surprise, he discovered the sages debating the Talmud just as they had done on earth.

"Is this the reward for Paradise?" the rabbi yelled. "There is nothing different here than upon the earth. They are still debating."

But a heavenly voice cried, "O foolish one, you think the sages are in Paradise. But it is just the opposite. Paradise is in the sages."

★Where does heaven reside? Is it an existence beyond this life? Is it a final peace? Does heaven lie within us?

These are the questions that people have debated and thought about for centuries. Teachers as diverse as Buddha and Confucius and Jesus have spoken of it. Jesus spoke of the kingdom as both present ("it is within you," "it has arrived") and future ("when the kingdom comes"). Perhaps, then, the heavenly realm is already visible if we look for it. Or we may have to work for it. Or perhaps we pray it into existence. Or ultimately it is God's doing.

One thing is sure, however. Heaven can only arrive when the heart is open—and the hand. We must be willing to give and to receive. This begins with humility and an awareness that we don't create all of the realities in our lives. Life's greatest blessings are gifts. And when we are praying for and honoring the gifts of heaven, we may discover that heaven has already arrived in forms we did not expect. New, perhaps. But heaven, nonetheless.

Simple Prayer (Jewish) A disciple asked his rabbi, "Tell me, rabbi, what is the one thing you do before you pray?"

The rabbi answered, "I pray that when I pray, that it will be with all my heart."

★One of the problems of any faith is when prayer becomes rote or devoid of thought and feeling. Prayer can become something we do, something we say just to say it. But prayer from the heart is where we connect with the divine. Nothing fancy is required. Just honesty. And this involves the whole self.

Where Wisdom Resides (Jewish)A woman asked Rabbi Yose Bar Halaftah, "Why does God only give wisdom to the wise? Wouldn't it be best for God to give wisdom to the fools who need it?"

Rabbi Yose told a parable to illustrate: "Suppose there are two people who desire to borrow money from you. One is wealthy. The other is poor. To which of the two would you be most likely to loan money?"

"Why, to the wealthy, of course," the woman answered.

"And why is that?" asked the rabbi.

"Because the wealthy man would be more likely to repay, while the poor man would likely struggle to repay the loan," she said.

"Listen to what you are saying," the rabbi said. "Why should the Almighty be any different? If God gave wisdom to fools, what do you think they would do with it? Wouldn't they squander it? That is why God has given wisdom to the wise and why the wise use it well in the study of the Torah."

★Jesus once remarked that he used parables in order to confound the wise. But he also noted that it was unwise to cast one's pearls before swine. Among the many parables found in the Talmud, this one attributed to Rabbi Yose offers some harsh but playful sage advice. It is always best to know one's audience and their willingness to receive before embarking on the arduous task of trying to communicate wisdom.

The Parable of the Linen and the Coat (Jewish)On a table lay a strip of new linen. The strip of linen said, "Someday I'm going to make a fine shirt." Suddenly, the linen noticed an old coat that had been tossed into a corner. The linen said to the coat, "What an ugly excuse for a coat you are."

Some days later the owner of the house used the new linen to make a new shirt. But when the man put the shirt on, he then put the old coat over the shirt before he went outside. The linen was jealous and asked, "How is it that you are more important than I?"

The old coat answered, "They first laundered me. And then the owner beat me with sticks to knock out the dust and the dirt. When he had finished this, I thought that I looked like new again. But then he put me in a kettle of water and boiled me. I was rinsed, dried, and pressed. And then I noted that I had been transformed into a beautiful coat. Before one can be exalted he must first suffer."

*Humility, and the acknowledgement of suffering as a path to enlightenment and exaltation, are a common theme among all faiths. For example, Jesus said, "Whoever exalts himself shall be humbled, and whoever humbles himself shall be exalted." Jesus also said, "The first shall be last, and the last shall be first." The Buddha instructed his disciples to "walk humbly" and in Taoism ("The Way") those who follow the teaching are instructed to make a humble path.

As this brief parable illustrates, humility is often born of hardship and difficulty. But difficulties develop character, even beauty.

The Merchant and the Parrot (Rumi) Once there was a merchant who kept a parrot in a cage. He loved conversing with the parrot and one day, before leaving on a business trip to Hindustan, the merchant asked his parrot if he had any message he would like to deliver to his relatives. The parrot responded by saying, "Yes, tell my relatives that I am confined to a cage."

So, while the merchant thought that this was a strange message, he nonetheless delivered these words to the first parrot he met in Hindustan. When the parrot heard the message, it immediately keeled over—dead.

The merchant was struck by this turn and wondered how the parrot's message could have such an adverse effect. So, upon his return home, the merchant told his parrot what had happened. As soon as the parrot received the news he, too, fell over dead. The merchant took the parrot from its cage and was preparing to bury it when, suddenly, it flew away. The merchant asked the parrot to explain its trickery.

"My relative feigned death so I would receive a message regarding my way to get out of this cage," the parrot explained.

*Rumi, the Persian Sufi poet, lived in the thirteenth century. His lengthy poem (mostly couplets) explores nearly every facet of life and faith. The poet also told parables, and his love poetry is generally regarded as one of the great works of literature. But certainly the heart of Rumi's poetry is love—love embodied, love explored, love lived. Like many other Sufi voices of his time, the center of the Sufi devotion was centered on Jesus (the Prophet of Love) perhaps more so than on the Prophet Muhammad.

Sufism, which is generally regarded as the mystic tradition of Islam, sought to embrace all faiths—or at least sought to see God everywhere, in the ubiquity of creation and human existence. To the Sufis, life is filled with mystery and awe, and the center of faith is not so much doctrine as experiencing love. (This couples nicely with the Jewish and Christian notions that the center of faith is to love God with all of one's heart, soul, mind and strength, and to love one's neighbor as oneself.)

Rumi's poetry and parables are filled with wonder and delight, inhabited by animals and the great mysteries of nature. In short, he worked in the metaphors of faith and did his part to give voice to the indescribable and the unknowable mystery of God.

In the parable above, Rumi makes a point for wisdom and a faith that leads to freedom and life.

Chapter Two

The Heart of Helpfulness

The Good do not grow old.
  —Dhammapada (Buddhist Sacred Text)

Do unto others as you would have them do unto you.
                                              —Jesus

Stories of helpfulness are a popular typology in legendary literature. These tales span the religious and cultural gamut, and have universal appeal. Some of these legends focus on cooperative effort, while other tales demonstrate our human need to assist others in daily tasks. These legends and teachings are very inspiring to anyone who has ever faced a difficulty or needed to find an outlet for helping others.

One of life's principal goals (if we are honest with ourselves) is to be helpful to others. In business, meaning is applied when customers are served well. In the home, family life works best when everyone pitches in and is helpful in their tasks and responsibilities. Communities thrive when people come together to create schools, hospitals, and entertainment. Religious institutions serve the common good when the good are serving others. And month by month we witness how people from all walks of life rally to help others in the aftermath of tragedies and storms.

We long to be helpful, but there is another strong pull in the human spirit to form our own individual kingdoms, too. Although John Donne once said that "no man is an island," we tend to live as if isolation and individualism are the greatest good—even the highest goal—in life. In this age of individualism and privacy we can easily become obsessed with our own happiness and security. But the more we focus on ourselves the more miserable, it seems, we become.

The stories and insights in this chapter play to a varied audience and will touch us in differing ways. We may glimpse how our gifts and talents can be used for the benefit of much larger purposes—and we may even feel inspired to stretch beyond our comforts to meet a need. Helpfulness is lived out in many forms and the insights gathered here have played across the ages.

We may also see how others have helped us—and that we are rarely the self-made products of our imaginations. Many others have invested their lives into our own, and it is true that it takes a village to raise a child. We are living proof.

In the end, we may also decide to make our own investments into the lives of others. This is the heart of helpfulness. The greatest investments we will ever make in life are rarely of the bank account variety, but are wholly invested in those we love, and those we might yet impact with our mentoring, friendship, and guidance.

An open hand is the only way we can give and receive.

Seeking and Finding (Buddhist)

There is a parable told in India of a mysterious medical herb that lay hidden under the tall grasses of the Himalayas. For years explorers sought for it in vain until, at last, a wise man discovered it by following the sweet scent it produced. Year after year the wise man collected the herb, cut it, and stockpiled it in a tub. But after his death the medical herb lay hidden in that distant and unknown spot in the mountains. Eventually the elixir turned sour and was actually harmful, for no one had discovered it.

★

Two things must happen in order for anyone to attain the true riches of God. First, a person must seek. Jesus once said, "Seek, and you will find. Ask and it shall be given. Knock and the door will be opened to you." Then, a person must be willing to use the blessings attained. These blessings can never be hoarded. Again, as Jesus once said, "It is better to give than to receive."

Similar teachings exist in Buddhism, Islam, and Judaism. When spiritual gifts go unused, they atrophy and become useless. And if we attempt to keep all of the blessings of God for ourselves, they waste away and cannot be of use to others—which is their intended purpose.

Blessings were never intended to be hoarded by the individual.

The Elm Tree and the Vine (Robert Dodsley)

An extravagant young vine wanted to impress a stately elm tree. In the spring the vine began to wrap itself around the elm tree with increasing determination, and as the summer neared, the vine began sprouting a profusion of leaves. Eventually the vine said to the stately elm, "Look at the abundance of my leaves—I seem to have more than you do!"

At this point the elm answered, "It is true, you have the outward appearance that seems now to be more impressive than my own, but you have dedicated all of your energies and efforts to making yourself look good instead of focusing upon the deeper roots. You look good for a season, but when the winter comes, you will wilt and die. I, on the other hand, have burrowed deep, and I shall withstand every test in the harshest of seasons."

★

An insightful parable for our times—when most people live well beyond their means and outward appearances so often belie a poverty within. Those who endure (economically or otherwise) focus more on depth than surface appearances. Possessing things is not security. And those who plan for the future have much deeper roots. Life itself is a test of seasons—and it is vital that we plan for the future as well as enjoy the present.

Just a Cup of Water (Sufi)

Moses once asked God to show him how he could help others. So God told Moses to visit a little village in the valley. There Moses encountered a poor man who was sitting at the gate—his clothes in tatters, his body plagued by insects and disease. Moses asked, "How may I be of help to you?"

The poor man replied, "I am very thirsty. If I could have just a cup of water."

Moses departed to look for water, but became distracted when he saw others who looked just as needy as the poor man at the gate. Moving from need to need, Moses attempted to meet many demands at once.

Some time later, Moses returned to the gate only to discover that the poor man had died of thirst.

Moses was distressed and asked God, "Lord Almighty, you fashioned human beings from the dust of the earth. Some of your creatures walk the path of paradise while others suffer. Some are happy while others are sad. But I do not understand why this poor man had to die of thirst."

God answered, "But Moses, the poor man asked you for a simple cup of water. Could you not have helped him before you became distracted by so many needs?"

★

One of the most important lessons we all learn in life is that we cannot meet all of the needs of the world. Human needs are overwhelming, and there is no end to the despair we can find in other people's lives if we go looking for it. But we can all do something to help others. Perhaps our circles of influence are small, and our abilities may seem insignificant, but we are all given some small responsibility to help alleviate the world's suffering.

Being helpful requires both a degree of concentration and focused effort. But it is easy to become distracted, to believe that we can solve other people's problems, or that we can make choices for them. Sometimes, in our willingness to help others, we lose heart, or we see another need that looks more compelling.

As this legend reminds us, the work of God is most often accomplished through our hands—even the smallest acts of kindness.

Why There Is Evil in the World (Tolstoy)

A Hermit lived in the forest, and the animals were not afraid of him. He and the wild animals used to talk together, and they understood one another.

Once the Hermit lay down under a tree, and a Raven, a Dove, a Stag, and a Snake came to the same place to sleep. The animals began to reason why evil should exist in the world.

The Raven said, "It is all owing to hunger that there is evil in the world. When we have as much as we wish to eat, we sit by ourselves on the bough and caw, and everything is good, and we are in every respect well off; but some other day we are famished, and everything is quite the opposite, so that we can see no brightness in God's world, and we feel full of unrest; we fly about from place to place and there is no rest for us. And even if we see some meat afar off, then it becomes still worse; for if we fly down to get it, either sticks and stones are thrown at us, or wolves and dogs chase us, and we are absolutely destroyed. How much trouble comes upon us from hunger! All evil is caused by it!"

The Dove said: "In my opinion, evil does not arise from hunger, but it all comes from love. If we only lived alone, we should have little trouble. Wretchedness shared makes one doubly wretched. And so we always live in pairs. And if we love our mates there is no peace for us at all. We are always thinking, 'Has she enough to eat? Is she warm?' And when our mate is away from us anywhere, then we are wholly lost; we cannot help worrying all the time 'If only the hawk does not carry her off, or men make away with her'; and we ourselves fly off in pursuit of her, and perhaps find the poor thing in the hawk's nest or in the snare. And if our mate is lost, then there is no more comfort for us. We cannot eat, we cannot drink; we can only fly about and mourn. How many of us have perished in this way! No, evil does not come from hunger, but from love."

The snake said: "No, evil arises neither from hunger nor from love, but from ill-temper. If we lived peacefully, we should not do so much harm; everything would be delightful for us. But now if anything is done to us, we fall into a rage, and then there is nothing gentle about us; we only think about how we can avenge the wrong on some one. We lose control of ourselves and hiss, and try to bite someone. We would not have pity on anyone, we would bite our own father and mother! It seems as if we could eat our own selves. The moment we begin to lose our temper we are undone. All the evil in the world arises from ill-temper."

The Stag said: "No, not from ill-temper, not from love, and not from hunger arises all of the evil in the world, but evil arises from fear. If it were possible for us to live without fear, all would be well with us. We are swift-footed, and have great strength. With our antlers we can defend ourselves from little animals; and we can run from the large ones. But it is impossible to escape fear. If it is only the twigs creaking in the forest, or the leaves rustling, we are all of a tremble with fear, our heart beats, we instinctively start to run, and fly with our might. Another time if a hare runs by or a bird flutters, or a dry twig crackles, and we think it is a wild beast, and in running away we really run into danger. And again we are running from a dog, and we come upon a man. Oftentimes we are frightened and start to flee, we don't know whither, and we roll over a precipice and perish. And we have to sleep with one eye open, with one ear alert, and we are always in alarm. There is no peace. All evil comes from fear."

Then the Hermit said: "Not from hunger, not from love, not from ill-temper, nor from fear come all of our troubles. But all of the evil in the world is due to our different natures. Hence come hunger and love, ill-temper and fear."

★

As with many Native American parables, or those of Greek origin, this Tolstoy fable uses anthropomorphic discourse to get to the heart of human nature. Here, as with the Greek adage "Know Thyself," we discover that we cannot presume to fix the evils of the world until we are first aware of our own deficiencies. Or, as Jesus once said, "First, remove the log that is in your own eye and then you can see clearly to remove the splinter that is in your brother's eye."

But we can rarely find the log.

Evil does arise from many sources—but all somehow reside within the human heart and condition. Perhaps this is why the "seven deadly sins" are ever present or, as classical Buddhist thought teaches, we must first empty before we can fill.

This beautiful story can refresh, however, with its playful and helpful insights about human inclination. There is enough diversity in hunger, love, ill-temper, and fear to keep us busy with ourselves for a long time.

The Comb (Kriloff)

A mother once bought a comb for her son. The boy loved his comb so much that he carried it with him wherever he went. He reached for his comb the first thing every morning and he carried it to bed at night. He carried it to the playground when he was at school. And he carried it home. But most of all, the boy loved his comb because it slid through his dark, slick hair so easily.

Then one day the boy mislaid his comb. He looked for his comb at home. He searched for his comb as school. But he could not find it.

Gradually his hair became tangled. But he had not noticed.

Then one day the boy found his comb. He was overjoyed. But has soon as he slid the comb through his hair tears came to his eyes. The boy was nearly pulling his hair out by the roots. He screamed at his comb, "What a worthless comb you are!" But the comb replied, "Why do you blame me? I am the same comb I always was. It is your own hair that has become tangled."

★

People have a strong tendency to pass the buck. We look for fault in others before we will look for fault in ourselves. The ability to look critically at oneself is a sign of maturity. Self-analysis is crucial for growth. And more importantly, the ability to gauge our strengths as well as our weaknesses is the first step in success.

This brief parable is also about neglect and the proclivity in the human condition to procrastinate or to cease practicing those disciplines that have been good to us. We can so easily make messes of our lives by overlooking the necessary practices that will produce the very goodness we seek. One shouldn't be surprised to find a tangled and messy life when apathy, neglect, and sloth are the highest aspirations. This would be true in work, marriage, parenting, or any walk of life.

In order to thrive one must live in the consistency of healthy practices. Or, as the maxim suggests: "Oh, what a tangle web we weave . . ."

On Being Truly Dead (Desert Fathers)

Two old men were talking one day. One said to the other: "I have died to the world." The other said, "Don't be so sure that you have died until you are really dead, for evil may still be present within you."

★

Over the first four centuries of the church, as people began migrating to large Christian centers such as Rome and Alexandria, there was a counter movement to refresh the church. This movement, often known as the Desert Fathers (but there were women and families, too), involved a Christian migration to the desert regions of Egypt (and also to regions in Syria) in the fourth and fifth centuries. The Desert Fathers also left behind a tremendous collection of oral teachings—later written down in Latin and Greek—that involved tales of the saints, teachings of the elders, and playful parables and stories that were meant to illuminate aspects of Christian devotion.

Much like the Sufi tradition and the wonderful tales told and re-told by the Sufi masters, the Desert Fathers corpus is a marvel to read. Moreover, the insights and applications found among the Desert Fathers corpus is remarkably fresh and contemporary, even timeless. These tales also possess a familiar ring to them, even a pliability, which people of all faiths and persuasions find helpful or meaningful.

Here, in this brief teaching, we discover a heart of helpfulness. Often, in one's pursuit for holiness, one discovers that such an austere spiritual undertaking is not as it appears. Regardless of one's faith—a person always brings his/her brokenness, failures, and weaknesses into the pursuit of the divine. Indeed, we are ever children of need and weakness—and no matter how strong we are or are revered, these broken places remain.

The Wisdom of Elders (Buddhist)

Many centuries ago there was a country which had the particular custom of abandoning its aged people on a remote mountain.

But a certain member of the State could not bring himself to follow this custom in regard to his own father. He could not bear the thought of abandoning his father in his old age. And so, in order to be a good son, he built a secret underground cave for his father and continued to care for him there.

One day the king of this country had a dream. He became vexed in spirit because in his dream he saw an approaching army that would destroy his country if he could not answer a riddle. The riddle was: There were two serpents—but how can one tell the sex of each?

Neither the king nor the wise men of the palace knew the answer, and so the king offered a reward to anyone in the kingdom who could solve the riddle.

The good son went to his father who was hiding in the cave and posed the riddle to him. The man's father said, "The answer to the riddle is simple. Place the two snakes on a soft rug. The snake that moves about is the male. The serpent that remains in one place is the female." Immediately the man returned to the palace of the king and revealed the answer.

In the weeks that followed, the king had other dreams with other riddles. But in each instance the king and the court sages could not answer them. But the good son, after consulting with his father, was able to solve every one.

Among the riddles that the old father solved were these:

Who is the one who, being asleep, is called the awakened one? And who, being awake, is called the sleeping one? The answer is: the one who is seeking Enlightenment.

How can you weigh an elephant? The answer is: load the elephant into a boat and mark a line where it sinks into the water. Then take out the elephant, and begin filling the boat with stones until you read the line. Weigh the stones and you have the weight of the elephant.

What is the meaning of the saying: A cupful of water is more than the water of the ocean? The answer: A cupful of water given in compassion abides for eternity, but the water of the ocean will one day come to an end.

Eventually the king asked the man how he always knew the answers to the riddles. The man told the king, "I receive the answers from my father, who is an elder of the people." This answer pleased the king so much that he gave a new decree that all of the elders should be brought home and no longer abandoned in the mountains.

★

It has been said that any people who lose a respect for their elders will soon lose their history and their soul. The memories of the old are like a path for the young, and without the past to guide the future, mistakes are bound to be repeated.

The Buddha nature is one of understanding the cyclical nature of life—a path of dying and rebirth which is far more than physical or existential. Rather, it is also memory that can shape the present need. The wisdom of the past is continually recycled into present.

The writer of Ecclesiastes once noted, "There is nothing new under the sun."

Indeed, even the latest inventions and ideas are in many ways recycled, or at least conceived upon the foundation of past knowledge and advancement. No people can afford to abandon the past. Doing so imperils the future.

Everyone needs to embrace the lessons and wisdom of their elders—and then pass this hope along to the young.

The Mountain and the Squirrel (Ralph Waldo Emerson)

The Mountain and the Squirrel
Had a quarrel,
And the former called the latter "Little Prig";
Bun replied,
"You are doubtless very big;
But all sorts of things and weather
Must be taken together,
To make up a year
And a sphere.
And I think it not disgrace
To occupy my place.
If I'm not so large as you,
You are not so small as I,
And not half so spry,
I'll not deny you make
A very pretty squirrel track;
Talents differ; all is well and wisely put;
If I cannot carry forests on my back,
Neither can you crack a nut."

★

Ralph Waldo Emerson, though not known as a teller of fables, was a moralist and philosopher. In this moralistic poem Emerson makes the necessary point that all have differing gifts. Some have gifts that are noticeable, monumental even, while others have gifts, nonetheless important, that are small but considerable to the good of the whole. It's a common nut—but one that folks have been cracking for a long time.

For Everything a Time (Bible)

I realized that there is nothing better for mortals than to eat and drink and find enjoyment in the labor. After all, for everything there is a season, and there is a time for every matter under heaven.

There is a time to be born, and a time to die;
A time to plant, and a time to be planted;
A time to kill, and a time to heal;
A time to discourage, and a time to encourage;
A time to weep, and a time to laugh;
A time to mourn, and a time to dance;
A time to throw stones, and a time to collect them;
A time to hug, and a time to part;
A time to seek, and a time to lose;
A time to keep, and a time to throw away;
A time to tear cloth, and a time to sew it;
A time to be silent, and a time to speak up;
A time to love, and a time to hate;
A time for war, and a time to make peace.
(Ecclesiastes 2:24, 3:1–8)

★

This familiar poem in the book of Ecclesiastes represents a parabolic teaching on the meaning of life and is reminiscent of the equally familiar Proverbs of the Bible. This wisdom tradition makes up the last third of the Hebrew Scriptures (Torah, Prophets, and *Writings*). The point of this poem has little to do with thinking about life as a series of choices, but is, rather, an observation about the ebb and flow of the natural eddies of life. All of these seasons are experienced, with the point being that, given all things as equal, we would usually prefer one over the other. It helps to be aware of one's surroundings, of course—and in the course of time, make those choices that are built upon the wisdom of the ages and for the common good.

A Swallow and a Spider (Abstemius)

A spider was watching a swallow catching flies. Being jealous of the bird's agility and the ease at which it caught its prey, the spider hatched the brilliant scheme to capture the bird in her web. She worked diligently spinning a web that she believed would ensnare the bird and prohibit it from catching the flies. But the swallow was too large, too fast and too strong, and easily broke through the spider's web. When the spider saw the folly of her scheme she said to herself: "I perceive that bird-catching is not my talent." And with that thought she returned to spinning webs that would catch flies.

★

Laurentius Abstemius, an Italian writer of the sixteenth century, was a fabulist and critic during the time of Pope Alexander VI. Like Phaedrus many centuries before him, Abstemius was keen on using the fables of Aesop as his template, even as he spun his own fables to teach morality lessons and offer under-handed criticisms of the church—especially the clergy.

Many of these fables—such as the one above—embody animals with anthropomorphic attributes as a teaching tool. Here, we see how the question of purpose comes into play. And the lesson here seems to be the futility of trying to accomplish a purpose that is beyond our means. A person is best served in discovering one's gifts and using those gifts well ... instead of trying to accomplish an improbable task, which leads to a life of futility. Why should one sing if one is not a singer? Why should one teach if one is not a teacher? Not all plans are worthy of our energies.

Cultivation (Confucian)

A disciple asked Confucius about the cultivated person. Confucius said, "Cultivate yourself by seriousness."

The disciple asked, "Is that all?"

Confucius said, "Cultivate yourself to make others secure."

The disciple asked, "Is that all?"

Confucius said, "Cultivate yourself to make all people secure. Even the sage-kings had trouble cultivating themselves enough to make all people secure."

★

Like the Buddhist cycle of life, Confucian thought advances the idea of foundational knowledge—a wisdom that, once built and realized, should be used for the good of humanity. Knowledge that harms or is horded by individuals is not wisdom. Wisdom is the knowledge this cannot be kept to oneself, but must be shared by all for the common good.

The Birds Elect a King (Pilpay)

One day an assortment of birds flocked together to elect a king and, since every species of bird present preferred its own persuasion, they were soon deep in argument. But when one bird nominated the owl—a species that some regarded as wisest but others as ugly—a fight broke out. The birds began clawing and pecking at each other until a new bird happened to fly into the mix and shout, "Enough of this! No more civil war! Why are we so eager to spill each other's blood over arguments? Come, let us elect a king who can serve as a judge over us. See, here is a buzzard flying overhead now. Let us elect him as king."

When the other birds heard this they unanimously elected the buzzard as king. But when the buzzard landed in the middle of the flock and realized what had happened it said, "Are you out of your minds? Why would you elect me to be your king—a species that lives upon the misfortunes of others? That's like electing a housefly to lead when you could have a Griffin. Shouldn't you, rather, have elected a bird like the Falcon, who is well-known for his courage and agility? Or how about the Peacock, who is at least makes a good appearance and carries the stars in its tail? Or wouldn't you have done better to elect the Eagle, the symbol of royalty? And if there were no such birds as these that I have just named who are willing to serve, than surely it would be better for you to have no king at all than to subject your-selves to a buzzard like me. Indeed, why would you grant power to one who will merely feast upon your misfortunes, fly above you while searching for opportunities to serve himself, and in the end, consume your own carcasses? Would it not be better for all concerned to have no king at all?"

★

Pilpay is the traditional author or translator of a collection of fables—originally written in Sanskrit—perhaps as early as the fourth century (India). These fables, as a collection entitled the "Panchatantra," are predominantly populated with animals and are much in the vein of Aesop or Phaedrus. Pilpay's work, however, migrates more easily into contemporary themes, and as the story above illustrates, can easily address the political attitudes of our own times—even strikingly so as one considers the wide dichotomy of political fire-branding evi-denced across a wide swath of cultures and nations. Indeed, as many political cartoons have illustrated through the centuries, the buzzard has become associated with the political arena and kings, presidents, and other leaders have, at one time or another, all worn the animated crown of scavenger.

Aside from the obvious political branding, however, this fable could also cross over into other worlds—even businesses and religious organizations—and could address the difficulties inherent in finding capable leaders who are not first and foremost focusing upon themselves. Eventually, as Pilpay would have it, the masses might actually come to the conclusion that no leader is better than a bad one.

Competition (Confucian)

The Master once said, "Gentlemen, never compete. You will say that in archery the do so. But even then they bow and make way for one another when they are going up to the archery ground, when they are coming down, and in the subsequent drinking-bout. Thus even when competing, they still remain gentlemen."

★

Since the spirit of competition runs high in modern times, this simple teaching of Confucius may bring some elasticity and common sense to the conversation. It is true that life is filled with many competitive endeavors, but it is equally true that many of these are corporate and team pursuits.

As Confucius taught, the competition itself is not the most important ingredient—but cooperation, mutual concern, and friendship. Often, we see how the sharing of knowledge and teaching benefits the whole, and can even improve the teacher. Being a mentor and having the ability to articulate one's expertise and craft to the young is an important aspect of learning. Likewise, those who are being apprenticed by the veteran need to have a heart of humility, which makes all learning possible. Whether it be business or community affairs, there is an attitude that serves the common good. Wise people look for this middle way that can lift the whole of the organization or the community. Without cooperation, much is lost. And, at the heart of all business relationships and success lies friendship. This is the true measure of achievement.

Oh, Rats! (Ambrose Bierce)

A rat that was about to emerge from his hole caught a glimpse of a Cat waiting for him, and descending to the colony at the bottom of the hole invited a Friend to join him in a visit to a neighboring corn-bin. "I would have gone alone," he said, "but could not deny myself the pleasure of such distinguished company."

"Very well," said the Friend, "I will go with you. Lead on."

"Lead?" exclaimed the other. "What! *I* precede so great and illustrious a rate as you? No, indeed—after you, sir, after you."

Pleased with this great show of deference, the Friend went ahead, and, leaving the hole first, was caught by the Cat, who trotted away with him. The other went out unmolested.

★

Ambrose Bierce, known primarily for his US Civil War era stories, was also a fabulist. Here he offers a rather humorous expose of a false helpfulness—a faux humility that borders on the exploitative. In business relationships, especially, it may be wise to test the waters of invitation. Some open doors may actually lead to traps.

Good Neighbors (Yiddish)

After King Philip of France ordered all Jews to leave the country (year 1311), there was a wealthy dealer in precious stones who entrusted his entire fortune—all of his precious stones—to the care of a Christian neighbor. The Jewish man thought, "Some day, the decree may be lifted and I will be able to return to my treasure."

The Christian neighbor promised to guard the Jewish man's possessions until his return. They parted. And the Jewish man took his family and the clothes on his back into exile.

Years passed, and eventually King Philip died. When his son ascended to the throne he revoked the decree of his father and allowed the Jews to return to France. The first thing the returning Jew did was look up his Christian neighbor in the hope that he had guarded this treasure well. But the Jewish man was heartbroken when he learned that his Christian neighbor had fallen on hard times some years before and had lost all of his worldly goods. Friends related that the Christian man had moved to the outskirts of the city and was very ill.

The Jewish man went to look for his friend and eventually found him in a small hovel, little more than a shelter, without any worldly comforts. The only thing that the Christian man possessed was a large trunk.

The Jewish man said, "I have returned, but there is no doubt that, since you have lost everything you owned, and have become gravely ill, you most certainly sold the precious stones long ago."

"On the contrary," the Christian man said, "I have guarded your treasure with my life. Although there were times when I thought that life was not worth living, and I even thought about killing myself, I nevertheless endured for the sake of your treasure. See, it is all inside this chest, just as you entrusted it to me."

The Jewish man said, "But why didn't you sell the stones and care for yourself?"

The Christian man said, "Because the stones did not belong to me. I had to keep my promise."

The Jewish man was moved and said, "It was a good thing that you endured and did not take your own life. But your hard days are over. You are my brother and half of my possessions belong to you."

So the Jew and his Christian brother lived side by side, as it once was, in everlasting friendship and love.

★

A beautiful story that speaks to Jewish–Christian relations, yes—but in the center we glimpse into the deeper truths evident in respect, honor, and concern among those who profess a faith in God. Even though there may not be a shared doctrine, there can still be love and peace—which is a core of belief and conduct of life. Likewise, as the old adage goes: Whoever knows one religion doesn't know any.

Friendship and conversation among people of faith only serves to foster understanding and an appreciation for one's own heritage. When people of faith are free to live out their own path, this is peace. We need not have to change another person to honor the individual. Being faithful to one's own beliefs is the beginning of understanding one another. And when two people look for the common threads in faith they will always find some.

The Buddha taught that there was a Middle Way. Jesus spoke of the narrow path. And the Tao offers yet another avenue among the many.

If we look deeply enough, we can discover where these paths cross, where they intersect. There in the middle is the way that leads to peace.

The Three Philosophers (Bierce)

A bear, a fox, and an opossum were attacked by a flood.

"Death loves a coward," said the Bear, and went forward to fight the flood.

"What a fool!" said the Fox. "I know a trick worth two of that." And he slipped into a hollow stump.

"There are malevolent forces," said the Opossum, "which the wise will neither confront nor avoid. The thing is to know the nature of your antagonist."

So saying the Opossum lay down and pretended to be dead.

★

This insightful parable—told by American short-story writer Ambrose Bierce—offers the kind of frontier wisdom and humor evidenced by the mid-nineteenth century philosophies that, later, writers like Mark Twain would exploit into full-blown satire. Here we find a parable that demonstrates the all-too-human approach to tragedy. Some people prefer to fight a difficulty head-on, others prefer to flee (or ignore), and still others are quite content to allow the problem to have its own way. The outcomes may be the same, but the approaches are quite different—and in the course of human drama, make all the difference in the world.

We are rarely so satisfied with ourselves as when we make a decision in the midst of hardship. Although choices are rarely cut from clarity and certainty, we nevertheless have to make choices that often have long-standing consequences. The point of the parable is to choose wisely—or to at least follow one's own natural path. Every person has a center from which he or she makes decisions—whether it be a philosophy, a theology, or a vision. But relationships are most important—and we can rarely go wrong when we make our choices from the heart.

The Earthquake (Traditional)

A wolf was pursuing a deer and, just as the wolf was about to seize its prey, an earthquake opened a deep chasm between the two. The wolf, sizing up the situation, said, "I refuse to recognize this inconvenience." At this word the wolf resumed the chase and, attempting to leap the chasm, fell headlong into it.

★

Sometimes we fail to recognize that missed opportunities in life may actually help us toward some greater end. We can often learn more from failure than success. By refusing to recognize these lapsed opportunities we often try to stay a course that is going nowhere. Some paths eventually lead to dead ends. But we can learn from those who have blazed the trails before us.

We should always allow a failure to instruct us. Indeed, each one has its lessons. And regardless of our age or station in life, we can continue to learn the lessons these teach.

The Ladder of Charity (Jewish)

According to Maimonides there are eight degrees of charity. They are:

1. Giving . . . but giving that is not from the heart. It is of the head only.
2. Giving cheerfully, but not proportional to the degree of the one who suffers.
3. Giving cheerfully and proportionally, but not unless asked to give.
4. Giving cheerfully, proportionally and without being asked, but placing the gift in the beggar's hand so to shame him.
5. Giving in such a way that the poor will know the person who gave the gift, but not have to interact with the one who gives—giving anonymously.
6. Giving in such a way that the person who gives is not aware of whom he is giving to—so that the recipient is anonymous.
7. Giving in such a way that both benefactor and recipient are anonymous.
8. Giving in order to prohibit poverty in the first place—by either providing employment to the marginalized, gifting or loaning money without interest, teaching a trade, establishing a business, or providing the means by which a person may earn a decent living. This latter is the fulfillment of the scriptures where it says: *If your brother has become poor or fallen upon hard times, you will support him, even if he is a stranger or a foreigner, and he will live with you.* (Leviticus 25:35)

★

There are many ways to remember truths, and creating lists is one way. Here, we discover that charity (and older word for "love" that encapsulates also the essence of generosity and concern for others) is not always as it appears. With each successive stage of charity, the heart grows larger, as does the intent and will. Charity at its lowest is simply giving money. But at the highest stage we see that charity is about giving ourselves to a greater cause.

Time, talent, treasure: these three constitute the triad of charitable work.

The Golden Rule (Jewish)

Once, a heathen came to Rabbi Shammai and said, "I would gladly accept the Jewish faith if you can teach me the entire Torah while standing on one foot."

Shammai became incensed at this request, picked up a ruler, and drove the man from his home.

Next, the heathen went to see Rabbi Hillel. He said, "I would gladly accept the Jewish faith if you can teach me the entire Torah while standing on one foot."

Although Shammai was wrathful, Hillel was gentle. He stood on one foot and said, "Don't do to others what you don't want them to do to you. This is the entire Torah. Everything else is commentary. Go and live it!"

"Do unto others, as would have others do unto you." (Jesus)

★

Much has been made through the centuries of the variety of this "golden rule" and the similarities of the teaching found in most faith traditions. There are variances, certainly, but a core of principle that can lead one to see that this is more than a religious precept, but a human one. There are few (if any) practices that, if taken to heart, would produce a much greater life.

Hillel's Piety (Jewish)

It has been noted that Rabbi Hillel was a gentle and pious man. Once, when his disciples were studying at the Rabbi's house, one disciple noted that Hillel used very little water to wash his hands before meals. The disciple asked, "Rabbi, why are you so stingy with the water?"

Hillel answered, "We should always strive for piety. But how can I accept this piety at the expense of making my servant girl work harder?"

★

This beautiful legend about Hillel speaks to true religion—which is helpfulness and respect for others . . . especially those who serve. Jesus taught many of these same ideas. Loving the neighbor. Praying for the enemy. Serving the hungry, the naked, the imprisoned. All of these demonstrate helpfulness to humanity even if born from a heart of faith and charity.

The principle that Hillel was after was simply this: Be aware of others first, show respect, and true piety will flow from the inside. We are washed clean by action and attitude, never by water alone.

The Prayer of the Pure Land (Tibetan Book of the Dead)

There is an obstacle in the path of liberation. Don't look upon it, and abandon all hate. Don't cling to it. Don't long for it. Have faith in the dazzlingly bright white light. Aim your intense willpower toward Lord Vajrasattva and make the following prayer:

Alas! When I roam the life cycle driven by strong hate,
May the Lord Vajrasattva lead me on the path
Of the dear light of the mirror wisdom!

•82•

May his Consort Buddhalochana back me on the way,
Deliver me from the dangerous straits of the between,
And carry me to perfect Buddhahood!

By praying in this way with intense faith, you will dissolve into rainbow light in the heart of Vajrasattva and you will go to the Pure Land.

★

The Tibetan Book of the Dead is an instruction book for the dead or the dying. Filled with vision, light and prayers, portions of this guide are often incanted over the deceased. Not all religions include rituals for the dying, but there are Last Rites in the Catholic Church and most cultures have words or practices offered after death that are meant to affirm the deceased and comfort the grieving. Among the prayers of the Tibetan Book of the Dead are those meant to guide the deceased into the Pure Land of light and peacefulness. These are nearly universal themes, and often in the prayers for the dead and the dying we are taught how to live. We can never love someone to death—but we can love them to life . . . and this is the greater choice. The pure light awaits those who live in full awareness of this joy.

The Little Parrot (Buddhist)

Centuries ago the Buddha was born as a little parrot. He flew among the trees, greeted the other creatures, and lived peacefully in his forest home. His one and only desire was to be of help to the other creatures of the forest.

One day, however, the little parrot noticed that the skies were growing dark. Soon smoke filled the air and great plumes of fire rose from the forest. The little parrot was distressed, thinking about all of the creatures of the forest who could not escape the raging flames. He loved his companions and he wanted to save them. Flying back and forth over the forest, the little parrot tried to warn all of the other creatures about the fire. But the flames were high and the winds were shifting—the creatures of the forest were confused and they could not escape.

Flying to a nearby river the little parrot dipped its beak and wings into the water and then flew back over the fire. As it struggled to see through the clouds of smoke it shook its wings, sending tiny drops of water down through the heat like shimmering jewels. Although the little parrot hoped that the drops of water might fall upon one of the creatures and provide relief from the heat, the drops were so small that they evaporated almost instantaneously before they reached the ground of the forest.

Nevertheless, the little parrot continued to return to the river. Time and again it dipped its wings into the water then flew back over the flames and shook its wings. As the parrot continued to do this, the parrot was also becoming black with soot and its wings were getting seared. Still, the little parrot did not relent from its concern for the creatures of the forest. The parrot continued to dive into the river and then send tiny drops of water into the flames.

Now it happened that many of the gods were watching this little parrot from their heavenly abode. The gods began to laugh at the futility of this little parrot as they watched it dart back and forth across the flames, shaking its wings to loosen even the tiniest drops of water. But one of the gods was moved by the compassion of the little parrot and decided to help.

Taking the form of a golden eagle, the god appeared at the forest fire. The eagle's wings were much larger than the little parrot's and its eyes were large and penetrating. When the little parrot flew back to the river for yet another futile attempt, the eagle said, "Your cause is hopeless, little bird. Fly away and save yourself."

But the little parrot did not listen to the eagle, but continued to fly over the flames and loosen the tiny drops of water over the fire. When the eagle saw that the little parrot would not relent from its task, the god was moved by the compassion of the parrot. The eagle could see the gods above reclining in their ease, enjoying their wonderful food, and the eagle felt a great strength from its privilege. So it decided to help the parrot.

Flying to the river, the giant eagle followed the little parrot's lead and dipped its wings in the water. But when the eagle returned to shake its wings over the flames, it was like a heavy rain. The water continued to pour from the eagle's wings, moistening the forest floor and extinguishing the flames. As the eagle flew over the forest the flames were reduced to smoke and eventually the creatures of the forest were saved. The little parrot was overjoyed. Soon after, the eagle disappeared and the god returned to his heavenly abode.

One more time the little parrot flew to the river, but this time when it returned with water on its wings, something amazing happened. When the little parrot shook its wings and the tiny drops of water descended to the scorched floor of the forest, grass and plants began to spout up from where the water landed.

A great cry rose up from the forest, "Hurray, hurray for the little parrot!" The little parrot returned to the forest once again, living in peace with the creatures it had saved.

★

In many early Buddhist texts the Buddha takes various forms to demonstrate the nature of compassion. Among the many teachings of the Buddha, helpfulness is a primary goal.

Consider also the early Buddhist teachings about the Buddha nature:

Buddha does not always appear as a Buddha. Sometimes he appears as an incarnation of evil, sometimes as a woman, a god, a king, or a statesman. Sometimes the Buddha appears in a brothel or a gambling house. So Buddha's mercy and compassion flow out in endless life, bringing salvation to people. The world is like a burning house or a forest fire—forever being destroyed and rebuilt. Thus, everyone must be dependent upon the Buddha's mercy and compassion. Buddha is father and mother to the world.

The Legend of Babushka (Russian)

Years ago lived an elderly woman named Babushka. She resided in a small Russian village. She was poor and lonely and spent her days carting wood and watching the caravans that passed along the roads on their way to the cities.

One evening in the dark of winter Babushka was sitting at home by the fire when she heard a strange noise echoing through the valley. It sounded like sleigh bells—but as she listened she realized that the sound was unlike anything she had heard before. The sound grew louder, and eventually Babushka opened her door and peered outside. Flecks of snow fell upon her face. She squinted into the moonlight. And there, coming up the road were three men who were riding on tall, humped beasts. Babushka had heard of camels, but had never seen one, and when the entourage stopped in front of her house she was startled by the presence of the three men. They dismounted from their camels and strode toward her door.

From the looks of them, Babushka could tell that the men were royalty. They wore elaborate robes and were adorned with gold. They introduced themselves. "We saw your light," they said, "and we were hoping to warm ourselves by your fire before we set out again on our journey."

"Where are you going?" Babushka asked.

"We are searching for a child," the kings said. "We have seen a star announcing his birth. The child is a king. And we wish to honor him with gifts and adoration."

Babushka invited the kings into her home, fed them, and listened to their stories about their arduous journey across the barren fields in search of the child. When the kings were ready to depart, they said, "We invite you to come with us, Babushka. Come join us in our search for the child."

But Babushka was old and she was afraid. She declined the invitation and watched the men as they packed their gifts and saddled their camels. Minutes later, they disappeared in the snowstorm.

That night Babushka was troubled. She dreamed of the child and grew despondent wishing that she had left her home and travelled with the kings as they followed the star.

The next morning Babushka packed a basket. She filled it with cakes and candies and her small gifts and decided that she would make her own journey in search of the child. Later that day she set out.

And legend has it that Babushka is still searching for the child to this day. If you listen closely enough, sometimes you can hear her outside a child's bedroom. She is still asking, "Is this the Christ child?" And sometimes children can still see Babushka in the form of an old lady who brings gifts in her basket, and places the gifts outside the home, as she is still following the star and searching for the newborn king.

★

This delightful legend has been retold in various forms through the years and is one of the most beloved of the Christmas legends in Russia. As with most legends of Christmas—whether they be related to St. Nicholas or the visitation of angels—the legend of Babushka relates the birth of Jesus in a way that children can understand, and it invites a spirit of giving.

While Christmas has always dressed itself in a variety of cultural attire, the central message of the gift of the Christ child has remained unchanged. The spirit of giving is also a spirit of hope. When we seek God's gifts first then we are made all the more generous through the generosity of God.

The Babushka legend is one that easily travels across time and culture, and regardless of one's faith, can inspire us to see the image of God in each other. This is what the word "incarnation" means—and when we believe that each person is made in the image of God we cannot easily dismiss the common humanity and experiences shared by all. If we are seeking God then we will often recognize the Christ in each other, and we may also discover that we have become the hands, feet, and voice of Christ himself.

Chapter Three

The Path of Humility

Humility is the Queen without whom none can checkmate the Divine King.
—Teresa of Avila

The baboon is a climber, but does not forget that he can fall.
—South African Proverb

There are many ways that we can respond to success in life. Success can be flaunted, even demonstrated so that others cannot miss the point. Success can be articulated in lofty and self-aggrandized words. Success can be made visible to the point that others are no longer inspired, but deflated.

Success can also be starved. And this is humility.

Humility and success, after all, go hand in hand. One who achieves greatness or good fortune has many choices. Like the baboon, we may climb very high in life—but it is best to remember that we can also fall. Or, as the old adage goes: *The bigger they are, the harder they fall.*

Here we can encounter many stories and parables about great success—but also the meaning behind humility. Humility is never just one way. Just as the Desert Fathers tradition in Christianity contains many fascinating legends about humble leaders, likewise there are many Sufi tales of mystics and famous personalities who have learned the gentle art of self-sacrifice. We can also see humility in the examples of contemporaries in many faiths and cultures. And there are legends that demonstrate the importance of humility and offer readers the opportunity to learn how to practice it.

Of course, one of the difficulties in studying humility is that humble people do not draw attention to themselves. As soon as one gains a glimpse of their achievements, they seem to vanish like the sun hiding behind a cloud. Humble people rarely tell their own stories. Rather, these insights are reserved for others—for those who have followed or studied the lives of the saints and the greatest leaders. This is, in part, where legend originates. These come later, after the fame has died away and the leaders have passed.

It may also seem ironic to study humility. After all, humility may also become a vice. "See how humble I am," is a mantra that can lead one down a path of self-deception.

Here the reader can encounter just enough humility, perhaps, to flee the other possibilities. It may be enough to bask in the glow of victory without flaunting it. Or perhaps we can look back and take note of our successes with a greater appreciation for them. This is gratitude. And gratitude is not far from humility. When one is thankful for the blessings, and realizes their true source, humility comes more naturally. We have not, after all, created a single day of our lives or created a single beautiful flower. These are reserved for a higher power. And in recognition we may find ourselves bending the knee.

The Shared Sacrifice (Upanishads)

Once, when Citra Gangayani was preparing to perform a sacrifice, he selected the priest, Aruni, to preside. Now Aruni had a son, Sveyaketu, who was in training. The father sent his son to perform the sacrifice.

But when Citra came to the temple to offer his sacrifice and noticed that the presiding priest was a young man he asked, "Tell me, are you sending me to a world that has closed doors, or will I have a path out? What if you send me to the wrong place?"

The young priest replied, "I am not sure how to answer your questions, I will have to ask my father and teacher."

The young priest returned to his father and repeated the concerns expressed by Citra. "What should I tell him," the apprentice asked.

The father said, "Even I do not know the answers to these questions. But let us return to the altar and offer our vedic recitations together."

Near the altar the father, Aruni, was carrying an armload of firewood. Citra was still there, awaiting an answer. Aruni came to him and said, "I present myself as your pupil."

Citra then said to him, "You have proven yourself worthy of the truth of Brahman, for you have not succumbed to pride. I accept the mentorship and will help you to find the way clearly."

★

Effective leaders need to possess humility. Why? Because without humility leaders cannot learn. The very heart of education is the willingness to accept new ideas, to be open to new concepts, to be coached. Spiritual leaders, in particular, may be susceptible to pride. For any faith, spiritual leaders may fall prey to the belief that they already possess the answers, that there is no need for further learning.

Everyone should have both a mentor and an apprentice. A mentor teaches us the path of humility, providing a forum to ask questions, to explore. An apprentice is needed so that we can teach the young and pass along our accumulation of knowledge. This is the yin and yang of humility.

Folded Hands (From *The Art of Happiness*)

The Dalai Lama removed his glasses, folded his hands in his lap, and remained motionless in meditation.

At the close of the session that day, as always, the Dalai Lama folded his hands together, bowed to his audience out of affection and respect, rose, and made his way through the surrounding crowd. His hands remained clasped together and he continued to bow as he left the room. As he walked through the dense crowd he bowed so low, in fact, that for anyone who stood more than a few feet away, it was impossible to see him. He appeared to be lost in a sea of heads. From a distance one could still detect his path, however, from the subtle shift in the crowd's movement as he passed along. It was as if he had ceased to be a visible object and had simply become a felt presence.

★

Humility is an art. It must be practiced.

In essence, humility is the ability to make ourselves "disappear," to become part of the larger whole, not the focus of our own desires, illusions, and cravings. This modern day story of the Dalai Lama demonstrates how folded hands and the posture of the body can be an indication of our willingness to recognize each other. When we turn our backs, look away from someone who is speaking to us, or generally seek to be the center of attention, we do not recognize the importance or value of the other person. And we all know what it feels like to be ignored or dismissed.

The humble heart is a seeking heart. Humility calls us to recognize the best in each other, and to, if for only a moment, recognize another person's presence and focus our attention on that face, that life, that need.

The Sower and the Seeds (Jesus)

A sower went out to the field to scatter seed. As he sowed, some seeds fell along unfurrowed rows, and the birds came and devoured them up. Some seed fell on rocks, and because they couldn't take root, when the sun came up, the seeds were scorched and they withered and died.

Still other seeds fell among thorns, but the thorns consumed all of the nutrients in the soil and the seeds could not grow. And then some seeds fell on fertile soil. These took root and brought forth their grain—some producing a hundred bushels, others sixty bushels, and others thirty. Whoever can hear this parable will understand. (Matthew 13: 3-9)

★

This parable of Jesus—very likely a common thread of story told by many rabbis of the first century—offers a glimpse of the common among the hillsides of Galilee and a teaching tapestry from which one may begin to understand the nature and difficulties of becoming a servant of God. There is much in life that can distract a person from being a disciple. Yes, there are worries and cares, but there are also the seductions of life—the alluring lights that seem so promising. One could create an entire commentary out of this simple parable, and that is exactly what the early church did.

But in its original form, the parable may have pointed out the disparities present in life and the hardships that often detract from the call. The path that the Buddha taught was called the "Middle Way," and was a call to eschew the extremes of life (neither right nor left, neither conservative nor liberal). Too much of any good thing creates an imbalance in life that can prove thorny. It is important to approach life with both a resiliency and a modicum of high opinion. Seeds must take root and grow. The beginnings of any movement are the most important. And when it comes to discipleship, the good soil is complete with nourishment. The best path to God is the simple way of humility and self-sacrifice. God will give the growth. The disciple must be willing to sprout.

Rock, Sand, and Water (Buddhist)

There are three kinds of people in the world. The first kind are like letters carved in rock. These people are easily consumed by anger, hold grudges, and retain their anger for a long time. Other people are like letters written in sand. They give way to anger, too, but their anger soon passes. Still other people are like letters written in running water. They are not influenced by passing thoughts, but allow thoughts of anger, revenge, abuse and gossip to pass through their minds unnoticed, for their minds are always pure and undisturbed by negativity.

★

A teaching of the Buddha. Still waters run deep, but stillness is also the ability to live unfazed by the noise and commotion of the world. Among the many teachings of the Buddha, this parable offers us a quiet center. When our lives our filled with too much noise we can lose our selves from too little thought, or we become slaves to the past by holding onto anger and thoughts of revenge. As the Psalmist once said, "Be still, and know that I am God." All faiths contain those practices that draw the faithful to those quiet centers, like a reflective pool, where one can not only see the self more clearly, but also the whole of their experiences. Do not be like rock or sand, the Buddha says, but become as water—allowing the difficulties and anxieties of life to flow across, through, and over the quiet center that remains undisturbed.

The Pumpkin (Lorenzo Pignotti)

A pumpkin plant was lamenting its nature, being required to trellis along the top of the soil for its nourishment and growth. "I must be the most vile of all the plants," it said to itself. "I am always covered with mud. I am ravaged by rain and mildew. I never get to breathe the higher altitudes of the fresh air."

But one day the pumpkin stretched for its tendrils and began to climb up the trunk of a magnificent oak tree. All summer long it climbed higher and higher until, at last, it was at the apex and was able to look down on the rest of the garden. The other plants asked the pumpkin, "How was it possible for you to climb so high?"

After much consideration the pumpkin answered, "I first learned how to thrive on the ground before I learned how to climb to the top."

★

A humble parable from the Italian fabulist, Pignotti, reveals the many lessons born of early experience. Indeed, as is true in the cycle of human life, we first must crawl, and then learn how to walk before we can run. Shooting stars are rare. Most success is gained through trial and error, or through long years of persistence and steady effort. This is the nature of humility and a willingness to learn from one's own weaknesses and errors.

Jesus told the parable about a grain of mustard seed—though smallest of the seeds it grows into an enormous bush. And Buddha also related the many parables about beginning efforts growing into mature discipleship. In the Qur'an we find the words: *Walk not boisterously upon the earth—neither making a hole in the earth nor attaining the mountains for height.*

A steady life of balance and persistence eventually leads to happiness and success.

The Way of Humility (Desert Fathers)

Once there was a hermit who was fasting for some weeks. But during this time he went to visit an old man in the community. While the old man was fixing a meal, several other pilgrims also stopped by. When they all sat down to eat, the man who was fasting took but a single pea off the plate and ate it. Afterwards, when they were alone, the old man took the hermit aside and told him, "My brother, when you go to visit a friend, do not make a show of your way of life. If you are fasting and need to keep to your way, then do not leave your cell. The hermit accepted what the old man said and after that he acted like others when he went to visit friends.

★

The delightful corpus of material attributed to the Desert Fathers—those ascetics who were leaving the cities in the early centuries of the church and traveling to north Africa and Syria—offers much in the way of understanding the path that leads to humility. Fasting, when used outside of the personal and the spiritual, is a sham, and in fact introduces the attitude of pride and demonstration into an action that is meant to produce the opposite effect. Fasting is a deeply personal discipline and is not meant for public display. No wonder the desert fathers made much of it . . . and Jesus spoke of it as well.

The Poodle and the Lion (Bierce)

A lion, seeing a poodle, fell into laughter. "Who ever saw so small a beast?" he said.

"It is true," said the Poodle, with austere dignity, "that I am small; but sir, I beg you to observe that I am all dog."

★

Philosophers and theologians have long pondered the meaning of a "full humanity." What does it mean to be alive? What are the aspects of living a full life?

Although it is easy to fall into the trap of focusing upon one's shortcomings and faults instead of one's strengths, encouragement comes at the point of full realization. Buddhism may refer to this as "enlightenment"—but there are other expressions as well: "Know Thyself," "You shall know the truth, and the truth shall set you free" (Jesus), "To thine ownself be true" (Shakespeare).

This concise parable offers a nugget of truth that may be applied in all walks of life.

The Mouse and the Elephant (Pignotti)

A young mouse had just arrived from studying in Athens where, with its limited brain-power, had required but a smattering of learning. Still, the mouse was proud of its accomplishments and set out to impress the other animals with its wisdom. When the mouse met an elephant it said, "I see that you are a large beast and believe yourself to be superior to me due to your size. But the way I see it, you are actually at a disadvantage. You are slow and sluggish and you have no nimbleness of movement, whereas I am light on my feet and very fast. Your size would also indicate to me that you are lazy and don't possess even a smattering of the intellect that I possess. When I look at you I pity—"

The mouse was still speaking mid-sentence when the elephant, which had grown tired of hearing the mouse's diatribe, squashed the mouse flat.

★

One doesn't have to look too deeply to see the metaphors in this parable. Pride, arrogance, and boasting rarely serve us well. Better yet, if one is going to boast of one's accomplishments and depth of knowledge, it is best to choose the audience wisely. As the old adage goes: *A little learning can be a dangerous thing.*

Anyone who undertakes a spiritual journey (or even an intellectual one) realizes that every new acquisition of knowledge or spiritual insight is accompanied by the realization that one lacks knowledge and spiritual insight. We learn best what we do not know. And if there is any boasting to be done it, this should rest on the laurels of those who have the deeper knowledge.

So often, as this parable implies, we hear the most from those who know the least. Those who have the deepest and most robust knowledge and insights often speak the softest. And whenever one does presume to speak of what one knows, it is best to make sure there are no elephants in the room.

The Eagle and the Bee (Ivan Kriloff)

An eagle was soaring through the air when it noticed, far below, a honeybee flitting about near a flower. The eagle descended to the bee and said, "O how I pity you! For all of your toil and skill you labor all summer long—just like thousands of your kind—to produce honey for the honeycomb. Nothing you do distinguishes you from any of the others, but you labor in obscurity all the days of your life. What a difference there is between us. For I spread my wings and suddenly I am borne upon the winds and I rise far above the other birds. Indeed, I am distinguished above others and there is no other like me."

When the bee heard these words from the eagle it answered, "Yes, there is glory and honor due to you. Indeed, I know no others can rise as high. But I know that my work is for the common good—and I do not attempt to distinguish myself from others. What consoles me is that a few drops of my honey might bring delight to those who taste it."

★

Like Tolstoy, Kriloff articulated the Russian spirit through his many parables. Here, the parable of the honeybee adds a sweetness to the gift of labor—and celebrates all who work for the common good. It is impossible for everyone to fly into the stratosphere of success. Most people, in fact, are content to be contributors to the greater enterprise. This parable also reminds us that there is much that we can accomplish together, which we cannot accomplish as individuals. There can be a joy in daily labor, in the gift of work, that adds not only a sweetness to our own lives, but to the lives of so many others.

Desert Ways (Desert Fathers)

It was Father Isadore who said, "Living without speaking is more beneficial than speaking without living. A person who lives correctly by example adds no more instruction by speaking, while a person who talks to much can often be a bad example. But when words and actions go together, it is the perfect philosophy for life."

Father Poemen once said, "We have all known those who are outwardly silent, but in their hearts they are critical of others. These people are actually talking all the time. But there are those who may talk from sunrise to sunset, but they speak only what is beneficial to others. These are the people who keep the true silence."

Mother Sarah once said, "If I were to pray that all people would be inspired by me, I would soon find myself asking forgiveness from all. So, [instead of praying that I would be an inspiration to others] I pray that I would have a pure heart toward everyone."

The elders used to say: "When we are tested by hardship we become more humble, for God knows our weakness and protects us. But when we are arrogant God removes this protection from us—and then we are most bereft."

A young brother asked an elder: "What is humility?" The elder replied, "Do good to those who have hurt you." The young brother responded, "But what if I can't do this, what then?" The elder said, "Then remove yourself from those who cause you pain and keep your mouth shut."

★

What a wealth of humble advice! In this age of incessant talking, one-ups-man-ship, and power-brokering on social media and in relationships, this sage advice still holds weight. The path of humility is more often paved with silence than with the arrogance of expertise. Those who think they know truth can most effectively convey that truth through action rather than words.

As Saint Francis once said, "Preach the gospel every day. And when necessary, use words."

Appearances (Jesus)

Jesus said, "So when you fast, do not look downcast and hungry like the hypocrites who love for others to know that they are fasting. They already have their reward. But when you fast, wash your face, put oil on your hair, and rest assured that your heavenly Father sees your fasting in secret and will reward you."
(Matthew 6:16–18)

★

A small portion of Jesus's long discourse commonly called *The Sermon on the Mount,* this saying illustrates the inner nature of fasting. Spiritual disciplines cannot work when displayed outwardly as a show of religiosity. In this age of bigger, better, and brighter, the heart of this teaching speaks to all outward forms of religion—organized or not—but especially those manifestations that need large audiences and affirmations to remain legitimate.

The Swan and the Stork (Abstemius)

A stork overheard the song of a dying swan and said to her, "It is contrary to the laws of nature for you to sing so joyously at the end of your life." But the swan replied, "On the contrary, I sing because I am entering another life where I will no longer be in danger of snares, guns or hunger. Who should not sing of such a hope?"

★

Jesus once noted that God takes care of the sparrows—and that people are of much more value than sparrows in the heart of God. This brief fable expresses the Christian hope of life eternal—but at the same time notes that death is a release from the heartaches and entrapments of this life. This is a theme that many faiths affirm—and in this beautiful message of the swan we see a hope that can carry us into peace.

Change of Mind (Hebrew Scriptures)

So when Balaam realized that it pleased the Lord when he blessed Israel, he did not use sorcery as he had in the past, but he journeyed ahead into the wilderness. When Balaam looked out across the valley and saw the tribes of Israel camping there, God's spirit came upon him and he gave this message to Balak the king of Moab:

How fair are you tents, O Jacob.
They appear as groves of palm trees
That stretch like a garden by the river.
Water shall flow from Israel's buckets
And his seed will have an abundance of water.
God brings him out of Egypt like a wild ox
And he breaks the bones of his enemies.
He crouched like a lion, and who would dare rouse him?
Blessed is everyone who blesses you
And cursed is everyone who curses you.

King Balak grew angry when he heard these words and he struck his hands together saying, "I brought you here to curse my enemies but instead, you have blessed them these three times. Go back to your house. I would have rewarded you handsomely, but the Lord has denied this reward by giving you this word."

Then Balaam said, "Didn't your messengers tell you that I couldn't be bribed. Even if you gave me a palace filled with silver and gold I could only say what the Lord tells me." (Numbers 24)

★

This well-known Biblical cycle tells the story of Balaam, a prophet who was at once opposed and supportive of the Jewish people. Prophets have this propensity. But here the prophet changes course (by changing his mind) and sees beauty where, before, he had seen only consternation and trouble.

How sad it would be to truly live a life "of no regrets"—a mantra often heard at retirement speeches, commencement addresses, and celebrations. But as another adage suggests—"the unexamined life is not worth living."

Changes of mind—as well as changes of heart—are essential if one is to grow in knowledge, in spirit, and in influence. A person who becomes entrenched in an unchanging mindset is not necessarily standing firm on principle, but may instead by standing in a stagnant pool. Change is growth. Change is knowledge. But change is difficult.

And the most difficult change of all is when we can see another person (and especially whole communities or peoples) in a new light.

The Snake (Magnus Lichtwer)

There was a snake which loved to bite every animal it met. Naturally, its bite was poisonous and the animals all became sick and died. One day the snake was slithering along when it came to a pool of water. Seeing its own reflection on the glazed surface, it thought it had encountered another snake, and so it bit itself and died.

★

The German fabulist, Lichtwer, here paints an intriguing picture of slander—or the personality who is always gossiping about others. Words can be venomous. Humility is the ability and willingness to be true to oneself. The humble person doesn't build himself up by tearing other people down.

The Wild Apple Tree (Gotthold Lessing)

A wild apple tree was always downcast about its fruit—as its apples were always knotted and holey, and there were few people who ate of it. One summer a swarm of bees made a nest in a hollow place in the tree's trunk and filled it with honey. The tree then became so proud of the sweetness residing in its interior that it began to boast about its fruit.

A nearby rose bush pointed out the obvious: "But is your fruit any better? You have merely a false sweetness, which does not reside in your fruit, as the nature of your apples hasn't changed one bit."

★

Another German fabulist, Lessing uses a common metaphor of fruit to propagate a sweet philosophy about humility. Pride can emerge from many sources within us, even from among the resources we did not create ourselves. Why should one boast about what one did not create? Self-awareness, even of one's limitations, is not a bad gift. One doesn't have to be the best at anything in order to take pride in an accomplishment.

The Promise (Hebrew Scriptures)

In the days when the judges ruled, there was a famine in the land, and a man of Bethlehem in Judah went to live in the country of Moab. The man, Elimelech, and his wife, Naomi, had two sons. The sons eventually married Moabite women—Orpah and Ruth. In time, all of the men died—Elimelech and his sons—and Naomi and her two daughters-in-law were left without husbands.

Naomi decided to return to her home in Judah and so she bid both of her daughters-in-law goodbye, bidding them to return to the mother's homes in Moab. Orpah decided to remain in Moab, but Ruth clung to her mother-in-law and wept. Naomi said to her, "Look, Orpah is returning to her family. You do the same."

But Ruth said, "Please do not force me to leave you. Wherever you go, I'll go; wherever you live, I'll live. From now on your people will be my people and the God you worship will be my God, too. And where you die, I will die—and be buried there, too. I take a vow that I will never be parted from you."

When Naomi saw that Ruth was determined, they went on together to the land of Judah. (Adapted from the book of Ruth)

★

There are many covenants mentioned in the Hebrew Bible. Some are between God and mortals, and others are promises made between people. The book of Ruth—the shortest book in the Hebrew Bible—is a period piece that is at once harrowing and promising. It begins with death but ends with life. What originates as loss is transformed into a greater promise for good.

These words, often used in wedding ceremonies and celebrations, have the ring of the familiar in them, as we have, either in attitude or actuality, often affirmed them. Where there is love there is the journey into the new country of promise—and sometimes even the harshest realities are transformed into beauty. This is what love does. And in and through such experiences we can also discover that we are fulfilling some greater work of God.

The Crusader (Traditional Christian)

There is an ancient tale about a hardened soldier who, during the Crusades, had accepted a wager that he could not carry a flame from the Church of the Holy Sepulcher in Jerusalem back to Paris—an arduous journey. The soldier, in his pride and arrogance, set out from the Church carrying the flaming torch, intent on proving himself to his weaker peers.

For many miles the soldier carried the torch, daring anyone—especially infidels—to stand in his way. In fact, his will was so hardened that he often carried the torch in one hand and his sword in the other, intent on frightening others who encountered him on the road.

One day, as the soldier lumbered along with the flame, it began to storm. Worried that the rain would extinguish the torch, the soldier was pressed to find shelter in a home. After knocking on the door he was aghast, however, to discover that he had arrived at a Muslim home and had to ask his enemies for shelter. He was surprised when the kindly Muslim couple opened their home, invited him in, fed him, and showed him hospitality. The soldier gritted his teeth and accepted their food and lodging, but he set out on his way the next morning at first light, eager to get on his way and travel beyond the territory of the infidels.

He continued with the light, dreaming of his arrival in Paris and the money he would make.

A few days later the soldier grew very weary and hungry in his journey and, after stopping to rest awhile under a shade tree, he suddenly was awakened by a gypsy caravan moving along the road. Seeing the plight of the stranger, the gypsies offered the soldier food and water, and even gave him provisions for several days.

Refreshed and re-energized, the soldier once again set out for Paris, certain that he would soon be among friends and people he recognized. He kept his sword close to his body and the flame stoked high, and as he traveled on he encountered a Jewish man who was begging on the side of the road.

"What are you doing here?" the soldier asked.

"Please, sir," the beggar said, "I have nothing for my family. If there is anything you can spare it will save us."

The soldier, realizing he had few provisions, felt compelled to give the beggar his remaining supply. Paris seemed closer, after all, and the soldier realized that he had been fortunate on his journey thus far. He said goodbye, and then lumbered on toward his destination.

In time the soldier came to a mountainous region. Here he was forced to depend upon a young boy who spoke another language, a child who knew the way through the mountain pass and served as his guide. The soldier, still carrying the flame from the Church in Jerusalem, used the flame to build warming fires by night, and then, in the mornings, he would set out again.

Day after day the soldier journeyed on, and each day, it seemed, he met someone along the road, or someone in a village, who offered him food, shelter, or help of some kind or another. The soldier knew he was getting close to Paris, but now the light itself seemed brighter, and fulfilling his destiny was more important than winning the wager he had set many months before.

Eventually he entered Paris with the torch, holding it high. But his friends did not recognize him. "Where is the man who set out from Jerusalem?" they asked.

"I am the man," the soldier said.

But the soldier did not look the same to his friends, nor did he did not act the same. His mannerisms, his demeanor, his attitude belied his former self, and now instead of the calloused and hardened soldier who had slain so many on the battlefield stood a man who was gentle, kind, and gracious.

The wager was no longer important, for the soldier now carried the light in his heart.

★

Spiritual awakening is the center of faith—becoming the person that God meant for us to be. This theme plays in many forms. To become a

Buddha one must empty. To confess Islam is to submit. To follow Jesus is to be born from above (John 3).

In this traditional parable of transformation and conversion, there sits at the center a journey of the spirit. The light carried becomes the light within. The closed heart becomes the open door. The fist becomes the embrace.

As the traditional maxim suggests, the unexamined life is not worth living.

It is only by stepping outside of our comfort zones, only by welcoming and accepting the new, that we grow in any way. Living among the familiar, the staid, the unyielding only serves to keep us in similar form. Spiritual growth occurs when we grow beyond our smaller selves and must adapt to the larger spirit within.

Just as there is a physical birth, so is there a need for a spiritual birth. In time, we do become unrecognizable to our old selves. The closer we grow to God and in our awareness of the needs of others, the more our appearance changes. At least others might notice. Some might even say it becomes angelic.

The Eight Qualities (Sufi)

It has been said that Sufism is founded upon the qualities exemplified by eight prophets. These are:

The Generosity of Abraham—who was willing to sacrifice his only son.

The Surrender of Ishmael—who submitted to God's will and sacrificed himself.

The Patience of Job—who endured sores and worms in order the question the Almighty.

The Mystery of Zacharias—about whom God said, "You shall not speak to anyone for three days except through signs."

The Solitude of John—who was a stranger in his own country and an alien to his own people.

The Detachment of Jesus—who was so removed from worldly things that he only possessed a cup and a comb, and these two he gave away when he saw a man drinking with his hands and another man who was using his fingers to straighten his hair.

The Garment of Moses—who served as an example by wearing wool.

And the poverty of Muhammad—to whom God sent the key to the all of the treasures that are upon the face of the earth.

★

There is much to glean from the Sufi path, including a deep respect for a great pantheon of prophets who preceded Muhammad. In the Sufi way, there are many attributes that one should willingly attempt to emulate.

Among the wisdom literature of the Bible—and especially the book of Proverbs—wisdom is personified as the highest of virtues, the virtue that makes all others beneficial rather than self-serving. As the book begins: "The awe of the Lord is the beginning of knowledge" (Proverbs 1:7) and "The beginning of wisdom is this: get wisdom. And whatever else you get, get insight. Prize her highly and she will exalt you; she will honor you if you embrace her . . . and will become for you a most beautiful crown." (Proverbs 4:7-9).

To be wise in the Sufi way, one should strive to emulate those who personified their respective attributes in superior ways, and by thus embracing, become a true servant of the Merciful.

Reflections (Upanishads)

Prajapati told his disciples: "Look at your reflections in a pan of water. What do you perceive about yourselves when you do this?" They poured water into pans and stared at their reflections. The teacher asked them, "What do you see?"

They said, "Teacher, we see our entire bodies. First the head, but we can see all the way down to the feet and even see details such as the fingernails."

Next, Prajapati told them, "Now go and dress in beautiful attire. Then return and look at your reflections in the water." The disciples retreated to their rooms, dressed in their finest robes, and returned to the pans filled with water. Prajapati asked, "Now what do you see?"

The disciples answered, "Teacher, we now see that we all appear beautiful. Our reflections are exactly as we are dressed—in our fine robes and our bodies adorned."

Prajapati told them, "What you see now is the self that is immortal. This is *Brahman*—the self that is free from fear." When the disciples heard this they departed with contented hearts.

★

Another reflective meditation reminiscent of the Buddha's parable of the flowing water. It is important that we see ourselves clearly, yes ... but all the more important that we see beyond our outward appearance. The immortal lies within. It is the spirit that makes us alive. Jesus once said, "What is born of the flesh is flesh, but what is born of the spirit is spirit." (John 3:6)

This passage from the Upanishads is a beautiful truth. Our greatest quest in life should be that of seeking the divine, the path that leads to God. In this we will also discover our true selves, our better selves—and that is when we reflect the divine.

Lightning Strikes (Zen)

There is a well-known Zen teaching about a master and his disciple who were walking on a treacherous mountain path. As they journeyed along one particularly dangerous slope a storm approached and overtook them. Remaining still on the path, they proceeded only after the lightning flashed. They would proceed but a few steps at a time in this manner, attempting to memorize the landscape each time there was a lightning flash. Eventually they arrived at their destination in this manner.

★

M. Scott Peck's bestselling book, *The Road Less Traveled*, begins with these three words: "Life is difficult." And so it is. Rarely can we proceed through life with one hundred percent certainty of our outcome. Rather, we tend to proceed in snatches of knowledge and wisdom as we are assured of the path we should take, the decisions we should make. The future has a tendency to be fearful (for it is dark and uncertain) and our destinations can seem distant to us—but we can only proceed one day at a time anyway.

As this Zen parable illustrates, our path is enlightened briefly at a time, but can still be sufficient for travel. Even if the light comes sporadically and in quick flashes of brilliance, we must press on.

Clarity (Jesus)

Jesus told them this parable: What do you think? Can a blind person guide a blind person? Won't they both fall into a hole? A pupil doesn't know more than the teacher, but anyone who aspires to learn will want to be like the teacher. And why would you look for a bit of sawdust in your neighbor's eye while ignoring a log in your own eye? Or how can someone say to a neighbor, "Friend, let me help you remove that piece of sawdust that's in your eye," when you can't possibly see well enough due to the log that's in your own eye? Don't be two-faced. First take the log out of your own eye and then you will have the clarity to help take the sawdust out of your neighbor's eye.

★

One cannot embrace life fully without clarity. And there are many attitudes that cloud our vision and our judgment: biases, hatreds, grudges, and fears. But as Jesus points out in this startling parable, clarity is not possible unless we first remove the blinders from our own eyes. One cannot be a healing agent to another unless first healed. And often, the very faults and failures we see in others are merely a reflection of those very same faults and failures in ourselves.

Two Trees (Jesus)

There's no such thing as a good tree that bears bad fruit—and it's silly to think of a bad tree that bears good fruit. Neither would someone try to gather up figs in a thorn patch nor harvest grapes from a sticker bush. That's how it is with people. Look closely: the good person has a wealth of good inside and actually does good things, but the evil person is bankrupt inside and does evil things. It's true: the heart betrays what comes out of people's mouths.

★

In this age of mass genocide, warfare, and long-smoldering animosities that are now erupting again, it is startling to note how an ancient teaching informs our contemporary consciousness. Often we are surprised when we see these old problems rearing their heads again. We think: I thought these ideas and hatreds were a thing of the past. But they are ever with us. Often, they just slip underground, only to emerge again in more virulent and violent forms.

What is the evidence of "good"? Jesus reminds us it is action, not words. How one lives and relates to others is the evidence of a person's goodness, not an outward appearance.

Good fruit is faith, hope, and love.

The Village (Jewish)

Once, Rabbi Tarfon, who was very wealthy, wanted to make an investment in some neighboring villages. He gave Rabbi Akiva four thousand dinars and said, "Invest it wisely." Rabbi Akiva took this money and distributed it among the poor.

Later, when Rabbi Tarfon asked him about his investment, Rabbi Akiva led him to one a yeshiva. But Rabbi Tarfon asked, "Where are my investments?" So Rabbi Akiva led him to another yeshiva. Akiva showed Rabbi Tarfon a child who was reading the book of Psalms. Akiva asked the child, "What are your reading?"

The child read aloud, "He has scattered abroad and given to the needy and his righteousness endures forever" (Psalm 112:9). Then Rabbi Akiva said to Tarfon, "This is your investment."

Upon hearing this, Rabbi Tarfon was moved. He stood up, kissed Akiva, and said, "You are my teacher and friend—my teacher in wisdom and my friend in right living." And he gave him more money to distribute to the poor.

★

Our greatest investments are in others. Often, when we speak of financial matters, we refer to "my money," "my investments," and "my account." But stewardship of the true riches is an awareness that we are merely caretakers of the gifts of God. God has entrusted to our care some portion of the world, and we get to decide what to do with that portion. In our time, there is a strong propensity to become hoarders. But when we invest in a child's education, in providing a jobs, or in the wholeness of another person, we are investing most wisely. Material possessions will eventually rot, but the investments that we make in others have an eternal weight.

The Dervish, the Raven, and the Falcon (Pilpay)

A young dervish was walking through the woods one day when he spied a Falcon that held a piece of flesh in its beak. The Dervish watched as the Falcon tore the flesh into strips and then flew to a Raven's nest and proceeded to feed the other bird. Upon seeing this the Dervish returned to his cell and contemplated: I have seen how the Creator provides for the helpless Raven and this is the humble path that God would have me take."

But that night the Dervish dreamed and God spoke to him thus: "It is true that all things in the world are created as I have ordained them, and wisdom may be gained by watching the natural order. But if you are going to imitate any of the birds, imitate the Falcon—for it is majestic and makes its way through the world. Do not imitate the Raven, which is a sluggard and waits only for the other birds to feed it, as it has come to expect that it will receive from the work of another."

Later, as the Dervish spoke to the teacher has asked, "Why is it, sir, that you advise us to create wealth for ourselves and to amass riches—but you do not inform us what we are to do with them?"

The Teacher said, "This is true—and all things considered, it is easy to acquire wealth. But the more difficult task is using your wealth for the good of others. Too many riches kill a man's spirit, but generosity gives him life."

★

The humble path is not the same as the lazy path as this Pilpay story illustrates. In the classic Christian list of "deadly sin," sloth is one of the seven and may, in fact, precipitate in all the others. Humility is not the same as poverty, nor is pride necessarily shackled to wealth. Rather, either can be a curse, and as Pilpay would remind us, often it is the impoverished who crave money most of all. Industry—having a purpose and an end—is the key to a satisfying life. Water that is flowing is can become pure. Stagnant water is of little value. Humility through generosity is the difference between them.

Chapter Four

The Quality of Mercy

Blessed are the merciful, for they shall receive mercy.
—Jesus

Where there is forgiveness, there is God Himself.
—Adi Granth (Sikh Sacred Text)

*I*n nearly every faith, there is a mystical tradition that attempts to counter the tendency toward formalism and institutional beliefs. This mysticism itself has also given birth to an abundance of legendary tales: stories of rebirth, devotion, and mercy.

Among the Cherokee people there developed a merciful philosophy centered on sharing. What good was it, for example, to know how to grow corn if one would not share it with the sick and the elderly? Likewise, in the ancient traditions of the Tao, it was noted that people loved the Tao because: "When you seek, you find; and when you make a mistake, you are forgiven."

How often mercy is seen as a weakness instead of a strength! Those who are forgiving and kind are often relegated to the back burners of history or, as in the case of luminaries such as Jesus,

Buddha, or Chuang Tzu—either crucified, shunned, or expelled. We do not live in a merciful world, but, as Jesus described, a world where eye for eye and tooth for tooth is deemed to be right and just. And often, we see how revenge takes not only an eye for an eye, but also the whole person, or consumes entire communities in its wake.

If we see God as merciful and benevolent, then the whole of our lives may be oriented around this divine gift. In the divine mercy, we ourselves may become merciful. As the Christian mystic Meister Eckhart once wrote, "The seed of God is in us ... and now the seed of a pear tree grows into a pear tree and a hazel seed grows into a hazel tree. A seed of God grows into God."

A Final Mercy (Bible)

When they came to the place called "The Skull," they crucified Jesus there between two thieves—one on his right and one on his left. And the soldiers mocked him.

One of the thieves also mocked him saying, "If you are the Messiah, then save yourself and us."

But the other thief said, "Don't you fear God, seeing that you are now condemned?" This thief said to Jesus, "Lord, please remember me when you enter into your kingdom."

Jesus said to him, "I tell you the truth, today you will be with me in paradise." (adapted from Luke 23)

★

One of the most moving points of the Passion Narrative is Jesus offering a final mercy to the dying thief. Such mercy may be an impossibility for us, but it strikes at the heart of the divine mercy. In the Dhammapada we encounter further thoughts about paradise: *Those of high thought and deep contemplation advance on the path, and in the end they reach Nirvana, the supreme peace and infinite joy.*

Mercy is a signpost along the way.

Jesus and the Donkey (Islamic)

Jesus had an old donkey that could not walk more than two miles a day. One night, when the donkey collapsed, Jesus made more than two hundreds trips to the well, carting water to the thirsty animal. But when the donkey refused to drink, Jesus stayed up all night attending to its needs.

The following day the disciples were bothered by their master's vigilance over the dumb animal.

Jesus replied, "The donkey has no tongue by which to tell me his needs. If he is thirsty, I must attend to him, as he has carried me faithfully throughout the day. How can I sleep until his thirst is quenched? Would I not have the Almighty to answer to?"

★

Typical of many of the wonderful Sufi teachings about Jesus, this one demonstrates the nature of selfless love. In the Sufi faith, Jesus holds a place of deep reverence and emulation, even devotion, and it was Jesus who demonstrated compassion toward all of God's creations. Empathy is often regarded as a purely human trait, but with Jesus, we see the divine love extending to even the beasts of burden

As with this legend, Jesus is often depicted alongside a beast of burden, a seeker, or one of the poor. His words and practices offer a glimpse of mercy that is often hidden in the world of self-aggrandizement and materialism.

God's Mercy (Jewish)

It is said that once Rabbi Akiva was going on a journey with his disciples, but when he came to their destination they discovered that there was no place to lodge in that town. Akiva said to his disciples, "Whatever God does is for the best." So that night Akiva and his followers slept in an open field. Now, Akiva had in his possession a donkey, a rooster, and a lamp. That night a lion came into their camp and ate the donkey, a weasel came and ate the rooster, and there was a strong wind that blew out the lamp. When the disciples pointed out this bad luck, Akiva again replied, "Whatever God does is for the best." The next morning word arrived that, overnight, a foreign army had besieged the town and carried away all of the inhabitants into slavery. When Akiva heard this he said to his disciples, "You see, we might also have been taken away had the armies heard the braying of the donkey or the crowing of the rooster or seen our light. Whatever God does is for the best."

★

There is a tendency to overlook casual events and circumstances as a portion of the divine mercy. But what if some circumstances are outcomes of God's protection? Such questions have been pondered for centuries and we need not jump to conclusions to accept that we lack understanding. What we may accept more readily is that we could very easily find ourselves in other, less austere, circumstances. Or, as one adage reminds us: "There but for the grace of God, go I."

A Final Compassion (Buddhist)

The Buddha would tell this story: that the most wicked of people, even those who had committed heinous crimes or whose minds were filled with greed, lust, murder, theft or lies, could take refuge in the compassion of Buddha. He said:

Suppose a good friend comes to people like this and pleads with them at the last moment saying, "You are now facing death and you cannot blot out your wickedness on your own, but you can take refuge in the compassion of the Buddha and Infinite Light by reciting his name."

Indeed, if even the most wicked of these people recite the name of Buddha in singleness of mind, all of their sins, which have destined them to the evil world, will be cleared away. Buddha will meet them, too, and will escort them into the Pure Land where they will be born in the purity of the white lotus.

★

Much like Christ's forgiveness on the cross, this teaching of Buddha points to a mercy that is deeper than our imaginations. The aim, of course, is to inspire compassion, to awaken us to flee from wrath and hatreds, and to see the divine in our midst.

The Fire of Mercy (Buddhist)

The world is like a burning house that is forever being destroyed and rebuilt. People, being confused by the darkness of their ignorance, lose their minds in anger, displeasure, jealousy, prejudice or worldly passion. They are like babies in need of a mother; everyone must be dependent upon Buddha's mercy and compassion.

(In the same manner) Buddha is father to all the world; all human beings are the children of Buddha. Buddha is the most saintly of saints. The world is afire with decrepitude and death; there is suffering everywhere. But people, engrossed the vain search for worldly pleasure, are not wise enough to fully realize this.

Buddha saw that this world of delusion was really a burning house, so he turned from it and found refuge and peace in the quiet forest; there, out of his great compassion, he calls to us: "This world of change and suffering belongs to me; all these ignorant, heedless people are my children; I am the only one who can save them from their delusion and misery."

So save them from suffering He preaches the Dharma, but the ears of people are dulled by greed and they are inattentive.

But those who listen to his teachings are free from the delusions and miseries of life. "People cannot be saved by relying on their own wisdom," He said, "and through faith they must enter into my teaching." Therefore, one should listen to the Buddha's teaching and put it into practice.

★

So often the Buddha used the metaphor of fire to describe the condition of the world. Although a metaphor created centuries ago, we live in one of the most incendiary ages of human history. Entire villages and buildings can now be obliterated in an instant, or even an entire people, and we understand that the real fire begins much earlier in the human heart.

A lovely thought—and a deep truth—that we may yet flee the fire and find sanctuary in the divine heart of mercy.

Sheep and Goats (Jesus)

When the Son of man shall come in his glory, and all the holy angels with him, then shall he sit upon the throne of his glory. And before him shall be gathered all nations: and he shall separate them one from another, as a shepherd divides his sheep from the goats. And he shall set the sheep on his right hand, but the goats on the left. Then shall the King say unto them on his right hand, "Come, you blessed of my Father, inherit the kingdom prepared for you from the foundation of the world: For I was hungry, and you gave me food; I was thirsty, and you gave me drink; I was a stranger, and you took me in; Naked, and you clothed me; I was sick, and you visited me; I was in prison, and you came to me."

Then shall the righteous answer him, saying, "Lord, when did we see you hungry, and feed you, or thirsty, and gave you drink? When did we see you a stranger, and take you in, or naked and cloth you? Or when did we see you sick, or in prison, and come to you?"

And the King shall answer and say to them: "Truly I say to you, inasmuch as you have done it unto one of the least of these my brethren, you have done it unto me."

Then he shall say also to them on the left hand, "Depart from me, you cursed, into everlasting fire, prepared for the devil and his angels: For I was hungry and you gave me no food; I was thirsty, and you gave me no drink; I was a stranger, and you did not take me in; I was naked and you did not clothe me; I was sick, and in prison, and you did not visit me."

Then they shall also answer him, saying, "Lord, when did we see you hungry, or thirsty, or a stranger, or naked, or sick, or in prison, and did not minister to you?"

Then he shall answer them, saying, "Truly I say to you, inasmuch as you did it not to one of the least of these, you did it not to me." And these shall go away into everlasting punishment: but the righteous into life eternal. (Matthew 25:31-46)

★

A grace-filled parable that is full of action and pull. Here we see the words of Christ's prayer come full-circle: "Forgive us our sins in the same manner that we forgive the sins of others."

Unlike the frequent-flier parables about forgiveness and mercy, this story shows the connection between our actions and our salvation. Redemption is not just a divine gift, but an active participation in the mercies of God.

Yama King (Buddhist)

Once Yama, the King of Hell, asked a man about his evil deeds in life, saying, "During your lifetime, did you ever meet three heavenly messengers?" The man replied, "No, Lord, I never met three such people."

Then Yama asked him if he had ever met an elderly man walking with a cane. The man admitted that he had, indeed, met many such people in life who were walking with a cane. Yama said, "You are suffering in this hell because you did not recognize in that old man one of the heavenly messengers who had come to warn you to change your ways and to realize that you, too, would one day be an old man walking with a cane."

Then Yama asked him, "Had you ever seen in life a poor, sick and lonely man?" Again, the fellow answered, "Of course, my Lord, I had seen many such men in life."

Yama said to him, "You are suffering in this present hell because you did not recognize in the poor, sick and lonely man one of the heavenly messengers, who had come to warn you to change your ways to realize that you were suffering from the sickness of self-centeredness and greed."

Then Yama asked him, "Did you ever see a dead man in your former life?" Again, the fellow answered, "Of course, I have seen many dead people."

So Yama said to him, "It is because you did not recognize the heavenly messengers in all of these people that you have come to this end. If you had recognized the messengers and heeded their warnings, you would not be in this present state of suffering."

★

All cultures and faiths have their visitations. Like presiding angels, or strangers who become friends, or messengers sent by God one must always be on the lookout for these momentary guests. Through them we may be receiving an answer to a problem or an opportunity to demonstrate the depths of faith.

These stories remind us that faith is not simply a spiritual affair but must be shackled to real flesh and blood in order to be effective. Christianity defines this as the incarnation—God in the flesh, but now the Spirit living through us (our hands and feet). In Judaism, this is known as the Torah. Buddhists insist that our relationship with others is an important part of the path.

We should be moved not by what is hidden in the spiritual, but by what we encounter in the flesh.

One Zen teaching tells the story of a master and pupil who were discussing revelation. The master noted that he was not hiding anything from the pupil, but was making all things clear. The pupil responded by saying, "Not so."

Later, as they walked together in the mountains they came upon a grove of cinnamon trees. The master asked, "There, do you smell the fragrance?"

"Yes," the pupil said.

"Then see," said the master, "I have hidden nothing from you."

The Burning House (A Parable of Buddha)

Let me tell you this parable. Once there was a wealthy man whose house caught fire. All of his children were in the house playing with their toys, and as the man called out to them from the street, urging them to jump from the window, they did not heed his cries. Finally the man yelled, "Children, listen to me! I have some new toys for you. Won't you come out and play with them?"

When the children heard this, they exited the burning house and were saved.

★

Much like the previous parable of fire, this Buddhist teaching offers enticement. What if our salvation arrives through encouragement and good news? We are, after all, rarely persuaded—and certainly not changed—by bad news. Hope, assurance, joy—these do have a powerful pull. In every heart is a desire to attain these delights. The path of faith begins with a single step.

Jealousy (Hebrew Scriptures)

Adam and Eve had an older son, Cain, and a younger son, Abel. Abel was a shepherd and Cain was a farmer. One day Cain brought and offering to God—the fruit he had produced. Abel also brought an offering—which was the first lambs born in his flock. The Lord seemed pleased with Abel's offering, but did not seem to respect Cain's gift. And so Cain became angry with God and jealous of his brother.

One day when the two brothers were out working in the fields, Cain rose up and killed his brother, Abel. Soon after, God appeared to Cain and asked, "Where is your brother, Abel?" Cain answered, "How should I know? Am I responsible for my brother?" (adapted from Genesis 4)

★

It is as old as time itself—one brother killing another. Knowing the source of these animosities is often difficult to come by, but the solution may be obvious. We are forever striving after peace.

The Captured Hawk (Abstemius)

A hunter once caught a hawk while it was pursuing a pigeon. The hawk began pleading for its life, saying, "You know, since I've never done you any harm, I hope you will be merciful to me."

The hunter replied, "But in what way has *the pigeon* harmed you? Surely you cannot expect me to treat you with a greater mercy that you would show the pigeon."

★

Many Christians pray the Lord's Prayer—"Forgive us our trespasses as we forgive those who trespass against us"—without noting the level of mercy implied. Jesus was saying, "For you will be forgiven with the same level of forgiveness you extend to others." Abstemius penned this simple fable to demonstrate as much, and as Shakespeare once wrote, "The quality of mercy is not strained . . . it droppeth as the gentle dew from heaven."

Indeed, the mercy we desire for ourselves should be the mercy we extend to others. Though difficult, this is one of the foundations that can lead to peace and understanding among all people.

Origins of Evil (Native American)

The Sky Woman gave birth to two sons. The first son became the Good Spirit. The second son was such a difficult birth that the Sky Woman died afterwards. This second son became the Evil Spirit.

The Good Spirit then took his mother's head and hung it in the sky. This is the sun. And from his mother's body he also created the moon and stars. What remained of his mother was buried under the earth, and this became the soil from which all life springs—which is Mother Earth.

But the Evil Spirit put darkness in the way of the sun, and the darkness always precedes and chases away the light.

The Good Spirit also created all things on the earth. But the Evil Spirit tried to counter this work by creating more evil. The Good Spirit made the tall trees. The Evil Spirit stunted the growth of others and covered them with poison vines and thorns. The Good Spirit made the helpful animals—such as the bear and deer. But the Evil Spirit created the lizard and the serpent. The Good Spirit made the pure springs of water. But the Evil Spirit poisoned the water.

In time, when the Good Spirit created people, he placed his protection over them and told the Evil Spirit that he must stop making trouble upon the earth. But the Evil Spirit refused. And so the Good Spirit fought a battle with his evil brother, and the Good Spirit prevailed. The Good Spirit was ruler of the earth and he banished his Evil Brother Spirit to a dark cave under the earth. Although the Evil Spirit can no longer roam the earth, he does have people who serve him.

★

Every culture, as far back in recorded history as history will take us, has realized that something is awry in the creation. There is, as some have said, "an evil greater than the sum total of our individual evils." This evil varies by name and intent.

To the Mohawk people—as with the most sophisticated theological questions—there is a mystery here that cannot be adequately described or explained. But there is a goodness, too. And in the end, perhaps it is equally as difficult to explain the goodness in the world as it is the evil.

Yin and Yang? Perhaps. Or just something inexplicable.

Overcoming Evil with Good (Buddhist)

There is one parable about the Buddha who, centuries ago, came to earth in the womb of a mother and was born a great king. He ruled his kingdom of Benares with justice and mercy and desired to rise above all difficulties to obtain perfection. He would ask his subjects, "Do you find any fault in me?" But no one came forward to express any fault in the king. The king thought, *but perhaps they are afraid of speaking the truth.* And so the king of Benares loaded in his chariot and set out to ask those who lived in the farthest reaches of the earth.

Along the way, however, he encountered the king of Kosala who was on the same quest—for this king ruled also with justice and mercy and was seeking to find if there was any fault in him. When their chariots met along the road, the king of Kosala said, "Move aside, for you are in the way of the king of Kosala."

But the chariot drivers of the two kings began to have a conversation about who should move aside. The chariot driver for the king of Benares asked, "But is your king wiser—of a more advanced age?" The compared notes and discovered that the two kings were born exactly on the same day. The other chariot driver asked, "Let us compare their mercies. Does your king deal equally with all subjects in his kingdom without regard to race or caste or wealth?" They again discovered that both kings treated their subjects equally. Next they compared morality—and at this juncture the charioteer of the king of Kosala described his king thus:

He is firm with the firm.

He overwhelms the kind with kindness.

He treats the good with good, and the evil he treats with evil.

When the king of Benares (who was actually the Buddha) heard this, he admonished his charioteer to point out that the king of Kosala had faults. The charioteer of the king of Benares then said of his king:

He overcomes anger with kindness.

He overcomes evil with good.

He showers the poor with gifts and the liar he overcomes with truth.

When the king of Kosala heard the superiority of the king of Benares, he stepped aside and let him pass, saying, "He is superior who can overcome anger with kindness, evil with good, and who can give gifts to the poor and speak truth to the liar."

★

In similar vein, Jesus also taught:

Do not resist an evildoer (Matthew 5:39); Give to everyone who begs from you (Matthew 5:42); Love your enemies (Matthew 5:44).

This Buddhist parable is likewise a compilation of many of Buddha's teachings on overcoming evil with good, generosity toward the poor, and countering anger with kindness. The path to enlightenment is made all the more difficult because of our faults. And as the parable points out, faults which we rarely see or can confess about ourselves.

The Prodigal Son (A parable of Buddha)

Once there was a wealthy man who had a son. One day the son ran away from home and was quickly reduced to poverty. But the father, out of deep love for his son, left his mansion to search for him. The father travelled for months, but could not find his son. Eventually he returned to the mansion.

One afternoon, a decade later, the father noticed a poor man living in the street. Suddenly he realized that this was his son. The father sent his servants to bring the son home. But no matter how much the servants pleaded, the son could not believe that he could live in the beautiful mansion and so he refused to be reunited with his father.

And so the father said to his servants, "Go back to my son and offer him a job working in the mansion. Perhaps he will become a servant and return to me."

This time the son accepted the offer and returned to the mansion, although he could not believe that the rich master was his father. Over the course of years, the master gave his son more and more responsibility and a greater salary, and in time the son had great wealth of his own. But the son still could not recognize the master as his father.

Eventually, when the father was dying, he called all of his servants together and said to them, "See, here is my only son. I have given him all things."

When the son heard his father's confession he came to his senses and said, "At last I have found my father and I accept that he has now entrusted all things into my hands."

★

Told centuries before Jesus's parable of the Prodigal, the Buddha related this parable of a son coming to his senses and a return home. The theme runs deep. We often forfeit our true joys and inheritance, squandering these for alluring objects and false promises. But we are never far from a welcome.

Life doesn't have to be so difficult—but in the simplicity of relationships and love we may discover our true home.

Lost and Found (Jesus)

So Jesus told them stories. He said: If any of you had a hundred sheep and lost one, you would certainly leave the ninety-nine sheep behind and go to search for the one that is lost. And of course, when found, you would put that sheep on your shoulders and bring it home rejoicing. You would say to your friends and neighbors, "Come celebrate with me because I have found my lost sheep." Well, that's how it is in heaven when one sinner repents.

Or, consider a woman who has ten silver coins. If she loses one, doesn't she light a lamp, sweep the house clean, and search every nook and cranny until she finds it? And when she finds that one coin she calls together all of her friends and says, "Celebrate with me for I have found my lost coin." Well, that's how much joy there is in heaven when one sinner repents.

★

Among the parables of the "lost and found," Jesus tells the stories of a lost sheep and a lost coin. Like the parable of the Prodigal Son, the end is salvation and celebration. To find ourselves is salvation, or salvation can also be a change of course. Fears as much as failures are the sins we fall to, even adore. What we discover in the return is the true peace— the Shalom—of transformation and new beginnings.

The Devil's House (Jewish)

There were two men who succumbed to the temptations and wiles of the devil. Every Sabbath eve they began to argue with others and were unable to be at peace. Rabbi Meir intervened, took the men aside, and bridged a peace between them. After this, the men heard the devil complaining, "This peace has driven me out of my own house!"

★

The Hebrew word "Shalom" is difficult to translate. It is both a greeting and a parting. But it is more than "peace." Shalom also contains the nuances of: "May God give you every good thing." It is a word of blessing and a word of hope.

As one sage has said, "If we want to drive the devil crazy, learn to live in peace."

But even if we are still on the road to salvation we can strive for these paths. Peace is understanding as well as intent. Peace is acceptance of differences. When both parties agree to strive for these ulterior ways, wonderful things happen.

The Gates of Hell (C. K. Chesterton)

A man who was entirely careless of spiritual affairs died and went to hell. And he was much missed on earth by his old friends. His business agent went down to the gates of hell to see if there was any chance of bringing him back. But though he pleaded for the gates to be opened, the iron bars never yielded. His priest also went and argued: "He was not really a bad fellow, given time he would have matured. Let him out, please!" The gates remained stubbornly shut against all their voices. Finally, his mother came; she did not beg for his release. Quietly, and with a strange catch in her voice, she said to Satan, "Let me in." Immediately the great doors swung open upon their hinges. For love goes down to the depths of hell and there redeems the dead."

The Pope's Visit (Contemporary Christian)

The story is that soon after Pope John Paul III was elected, he put on his red shoes and went walking through the streets of Rome. People ran to him, kneeling at his feet to receive the blessing of the Vicar of Rome. The Pope visited an orphanage and blessed the children. He visited a hospital and blessed the sick. He visited the poor houses and blessed those in poverty.

At last he came to the Roman prison and asked for entry so he could bless the prisoners. The warden was hesitant, reminding the Pope that the prison housed some of the worst offenders. But the Pope insisted, and the warden relented. The Pope walked the halls of the prison, blessing those prisoners who reached out from behind the bars. Eventually he came to a large iron door. "I would like to go in there," the Pope said.

The warden refused. "You cannot go in there. Behind that door are the worst criminals in the country. Men who have committed despicable crimes: murderers, rapists, the most violent of types."

But the Pope persisted.

The warden begged the Holy Father to reconsider.

At last the Pope said, "But I must go in. I must see these men."

When the iron door opened, the room was pitch black, save for a small shaft of light from above. As the Pope stepped into the small room, one man recognized the Holy Father, screamed, and then rushed toward him with his arms outstretched. One of the Swiss Guards who served as bodyguard to the Pope drove the man to the ground with a blow. Dazed and bloodied, the man eventually trembled to his knees, wrapped his arms around the Pope's waist, and wailed, "O Father, Father, tell me . . . is there any hope for me? Is there any hope?"

The Pope stretched out his hands in blessing and said, "My son, there is hope for us all."

★

Is reconciliation possible? Outside of a church in Coventry, England, one can find this remarkable prayer:

The hatred which divides nation from nation, race from race, class from class . . . Father Forgive.

The covetous desires of people and nations to possess what is not their own . . . Father Forgive.

The greed which exploits the work of human hands and lays waste to the earth . . . Father Forgive.

The envy of the welfare and the happiness of others . . . Father Forgive.

Our indifference to the plight of the imprisoned, the homeless, the refugee . . . Father Forgive

The lust which dishonors the bodies of men, women and children . . . Father Forgive.

The pride which leads us to trust in ourselves and not in God . . . Father Forgive.

The Way Out of Hell (Hindu)

There is an episode taken from the life of Ghandi that goes like this. Once, during his hunger strike, when India was erupting with violence—Muslim against Hindu, Hindu against Muslim—two men, one of each faith, came to Ghandi and pleaded with him to end his hunger campaign and speak to the people. Ghandi refused, saying he would not eat until India was at peace. The Muslim man asked, "But how can this happen? We are in hell."

"Ghandi answered, "But I know a way out of hell."

"And how is that?" the Hindu asked.

Ghandi turned to the Muslim and said, "Find an orphaned child and raise him as a Hindu." And to the Hindu he said, "Find an orphaned child and raise him as a Muslim."

"This is the way out of hell," Ghandi said.

★

Instead of creating our hells on earth, what if we worked to create heaven? Ghandi's teaching demonstrates that it is possible for one person to honor another's beliefs and traditions. It is possible for people with different beliefs to live together. No doubt the world needs a deeper understanding, a greater hope, even compassion. By following this path we discover our humanity.

Getting Dirty (Chassidic)

A rabbi wanted to instruct his students about the nature of redemption. He said, "If you want to lift a person from the mud and filth of life, it is not enough to stand on top and reach down with a helping hand. You must climb into the mud and filth yourself, take hold of your brother, and pull him out to the light of day."

★

There are many expressions of this traditional Native American maxim: *Before you can understand another person, you must walk a mile in his moccasins.* Here, in the case of the Chassidic tradition, we discover that helping another person is often dirty work. In fact, our human difficulties are often quite messy and convoluted, and anyone who sets out to help another person quickly discovers that problems are rarely so easy to solve as they first appear. In the case of the Muslim tradition, God has sent the Prophet to instruct and lift from the mire. In the Christian gospel, it is Emmanuel—God with us—who has entered the world of corruption, sin, and death to redeem humanity. And in other traditions the instruction is no less clear: that in order to understand the plight of another we must first be willing to enter into the fray on a personal level. Service at a distance solves little. Service that is at one with the suffering changes life—especially the one who serves.

The Measure of the Kingdom (Jesus)

Jesus said, "What is the kingdom of God like? What can it be compared to? It's like a mustard seed that someone planted in a garden. That tiny seed grew and became a magnificent tree and the birds of the air made their nests in its branches.

"What else is the kingdom of God like? It's like a woman who mixed yeast in three measures of flour, and kneaded it until the whole loaf was leavened."

★

Every person begins his life with infancy. And from that infancy all of life grows—whatever, in fact, it will become. So it is with faith. Small acts, seemingly insignificant decisions, even mundane choices made on behalf of others—all of these can have a much larger and deeper impact than our minds can comprehend. Jesus equates the signs of God's presence with these small acts of faith—open hands, open hearts, and open minds.

Just as one would never overlook the potential inherent in a seed, we should never doubt that a garden can grow from these small decisions. A garden requires a degree of nourishment (water and nutrients), sunlight, and some attention.

God desires to grow a garden in the human heart.

The Legend of the Pelican (traditional)

A Pelican, the most majestic of birds, once flew far and wide over the ocean looking for food for her young. The Pelican endured raging winds, scorching sun, and the hardships of flying so far over the water without relief. At last, exhausted from her search for food she returned to her nest, but had nothing to feed her young. Her three young birds cried out for food. Moved by love, the Pelican pricked at her breast with her bill, opening a wound from which she nourished and saved her young.

★

The legend of the Pelican predates Christianity, but the image of the Pelican feeding her young from her bleeding breast was adopted by the early church and expanded during the Middle Ages as a Christ symbol. St. Augustine (fourth century) used the legend of the Pelican, and many other mystics and saints adopted the legend in various forms.

Another legend of the Pelican relates how, because of her large bill, a female Pelican can sometimes accidently wound or kill her young. Then, after mourning for three days, she plucks open her breast and bathes her young with her own blood, miraculously reviving them to life.

Chapter Five

Simplicity of the Saints

Paradise is found at the feet of the mothers.
—Muhammad

Nothing is more conducive to righteousness than solitude.
The one who is alone sees nothing but God.
And when nothing is seen but God,
then one is moved by the will of God.

—Sufi

*E*ach generation, it has been said, must rediscover the meaning of faith for itself. Often, this faith is rediscovered in retrospect: by pondering the saints who have come before. And often, we discover various types of simplicity in these lives.

This simplicity, however, is not crudely defined as poverty, or ignorance, or even narrowly-defined faith. Rather, the saints embody a broadness to their thinking, their logic, and in their abilities to let go of so much baggage. Their gifts could, then, be defined as freedom without excesses. In the words of the old Quaker song:

"'Tis a gift to be simple, 'Tis a gift to be free."

In our time, which may broadly be categorized as an era of excesses, people often discover their renewal or awakening by parting ways with these desires that seem to drive humanity into greed, accumulation, and lust for power and domination. We can see these excesses in work, relationships, and even in our play. Nothing is good enough unless it produces success and victory—which is often narrowly defined as more consumption, larger salaries, larger or more expensive toys, or even prestige. Everyone wants to "win"—and by consequence, we also need to believe that there are losers, too.

Peering back at the lives of saints and sages, however, affords us an opportunity to glimpse the simplicity of their lives and their attitudes. So often their success would have been defined as wealth of friendship, influence, or the impact of their teaching. Their freedoms were found in these meaningful and lasting friendships and the startling revelations of their instruction.

We may yet discover—in these tales about, and teachings of great saints and mystics—how certain men and women walked closely with God or offered new understandings of the world. Some lived humbly yet possessed a power in their words. Others were ordinary people but told stories that contained great truths. And yes, some possessed wealth but demonstrated enormous generosity and an ability to see that all good things are blessings from above.

The sages and saints of old seemed to understand that everything in life—all possessions and loves and joys—were merely on loan. We bring nothing into the world. We shall take nothing out of it. What we do with our loan during this life most accurately defines the kind of people we will be. There are a great many teachings of the saints that can help us. A few are here.

In classical Hindu teaching (a passage from the Basavanna) a series of questions strike at the heart of our time—as hatreds have swelled and the world seems to be sitting on a tender-box of explosives:

Why do you become angry at someone who is angry at you?

What will you gain by it?

What will he lose by it?

Your anger merely brings dishonor to yourself and disturbs your mind.

So how can a fire inside of you consume your neighbor's house without also burning down your own?

Simplicity. It is difficult to obtain. But, as the Zan masters taught: *The journey of a thousand miles begins with a single step.* Let us take it.

Riversides (Buddhist)

Once there was a man who was going on a long journey. After he had set out and had walked for many days he came to river. He noted to himself, "This side of the river is very dangerous and difficult to navigate, but the other side of the river looks much better and easier to walk on." And so he built a raft made of branches and covered it in stalks. He crossed safely to the other side and was very pleased with his ingenuity. But then he thought, "Since I built this nice raft, I might as well carry it with me on the remainder of my journey. It would be a shame to waste it."

And here is the question: Could we call this man wise?

★

What do we carry with us through life? Are these "things" necessary? Or are they merely burdens? This wonderful teaching (attributed to the Buddha) invites us to consider both our self-absorption and our excesses. We are, in fact, on a journey and there are always more detours and pitfalls in our futures. What we carry with us can often be as much a distraction and a burden as a blessing.

The wisest learn how to find the balance between enough and too much and then, as needed, shed what is no longer expedient to the destination.

The Harp (Buddhist)

There was a young man named Srona who came from a wealthy family, but had always suffered from ill health. Nevertheless, he was eager to be one of Buddha's disciples. He labored so hard on the path to Enlightenment that his feet bled.

But Buddha took pity on him and said, "Dear Srona, didn't you study the harp at home? You know that a harp does not make beautiful music if its strings are either too tight or too loose. It only makes the music when the strings are stretched just right and in tune. So, is one's training for Enlightenment. You must not stretch your mind too tightly or too loosely in your seeking, but you must be contemplative and act wisely."

★

It is important to remember that any goal, any pursuit, can become a burden—even spiritual ones. Faith has often been described as the ability to relax in the presence of the divine. Faith that adds stress to one's life is not helpful. Religious disciplines or beliefs that detract from our connection with the divine and with others are hindrances. A philosophy or way of life that adds only to our individual welfares without making provision for the welfare of others is destitute.

Here the Buddha offers the simple way—all things in moderation. Do not stretch too far or too tightly . . . and be willing to let go.

The Teaching River (Abstemius)

One day, as a man walked by a river, he noted the following: that where the river ran smooth it was deepest, and where it made the most noise, it was shallow.

★

This is a truth: still waters run deep, and trouble reveals shallowness. The same holds true for people. Deep reflection leads us to tranquility and

SIMPLICITY OF THE SAINTS

a peaceful life. Shallow thoughts lead to trouble. Often, in fact, those who make the most noise, or cause the most trouble in life, are not deep individuals. But going deeper requires time and attention. Anyone can make the jump and the journey—and it is not just the individual who benefits from the still waters, but society as well. Saints and mystics have learned this through the centuries, and still the deep waters are where we need to sail.

The Three Hermits (Traditional Russian Christian Tale)

Many centuries ago an archbishop was sailing across the ocean when his ship drew near to a seemingly deserted island. After disembarking, the archbishop was surprised to find three men approaching on the shore. "And who are you?" the archbishop asked.

The men answered, "We are three hermits who have lived on this island by ourselves for many years."

"And how do you pray?" the archbishop asked.

One of the hermits answered, "Sir, we have forgotten the traditional prayers. All we know to pray are the words, 'Lord, have mercy on us sinners.'"

The archbishop was flabbergasted at their ignorance. "Do you not know the Lord's prayer?"

They answered, "We do not remember it. Could you teach us again?"

The archbishop spent the day with the three hermits, reciting the Lord's prayer to them time and again. But each time the archbishop thought the hermits had memorized the prayer, they would forget a phrase. At last, convinced that he had taught the Lord's Prayer to the three hermits, the archbishop returned to his ship and set sail.

Later that night, on deck, the archbishop noted three figures walking on the water toward the ship. It was the three hermits. "We have forgotten the words of the prayer you taught us," they cried. "Can you teach us again?"

Humbled, the archbishop prayed to himself, "Lord, have mercy on us sinners." And then he said to the hermits, "Return to your island and pray the simple prayer as you did before."

★

Must prayers be powerful to be effective? What if the heart of God is touched by simplicity itself? These are the questions addressed by this wonderful Russian parable.

Prayer is not effective by one's recitation or knowledge, but by one's humility. Information is not the purpose of prayer, but *transformation*.

Praying the Mystery (Sikh)

How can I describe the greatness of your name? O Nanak, if I had hundreds of thousands of stacks of paper, and if ink were never to fail me, and if my pen were able to move like the wind, and if I were to read and recite and embrace love for the Lord—even so, I could not estimate your value. How can I describe the Greatness of your Name?

You have so many creative powers, Lord; your bountiful blessings are so great. So many of your beings and creatures praise you day and night.

★

These Sikh prayers from the *Sri Guru Granth Sahib*, are expressive of the Sikh religion—the fifth largest faith in the world. Sikhism began in the fifteenth century in the Punjab region of India. This document, the *Sri Guru Granth Sahib* is a collection of the Gurus' teachings, but are not considered "scripture" in the same vein as other faiths. Rather, Sikhism sees truth in all religious traditions and sees no differentiation between a religious and secular life—for all of life is under the care and discretion of the One God—who is indescribable and unnamed.

The morning prayers of a Sikh, taken from the *Japji Sahib*, are praiseworthy and con templative and speak of the mystery and majesty of God:

God is only One.

His name is True.

He is the Creator.

He is without fear.

He is inimical to none.

He never dies.

He is beyond births and deaths.

He is self illuminated.

As with many of the Sikh prayers, the beauty of the poetry is rarely exceeded by those found in other traditions. Reminiscent of the Psalms, as passionate as Rumi, *the Japji Sahib* (morning prayers) and *Kirtan Sohila* (bedtime prayers) form masterful bookends to the day. At the heart of these prayers is humility, and a wonder that fills all of the life with an inexpressible joy of the love and beauty of the Creator.

Gold Diggers (Jewish)

There is a story about a disciple of Rabbi Simeon ben Yohai who journeyed into a far land to make his fortune. When he returned, he was indeed wealthy. When the other disciples saw how wealthy he had become, they were envious and they sought permission from the rabbi to travel afar to make their fortunes as well.

But Rabbi Simeon took them to a nearby village and prayed, "O Valley, fill up with gold denars!" Right before their eyes the valley began to glisten with gold. Then Rabbi Simeon turned to this disciples and said, "If it is gold you want, go and take it. But also know that whoever takes the gold now will be taking his share of the world-to-come, since the reward for studying Torah is not of this world, but shall be found in the world-to-come.

★

There are many attractions in life, including a desire to make a way in the world—perhaps, even, a fortune. But the spiritual life requires other types of wealth including relational, social, and intellectual investments. As this parable describes, our desires are often influenced by the prevailing winds of culture and the times. It is difficult to rise above the common practices.

Buddha and Jesus also taught that the true riches were to be found in these spiritual disciplines of helpfulness, peace, and love. It is not easy to trade the common for the uncommon; nor is it easy to fulfill promises made. Those who set out to enrich their spirit will frequently discover setbacks, pitfalls, and detours along the way. It is not easy to focus on the true riches.

Perhaps, as Jesus taught, the secret to wealth is not in the accumulation, but in the distribution. Or, "It is more blessed to give than to receive." Good news, really, not only for the poor but for those who have been blessed with great opportunity to be blessing to others.

The Twelve Apostles (Christian legend)

Many years before the Messiah was born, there was a mother who had twelve sons. They were a poor family, and every day the mother worried about feeding her children. Most of all, she hoped that her sons would be able to live on earth with the Messiah.

When the oldest son, Peter, came of age, he set out to make his fortune in the world. He wondered in the forest for a long time and became very despondent. One day, when he was feeling dejected and hungry, he lay down under a tree for a nap. When he awoke he saw a young man standing next to him. "What are you seeking?" asked the young many dressed in dazzling white.

"I am hoping to find the Messiah," Peter said.

"Come with me," said the young man. He led Peter to a cave that was filled with glittering jewels and gold. Further in the cave Peter noticed twelve cradles. "And what are these?" Peter asked.

"Lie down," said the young man, "and I will rock you to sleep."

Peter placed himself in the cradle and was rocked to sleep. In time, all of his eleven brothers came to the cave also. The young man, who was an angel, rocked them all to sleep. They slept for many years, and when they awoke, they were with the Messiah. They became the twelve apostles.

★

This legend, likely based on a Grimm's tale, is indicative of many European legends about the twelve apostles. As the saints were referred, and large cathedrals built to their memories, the lives and deaths of the apostles took on mythical proportions. But the legends themselves point to a simple faith that would uphold people in their hardships and poverty. As in many faiths, these legends were meant to provide hope to people in their difficulties.

Two Horses (Bierce)

A wild horse meeting a domestic one, taunted him with his condition of servitude. The tame animal swore that he was as free as the wind.

"If that is so," said the other, "pray what is the office of that bit in your mouth?"

"That," was the answer, "is iron, one of the best tonics known."

"But what is the meaning of the rein attached to it?"

"That keeps it from falling from my mouth when I am too indolent to hold it."

"How about the saddle?"

"It spares me fatigue: when I am tired I mount and ride it."

★

Human beings have the capacity to believe anything—even lies about ourselves. In fact, we can view life through rose-colored glasses. How difficult it is to view ourselves through an introspective lens, with real honesty and openness toward change. Human beings have a remarkable propensity to overlook the excesses that enslave us—or the attitudes and practices that destroy our own freedoms. Freedom is no easy task. And as many have pointed out, the most difficult work we will ever accomplish in life is the work we will do on ourselves.

The Good Samaritan (Jesus)

Jesus told them a parable:

As a man was traveling from Jerusalem to Jericho he was accosted by thieves who beat him, took the clothes from his back, and left him for dead. Soon afterwards a priest walked by, saw the man in distress, but passed by on the opposite side of the road.

In much the same way a religious leader also walked by, even stopped to look at the man, but then abandoned him.

Finally a Samaritan—a despised and sinful man—happened to be passing along that same road. He stopped, helped the man, bound his wounds, and then loaded him onto his donkey. Further up the road he left him at an inn and told the help there, "Please take care of my new friend, and if he owes anything after he is able to get back on his feet, charge that to my account. I'll be back in a few days to pay the bill."

Jesus asked, "Which of these was a true friend to the man who had been injured?"

★

There are certain parables that not only have timeless appeal but carry over into all walks of life. This parable—perhaps one of the most familiar and impactful that Jesus told—is not about beliefs or doctrines or creeds. Rather, it is about practicing the very heart of God by demonstrating God's love through action, not lip service.

Concern for others should cross boundaries. Take us out of our comfort zones. Make a new day possible.

Brother Anthony and the Bow (Desert Fathers)

Anthony and some brothers decided to walk in the woods. After a while, they grew tired and stopped for a rest. They sat down on the ground and were soon talking among themselves and laughing.

Suddenly a hunter appeared in the thicket and saw this display of frivolity among the saints. The hunter scowled his disapproval.

Brother Anthony asked him, "Why do you judge us so harshly?"

"Because," the hunter said, "It is unseemly for holy men to laugh."

"I see," said Brother Anthony. "But let me show you something." Here he asked the hunter to place an arrow in his bow and shoot it. The hunter obliged. "Now shoot another," Brother Anthony said. "And another. And another."

Finally the hunter stopped and said, "This is nonsense. If I bend my bow all of the time, it will break!"

"And so it is with the work of God," said Brother Anthony. "If we push ourselves constantly, we will soon collapse. It is only right, therefore, that from time to time we should relax our efforts."

★

When asked to define the word "Puritan," a seminary student once answered: " A Puritan is a person who is deeply troubled by the very thought that someone, somewhere, might be having a good time."

In truth, we have all known such sour people. But sour people only produce sour grapes.

Those who desire to make the best of life—and even do their best work—must learn how to relax, how to get away from the grind of constant labor and stress. Perhaps the Latin American siesta is in order, or the ritual Sabbath of the Jewish orthodox. Regardless of the names, however, the need for a period of rest is built into the very fabric of our beings. People are not machines. We wear out. And the harder we drive ourselves, the more likely we are to experience disorders of the body, mind, and spirit.

The best prescription for a happy and productive life is, of course, focused labor (maybe even long labor) followed by scheduled periods of rest and renewal.

It sounds simple but the ends are difficult to achieve. Don't forget to make laughter a part of your life.

Polycarp and the Kingdom of Truth (Christian)

The excellent Polycarp, Bishop of Smyrna, had, when persecution prevailed, left the city and repaired with his faithful disciple, Crescens, to the country in the vicinity of Smyrna. In the cool of the evening he went out under the shade of a noble tree which stood in front of the farm-house. Here he found Crescens under an oak, supporting his head upon his hand, and weeping.

The old man approached and asked, "My son, why do you weep?"

Crescens raised his head and replied: "How can I not mourn and weep? I am thinking of the kingdom of God on earth. Storm and tempest are thickening around it, and will destroy it in its youth. Many confessors have already fallen off, and have denied and disgraced it; and thus prove that unworthy persons also profess with the mouth, although their heart is far from it. This fills my soul with mourning, and my eyes with tears."

Polycarp answered, smiling, and said: "My dear son, the heavenly kingdom of truth is like a tree which a countryman planted. Secretly and quietly he deposited the gem in the earth, and went his way. It sprouted and shot up among the weeds and briars, and lifted its head above them, so that the briars died of themselves; for the shade of the tree above caused them to wither away. But the tree grew, and the winds raved around it, and caused it to quake; so much the deeper did its roots strike into the ground, and fasten themselves about the rocks of the earth far down, while its branches reached up towards heaven. So the storm made it more firm. And when now it became higher, and its shadow was spread far and wide, the weeds and briars grew up again beneath it. But it regarded them not in its loftiness, and stood there in still and quiet state, a tree of God!"

Thus spake the incomparable bishop; and then he reached his hand to his disciple, and said, smiling: "Why are you troubled, when you look up to its top, by the weeds which creep about its roots!"

Then Crescens arose, and his spirit was serene; for the old man walked beside him, bowed with years, but his spirit and his countenance were those of a youth.

★

Polycarp, bishop of Smyrna, was a second- century Christian martyr who, according to tradition, was burned at the stake. Many early Christian teachings and stories formed around Polycarp, including this one that is reminiscent of the parable of the wheat and the tares (told by Jesus). Buddha is said to have taught a similar concept—admonishing his disciples to leave behind the "burning buildings" of the world and focus upon the enlightenment.

Another way of thinking about life is this: Why would we focus on the ugly when we can be inspired by the beautiful? So much of life is perspective—and beautiful thoughts lead us to beautiful places.

Simple Prayers (Jesus)

Jesus told them this parable:

Two men went to the temple to pray—one was a religious leader and the other was a man who collected taxes for the government. The religious leader, standing off by himself, prayed this prayer: "God, I'm so thankful I'm not like these other people who are thieves, deceivers, adulterers, and tax collectors. I fast twice a week, a give a tenth of my income to God's work."

But the tax collector could hardly lift his face to heaven. He was distressed and pounded his chest saying, "Please God, be merciful to me. I'm just a sinner."

I tell you, the tax collector went home justified before God instead of the religious leader—for everyone who exalts himself will be humbled, but whoever humbles himself will be exalted.

★

Whatever this parable is about, it is certainly about the divine mercy and a warning against self-righteousness and spiritual arrogance. Jesus always recognizes human need and weakness while also embracing hope, and holding out the power of transformation. Transformation is born of relationship. And in relationship with God we discover that we are already accepted despite our failures. In short, there is no place for arrogance when it comes to a life—or any path—of faith.

Three Ways to Pray (Jewish)

Once, the Emperor Antonius asked Rabbi Ha-Kodesh about prayer. "Is it a good thing to pray frequently to God?"

The rabbi answered, "It is not a good thing."

"But why?"

"One should not become too familiar with God," the rabbi answered.

The rabbi's answer, however, did not seem to sit well with the Emperor.

Early the next morning, when the rabbi entered the palace, he greeted the Emperor with, "Peace be with you, O Mighty Caesar."

A little later that morning, the rabbi greeted the Emperor with these same words. And a few hours later, the rabbi greeted for a third time with the words, "Peace be with you, O Mighty Caesar."

The Emperor grew perturbed by the rabbi's constant greeting and said, "Why are you bothering me with so many words? Are you trying to make me the blunt of your joke?"

The rabbi immediately responded, "O that the Emperor might hear his own words and learn from them. If you, and flesh and blood ruler, have grown weary of hearing so many greetings and petitions, might not the Lord of the Universe grow weary from hearing so many prayers?"

Another time, Rabbi Eleazar was leading a group of students in worship, and it was noted that one of the students was reading the prayers too slowly. Rabbi Eleazer responded, "But is this student praying any longer than our teacher, Moses, who prayed upon the mountain of God for forty days and forty nights?"

Later that week, it was noted that another student was praying too quickly.

Rabbi Eleazer responded, "But is this student praying with any more brevity than our leader, Moses, who, when he prayed for his sister Mariam, used the words, "Heal her, O God'?"

Yet another time Rabbi Hanina Ben Dosa was on his way home when a heavy rain began to fall. He prayed, "Lord of the Universe, is this fair? Everyone else sits at home, warm and dry, while Hanina gets drenched!"

Immediately the rain ceased.

Later, at home, Hanina prayed again, "Lord of the Universe, I am at home, warm and dry, but is it just that there is no rain falling upon the fields?"

Immediately it began to rain.

★

All of these tales, adapted from the Talmud, are examples of Jewish parable and demonstrate the ability to see the tensions at the heart of prayer. On the one hand, God already knows our need, so what is the purpose of asking God or pointing out the obvious? But on the other hand, prayer affords us the opportunity to commune with the Creator, and nearly all faiths emphasize the need for people to express the obvious and to ask God for help. On the one hand we can never pray too much, but on the other we know that action is often required, and it is movement that may be, in fact, the answer to our prayers.

These are tensions that have been played out in all religions, and it could be observed that teachings on prayer form one of the central themes of faith. But what is prayer? Is prayer a recitation of words (such as the Shema Prayer of Judaism or the Lord's Prayer, the "Our Father" of Christianity)? Is prayer an individual endeavor? Or is prayer best experienced and expressed in a corporate or communal way with others?

Does prayer change God (and can God be influenced)? *Or* does prayer change the one who prays? Is prayer magical (i.e., we get things, or change the universe, when we pray)? Or is prayer relational (i.e., the center of prayer is love and devotion and humility)?

These are not insignificant thoughts, but questions that people have struggled to answer for centuries. And it should be noted that there are as many ideas about prayer as there are people who pray.

These ancient Jewish samples on prayer lean toward a playfulness and a mystery to prayer. And perhaps this is the best place to begin . . . and perhaps to end.

Or, as the following parables and teachings of Jesus confer, prayer is something we should do—even if we don't know the outcomes. At the very least, prayer matters to the one who prays.

More Prayers (Jesus)

Jesus said, "When you pray, don't stand in the public places to be seen and heard by others. But find a private space and pour out your heart to God there.

"And don't use empty phrases or rote words that have no meaning to you . . . but pray in secret. And your heavenly Father who sees all things will reward you."

Jesus said, "Once there was a woman who was being harassed with a bogus lawsuit. She went to the judge to plead her case, but the judge wouldn't give her an audience. But she didn't give up, she kept returning, time and time again, and eventually the Judge grew weary of her persistence and allowed her to state her case."

Jesus said, "Which of you, if your child asked you for a loaf of bread, would give him a scorpion to eat? Well, if you want to give good things to your own children, why would God, the Creator of the Universe, be any less loving?"

Jesus said, "There was a man who received unexpected guests. But he did not have enough food on hand to feed them all. However, since he wanted to be hospitable he went next door to a neighbor's house at midnight and knocked on the door. When the neighbor answered the man said, 'Please open the door and give me some bread so I can feed my friends.' But the neighbor answered, 'No! Go away! Do you have any idea what time it is? Come back in the morning and I'll give you what you need.'

"But the man kept knocking. He didn't relent. And eventually, because of his persistence, the neighbor opened the door and gave him the bread he needed."

Once, the disciples came to Jesus and said, "Teach us how to pray."

Jesus said to them, "Pray like this: Our Father in heaven, your name is to be revered. We want your kingdom to come upon the earth, and your will to be accomplished, in the same manner that it exists in heaven. Give us today all that we need. Forgive us our sins in the same manner that we forgive those who have sinned against us. But please don't test us in our weaknesses, but deliver us from all that is evil. For all of the kingdom, glory and power belongs to you and you alone. Amen."

★

Jesus had many teachings on prayer—and these teachings, adapted from the gospels of Matthew and Luke, clearly reflect the Jewish playfulness and mystery of prayer itself. On the one hand Jesus gives his followers a prayer to repeat, but on the other hand he asks them not to use rote phrases or words emptied of meaning through their familiarity. On the one hand Jesus teaches the public nature of prayer—praying in community with others—but he also notes that God sees, and even desires, the unseen and intimate prayers of individuals.

These are tensions that have always existed within the Christian faith, too. While hermits and mystics (and many in cloistered communities) have sought to define prayer as a community apart from the world, others have navigated prayer as tradition, or some combination of the corporate and the private.

We may never answer the question, "What, exactly, is prayer . . . and what does it accomplish?" But we can note that prayer can be woven into the fabric of life. Prayer is, at least in part, built on the foundation of a love, devotion, and humility that leads us closer to the divine.

Saint Francis and the Vineyard (Christian)

Once when St. Francis was suffering grievously in his eyes, the Lord Cardinal Hugolin, the Protector of the Order, because he loved him dearly, wrote to him, ordering St. Francis to come to him in Rieti, where there were some very good eye doctors. And when St. Francis received the letter of the Lord Cardinal, he went first to San Daniano, where the very devout spouse of Christ St. Clare was. For he intended to visit her and console her before he left, and then go to Rieti.

And the first night after he went to San Damiano, his eyes became so much worse that he could not see any light. Since he was unable to leave, St. Clare had a little cell made for him out of reeds and straw, in which he might stay in the seclusion and get more rest.

And St. Francis stayed there for fifty days which such pain in his eyes and so greatly disturbed by a large number of mice instigated by the devil that he was unable to obtain any rest at all, either by day or night. And after he had been enduring that trial and tribulation for many days, he began to reflect and to realize that it was a punishment from the Lord for his sins. And he began to thank God with all of his heart and to praise him, crying in a loud voice: "My Lord, I deserve this and much more." And he prayed to the Lord, saying: "My Lord Jesus Christ, Good Shepherd, who have shown Your very gentle mercy to us unworthy sinners in various physical pains and sufferings, give grace and strength to me, Your little lamb, that in no tribulation or anguish or pain may I turn away from You!"

And when he had uttered this prayer, a Voice came to him from Heaven that said: "Francis, answer Me. If the whole earth were made of gold, and all the oceans and rivers and springs were balsam, and all the mountains and hills and rocks were precious stones, and you found another treasure that was as much more valuable than all those things as gold is than earth, and balsam than water, and gems than mountains and rocks, and if that most valuable treasure were given to you for this illness of yours, should you not be very happy and rejoice greatly?"

St. Francis answered: "Lord, I am not worthy of so precious a treasure."

And the Voice of God said to him: "Rejoice, therefore, Brother Francis, because that is the treasure of eternal life which I am keeping for you. And right now I invest you with it. And this illness and affliction are a pledge of that blessed treasure."

Then St. Francis, thrilled with joy by that glorious promise, called his companion an said, "Let's go to Rieti—to the Lord Cardinal!"

And after first consoling St. Clare with holy and honey-sweet words and saying good-by to her humbly, as he usually did, he set out for Rieti.

But when he arrived near Rieti, such a great crowd of people came out to meet him that he therefore did not want to go into the city, but turned aside and went to a certain church that was about two miles away from the town. But the people, knowing that he was staying at the church, flocked out to see him in such throngs that the vineyard of the priest of that church—for it was vintage time—was completely ruined and all the grapes were taken and eaten. When the priest saw the damage, he was bitterly sorry and he regretted that he had allowed St. Francis to go into his church.

The priest's thoughts were revealed to the Saint by the Holy Spirit, and he summoned the priest and said to Him: "My dear Father, how many measures of wine does this vineyard produce in a year when it produces well?"

The priest answered: "Twelve."

And St. Francis said: "Then I beg you, Father, to bear patiently my staying here in this church of yours for some days, because of the rest and quiet I find here. And let everyone take the grapes from this vineyard of yours, for the love of God and your poor little self. And I promise you on behalf of my Lord Jesus Christ that this year you will get twenty measures."

St. Francis did this—staying on there—because of the great good which he saw the Lord performing in the souls of the people who came there, for he saw that many of them, when they came and went away, were inebriated with the love of God and converted to heavenly longings, forgetting the world. Therefore it seemed to him better that the material vineyard should be damaged than that the vineyard of the Lord of Hosts should be sterile in heavenly wine.

So the priest trusted in the promise of St. Francis and freely let the people who came there take and eat the grapes. It certainly is a wonderful thing that the vineyard was completely stripped and ruined of them, so that only a few little bunches of grapes remained. But when the vintage came, the priest, trusting in the Saint's promise, gathered those little bunches of grapes and put them into the wine press and pressed them. And as St. Francis had promised, he obtained twenty measures of the very best wine that year.

By that miracle it was clearly shown that, just as through the merits of St. Francis the vineyard with its ruined grapes had produced an abundance of wine, so the Christian people, who were sterile in virtue because of sin, through the merits and teaching of St. Francis frequently brought forth good fruits and penance.

★

Born the son of a wealthy merchant in Assisi, Italy in 1182, Francis had a brief and disappointing military career as a young man. But after a visit to Rome, where he visited the poor and was deeply moved by human suffering, he soon renounced his worldly goods and took up a life of direct assistance to the poor and marginalized. Tradition has Francis preaching to the birds of the air and the beasts of the field, and after 1220, while suffering from malaria and glaucoma, Francis was said to have received the stigmata of Christ, which are the visible scars of the crucified Jesus on his hands and feet.

Soon after Francis's death, many traditions and stories emerged about him. Many were written down, including this tradition regarding St. Francis and the vineyard.

As the story relates, Francis had a deep humility and awareness of his own sins—a mark of many saints—but also a life attached to the miraculous and the abundant. Small gifts become large blessings in the world of the saints, and as Jesus said, small faith often produces great abundance.

One of Francis's famous sermons—the sermon to the birds—is, of course, meant for people. Francis hoped that the teachings and metaphors used to describe the birds of the air could also describe our blessings and our needs. The sermon goes in part like this:

My little sisters, the birds, you are such beloved by God, your creator, and in every place you should praise him with your song. Remember that he has doubly and even triply dressed you and you can go where you wish. God gives you food to eat and provides springs and rivers for you when you are thirsty; there are hills and valleys for your refuge and trees to make your nests. You do not have to sow or weave, for God gives you and your offspring amply clothing. For love your creator, for he has done much for you. Finally, my little sisters, beware of the sin of ingratitude. Be ready always to give praises and thanks to God.

Asking and Receiving (Jesus)

I say to you, "Ask, and it will be given to you. Search, and you will find. Knock, and the door will be opened. For everyone who asks receives. And everyone who searches finds. And everyone who knocks will discover an open door. Is there anyone among you who, if your child asked you for a fish would give a snake instead? Or if your child asked for an egg, would you give a scorpion? If you then, who are evil, know how to give good gifts to your children, why wouldn't God give even greater gifts to those who ask?"

★

As with many parables told by Jesus, we discover that metaphors are powerful images. An open door, a loving parent, gifts given to children . . . who would fail to understand or be moved by these ideas?

Persistence is a key ingredient in life—a perseverance that sees one through great difficulties but also invites new opportunities. No one can discover anything new about themselves, about others, or about the divine, without first being willing to try. The other side of the door represents a closed life, a closed mind—and in the end, a closed heart.

What this parable teaches is a generosity of spirit, an adventurous faith, and love that keeps on giving. Without these we are little more than bodies walking. With them, we are living souls.

Practice Makes Perfect (Desert Fathers)

Father James once said, "We must not desire words alone—for there are already too many words in the world as it is. What we must desire is action—for that is what others are looking for and not just words that are like dry fruit."

St. Francis once said, "Preach the gospel every day, and when necessary, use words." It is the practice of faith, not the confession of it, which determines the depth of our lives and commitments. Faith is a verb, not a noun. Acts speak much louder than words—as Father James noted.

One's expressions of faith through service, generosity and self-sacrifice are more powerful than words. One should not work so hard on memorizing beliefs and facts as on living out one's creed in acts of kindness. One's creed should not be contained in a book, but in the heart.

The Seed (Tolstoy)

Many years ago two children were talking down a road when they happened upon a small round object—a grain seed unlike any they had ever seen before. They picked up the seed and took it to the Tsar for examination.

Now the Tsar was deeply fascinated by this seed and his first thoughts were that it might be a new kind of grain that could produce enormous wealth. He gathered his wise men together and asked, "Have you seen this seed before? Can any of you identify it?"

But, alas, none could. One of the wise men said, "Perhaps there is someone in the kingdom who is older, who can identify this grain for us."

And so the Tsar summoned an old man from the peasantry into the palace for questioning. This old man arrived in the palace, limping and walking with two canes. He also had no teeth. The Tsar said, "Tell me . . . have you seen this seed before and do you know what type of plant it might grow?"

The old man studied the seed for long minutes and then said, "Your highness, I have never seen such a seed before in my life. I am sorry I cannot identify it. But my father is still living, perhaps he can be of help."

The Tsar, startled to learn that there was one older yet in the kingdom, then summoned this man to the palace. Now this man was very old, and when he arrived at the palace he was walking with one cane, and he had two teeth. The Tsar showed him the seed and asked, "Tell me . . . have you seen this seed before and do you know what type of plant it might grow?"

The old man studied the seed for long minutes and then said, "Your highness, I have never seen such a seed before in my life. I am sorry I cannot identify it. But my father is still living, perhaps he can be of help."

At this word the Tsar was truly astounded, but he realized that there was yet another who was older. He summed this man's father to the palace. When the man arrived he was very old, indeed, and yet he walked without a limp and his smile shone bright with teeth. The Tsar was most intrigued, but he showed the old man the seed and asked, "Tell me . . . have you seen this seed before and do you know what type of plant it might grow?"

The old man studied the seed briefly and then said, "This is the grain that I knew in my childhood, and it grew freely among the hills and the fields. It produced abundantly, and everyone had more than enough to eat."

The Tsar was thrilled to hear this, and yet he was more than intrigued by the old man. The Tsar said, "When I summoned your grandson, he appeared in the palace walking on two canes and had no teeth. Your son, who was older, walked with one cane and had two teeth. But you appear before me, the oldest of all, with a spring in your step, still an energetic man—and you still have all of your teeth. Tell me two things: How is this possible, and why does this grain no longer grow in the kingdom?"

The oldest man smiled and answered, "These two are related. When I was young the earth belonged to everyone and no one labored alone, but for the good of all. There was no greed, and everyone lived according to God's word. These practices made us healthy, but now everyone is poisoned by their own greed and corruption."

★

This marvelous story paints a beautiful tapestry of the common good and offers the sage advice of the elders. Where there is satisfaction and shared interests, greed cannot take root. Even the things which sustain life can become corrupted and ineffective when self-interest and personal profit replaces the good of the whole. The earth itself can become sick.

Although Tolstoy lived decades ago, this parable, adapted from his many teaching stories, seems contemporary. The marvel and the wonder of old age is wisdom gained. Somewhere in our time we can also listen to the sages. They would have much to teach us.

Chapter Six

Crisis and Courage

How can you buy or sell the sky? The land?
The idea is strange to us. If we do not own the freshness
of the air and the sparkle of the water, how can you buy them?
—Chief Seattle

I awake today in Heaven's might and in the brightness
of the Sun . . .
—St. Patrick

Many of the world's most powerful narratives emerge during periods of crisis—as leaders rise up to lead a people, or communities learn valuable lessons through hardship and triumph. Consider, for example, the Biblical stories of the Exodus from Egypt and the Passover narrative, or the Passion Narrative of the New Testament, or many of the parables of Buddha. Crisis often creates courage, and humanity has often gleaned victorious lessons from periods of hardship and testing. Many of these larger-than-life achievements are also recorded in legend, poem, and song. These reflect both courage and conviction.

Among the many sayings and stories attributed the Desert Fathers—those Christian ascetics who removed themselves from the urban sprawl of the fourth and fifth centuries, we discover a wealth of courageous insights about simple living and the joys of seeking the divine. The Syrian and Egyptian deserts offered a blank and reflective canvas from which to create new approaches to crises, and thus discover new aspects of faith and courage.

One such saying, attributed to a sage known as Abba (Father) Pior goes like this: "Every day he would make a fresh beginning." This seems simple enough—even obvious—but from a spiritual perspective we discover many deeper truths.

It does take courage to face every new day "fresh"—to leave behind the old anxieties, the common experiences, the usual worries. This also involves creativity. What if we were able to face every new day as a blank canvas, free from the constraints of yesterday's brush strokes? What if, every morning, we felt that we were shedding the old shackles and were free to run a new race with joy? This is easier said than done. More commonly, we face each new day with the same worries, the same cares, and the same hum-drum approaches to the same problems as the day prior. A new day doesn't mean that we are willing to change. Most of the time, we just stand pat and wallow in the leftovers from the day before.

Courage may be the conviction to march toward a new horizon. In this definition, few have this type of approach to life.

The parables, teachings, and tales in this chapter may introduce us to new ways to handle crises in our lives and in our world. We may not have all the answers—but some of these beautiful words may introduce us to new thoughts and approaches. We may also discover that we have more in common with others than we at first imagined. Regardless of nationality or language or culture, human beings are essentially seeking the same happiness and goals.

In these wonderful stories we encounter ourselves doing courageous things. Some of these words are about us. And if we read closely, we will discover that we can make choices that will not only impact our own lives, but the lives of those around us. There is nothing magical here—but something wholly mystical and encouraging, even (and perhaps especially) blessed. Regardless of our age or station in life, we all need courage to see us through. And may we all find some additional strength from these sage teachings.

The Fugitive (Buddhist)

Once there was a man who was a fugitive from justice. He attempted to escape into the forest, but in his haste he fell into a pit. Grabbing hold of a vine as he descended, the man escaped death, as he noted that there were two large vipers at the bottom of the pit. However, as he clung to the vine, he also noted that there were two mice above him that were eating away at the vine that was supporting him. He could neither descend nor ascend to safety. Suddenly, he spied a bee's nest above him at the rim of the pit. As the bees flew in and out of the hive, honey began to drip down upon his lips. He tasted the honey, and for a moment he forgot his troubles and was swept away in the sweetness of the blessing.

★

Buddhist parables—much like the parables told by Jesus—are weighted with metaphor and hold up well across time, cultures, and traditions. Here is a story about life itself—a life that we know is filled with pitfalls and detours, with dangers and entanglements. We often live in fear of abandonment, or helplessness, or even in holes of depression or anxiety. But then, in the midst of these troubles, if we are perceptive we can always discover the sweetness of the universe. Even in times of trouble we can be thankful. Closing ourselves off to these mysteries and joys is not the answer. Rather, it is being open to these blessings that enables us to receive them: blessings that we can often miss or disregard because of our fear or attachment to our troubles. We dare not prefer misery (or making others miserable) over a life of harmony and joy.

★

Another tale from the Desert Fathers aptly illustrates this idea:

As he was dying, Father Benjamin left these final words: "You will be saved if you rejoice always, pray constantly, and give thanks in all circumstances."

Gratitude, indeed, is difficult . . . but those who live a life of thanksgiving soon find themselves on the mountaintop of joy instead of lingering in the sinkhole of misery.

The House Mouse (Abstemius)

A mouse that had lived inside a cedar chest its entire life one day happened to peer through the crack in the lid. Spying a morsel of crumbs on the floor nearby, it ventured out of the chest for the first time in its life to enjoy the food. Overcome by the awe of its new surroundings the mouse said to itself, "I never knew that such a world existed. What a fool I have been for limiting myself in the box."

★

This beautiful parable from Abstemius is pure metaphor (and maybe a little Dr. Seuss?). Whatever this story is about, it certainly touches upon our limited human experience, our proclivity toward individualism, and our fear of risk-taking. The boxes that limit us could be anything: bad habits, sloth, narrow-mindedness, fear, or even an inability to imagine anything better for ourselves. But we often don't have to venture far to experience a new world of possibilities.

This brief parable has implications not only for the spiritual life—and our relationships and families—but also for businesses and all manner of envisioning a better world. In truth, many of the oldest insights have a contemporary pull.

The Hazel Branch (Christian legend)

One day Mary placed the infant Jesus in his cradle, and after he had gone to sleep, she said, "While you are sleeping, child, I will go out into the woods and gather some delicious strawberries." And so Mary left Jesus and journeyed into the woods. She soon discovered a bed of strawberries and began to pick them. But a serpent crept up upon her and was about to strike when, startled by its hiss, Mary noticed the serpent and ran away. The serpent pursued her, but she hid behind a hazel tree. After the serpent passed by, Mary returned to gather up the strawberries. As she was returning home to said, "As the hazel tree has protected me from evil, so shall it protect others in the future."

★

Another early Christian legend, most likely from the late Middle Ages, relates the common practice of attaching an artifact to an event. Here is a story associated with the hazel branch (purported to ward off snakes).

All faiths eventually associate events with holy places or holy items. Some of these items are meant to invite others into a deeper devotion to, or memory of a saint. Likely, this story was told to children—another way that faith was passed from one generation to another.

But at their core, such artifacts were meant to invoke a sense of the divine presence in the midst of difficulty. Relics, however, are not required. A mountain will do, or the ocean, or even a bed of flowers in the back yard. Anything that excites our imaginations and our awareness of the divine is a holy moment.

The Dream (Buddhist)

There is a story about a king who placed four vipers in a box and gave them to his servant. He told the servant, "If you anger but one of the vipers, you will be put to death."

Fearing for his life, the servant decided to discard the box and flee. He sought sanctuary in a nearby village. Soon afterwards, the king sent five guards to go and search for the servant. When they found him in the neighboring village, they attempted to lure him into a trap by being friendly, but the servant mistrusted their intentions and fled to yet another village.

But in this village the servant had a dream. In the dream he was warned that there would be six bandits who would attack him. When the servant awoke from his dream, he fled to the edge of the river, but it was wild and he had to make a raft. Working diligently, the servant built his raft, crossed the turbulent water, and eventually was able to live the rest of his life in peace and security.

★

In this Buddhist parable we encounter a metaphor of enlightenment, which the Buddha often likened to escaping from a burning house or forging a wild river. Life itself can feel this chaotic and uncertain. Those who seek the path of enlightenment, and find it, are like those who escape from many dangers and find peace on the other side. Jesus likened this to "a narrow path," and Chuang Tzu called his method "the Way" or "Tao." Everyone is walking a road—but as these great teachers enjoined, not all roads lead to life. To find this truth, one must be willing to leave behind the deadly vices, the pursuits of evil, and at last cross through the enticements and strong currents of desires that threaten to sweep us away. In some traditions these enticements may be called sins or lusts. In other traditions they may be known as vices. Or still others, as weaknesses or the human condition. Regardless, whenever we can escape them, another life awaits on the other side of these transformations.

The Great Adventure (Based on a Greek Legend)

Once, when Hercules and a companion were passing through a far country, they came to a sign upon which was written the following inscription: *To the Brave Adventurer—if you wish to obtain a great treasure, here cross the waters of the river, proceed into the mountains carrying an elephant on your shoulders, and summit.*

When the companion read these words he said, "What a ridiculous adventure this is. There is no telling how deep the water is, or how high the mountain. And as for carrying an elephant on one's shoulders while advancing to the summit, this is impossible." At this word the companion turned back and returned home.

Hercules, however, crossed the river at once—and discovered that the waters were not deep at all. On the other side of the river he found the elephant tied to a stake. He loaded the heavy beast on his shoulders and proceeded on his quest. Much later, when he came to the summit carrying the elephant, he noticed a town in the valley below. Great shrieks went up from the town when the people saw Hercules carrying the elephant.

And so it was when Hercules entered the town, they hailed him as a hero and welcomed him as king.

★

This ancient Greek legend offers a prize to those with an adventurous spirit. Those who spend much time calculating the risk often lack commitment to a cause. Hesitation can be costly. And sometimes, opportunities forfeited can never be recovered. The greatest prizes of life are often those born of daring achievement, or earned under duress or enormous sacrifice.

The old adage "He who hesitates is lost" may well apply here. But equal to the cause would be: "From great sacrifice comes great reward." Indeed, a crisis can be the perfect opportunity to demonstrate great courage.

The Land Crisis (Talmud)

Two men were fighting over a piece of land. Each claimed ownership and tried to prove his case. At last, in order to reach a conclusion, they agreed to allow a rabbi to hear their case. The rabbi listened, but was unable to reach a verdict because both men had presented ample evidence for their cause. Finally, the rabbi said, "Since I cannot decide this case, let us ask the land." He put his ear to the ground and after a few minutes stood up and said, "My friends, the land says that it belongs to neither of you—but that *you* belong to *it*."

★

Space and ownership have always been driving forces between people—and between nations and ideologies. Many a crisis comes from our connections to the earth. But there are many traditions—including Native American—that point to the fallacy of our ownership of the natural order. Rather, stewardship and caretaking are affirmed as our primary relationship to the earth. As the Psalmist once proclaimed, "The earth is the Lord's and the fullness thereof." And in the beginning (Genesis) it is God who affirms: "Be fruitful and multiply and fill the earth and tend it, for I have made you caretakers over the fish of the sea and the birds of the air and everything that moves upon the earth."

Today, it takes courage to be a steward, to care for that which others may abuse or destroy for profit.

As Chief Seattle affirmed, the earth is sacred to all people. We are part of the earth and the earth is part of us. Or, as Lao Tzu (*Tao Te Ching*) noted: "The highest good is like that of water. The goodness of water is that it benefits the ten thousand creatures; yet itself does not scramble, but is content with the places that all men disdain. It is this that makes water so near The Way."

And, although not all may be able to affirm the noble path of caring for the earth, perhaps some may affirm the prayer:

Oh Great Spirit, whose breath gives life to the world and whose voice is heard in the soft breeze, we need your strength and wisdom. May we walk in Beauty. May our eyes ever behold the red and purple sunset. Make us wise so that we may understand what you have taught us. Help us to learn the lessons you have hidden in every leaf and rock. Make us always ready to come to you with clean hands and straight eyes, so when life fades, as the fading sunset, our spirits may come to you without shame.

The Cat and the Sparrow (La Fontaine)

A cat and a sparrow lived in the same house. In fact, though their natures were different, they were actually the best of friends. Others marveled of their friendship and could not understand why the sparrow did not fly away, nor why the cat did not eat the sparrow.

One day another sparrow flew into the house and unsettled this arrangement. The new sparrow pointed out the dangers of this arrangement and attempted to persuade the other sparrow to leave. "Don't you know that cats eat birds?" it said. "Your life is in danger. I implore you to leave this arrangement at once."

When the cat heard what this other sparrow was saying it answered, "I have no desire to eat the sparrow. We are the best of friends." But when the other sparrow persisted with its warnings, the cat grew weary of it and gobbled it up. Then, upon tasting sparrow for the first time in its life, it understood its nature and proceeded to eat the other sparrow, too.

★

The French writer, La Fontaine, was a deft commentator and fabulist. Here he weaves a fascinating tale about human nature and the weak bonds that often form the basis of friendships between nations and ideologies. Whatever this parable is about, it strikes us as truthful from the vantage point of human experience.

Blood is thicker than water, as they say—and we often see the faulty logic that certain agreements and relationships are built upon. Experience is the best teacher. And we so often see how quickly animosities can erupt when there is misunderstanding and mistrust. It takes courage to be a peacemaker.

The Trout and the Sucker (Dodsley)

A fisherman went down to the Thames and cast an artificial fly into the water hoping to catch a trout. As it happened, a mother and her baby trout were swimming by at that very instant. The baby trout, eager to get at the meal, was about the strike the artificial lure when the mother trout intervened. "Be very careful, my child," she said. "It is not wise to rush too swiftly to judgment or to risk the possibility of danger based upon appearances. How do you know if this is a real fly, or if it is a fisherman's lure? Better to let someone else take the risk and then follow. If this is a real fly, it would very likely elude your attack, and then you can always make a second attempt. Be wary of first impressions."

Just as the mother trout was finishing her speech, a sucker came swimming by, saw the bright colored lure, and bit it. It was immediately drawn up out of the water and tossed into the fisherman's net.

★

Many a crisis has been averted through sound reason and patience. Sleeping on an opportunity rarely hurts, and if the proposition is sound, it will be waiting the following day. Patience is, indeed, a virtue . . . and so is the ability to look beyond first impressions. Appearances, after all, can be deceiving. A little caution and risk-aversion rarely hurt anyone, but those who live by their impulses usually end up getting burned in the end.

The Vision of Peace (Isaiah)

The wolf shall live with the lamb, the leopard shall lie down with the kid, the calf and the lion and the fatling together, and a little child shall lead them. The cow and the bear shall graze, their young shall lie down together, and the lion shall eat straw like the ox. The nursing child shall play over the hole of the asp, and the weaned child shall put its hand on the adder's den. They will not hurt or destroy on all my holy mountain; for the earth will be full of the knowledge of the Lord as the waters cover the sea. (Isaiah 11:6-9)

★

Sometimes—in the midst of a crisis—it helps to have a different vision. The book of Isaiah provides many such sobering and poetical metaphors. Images like this one provoke a sense of longing, and can help us to work toward a deeper reality.

The Three Friends (Buddhist)

Centuries ago the Buddha dwelt upon the earth in the form of an antelope. Deep in the forest, he was friends with the woodpecker and the tortoise.

One day the Buddha went out for a walk at the morning light and became ensnared in a hunter's trap. When the woodpecker and the tortoise saw this they said, "What shall we do? We must save our friend."

The tortoise said, "I will go and gnaw on the leather straps of the trap with my sharp mouth while you distract the hunter."

And so the tortoise crawled to the trap and began gnawing while the woodpecker flew toward the hunter's house. Just as the hunter was exiting his home with his knife in hand, the woodpecker flew down and hit him in the face, distracting him and causing him to return to his home momentarily as he thought, "This bird is a bad omen."

After a few minutes, however, the hunter again exited his home with his knife in hand and began his trek toward the trap in the forest. The woodpecker flew back to warn the tortoise, who had managed the chew through the leather straps, releasing the Buddha antelope. But when the hunter arrived to find the trap empty, he also noticed a tortoise that seemed completely spent of energy. The hunter tossed the tortoise into a sack and thought, "This will make a nice stew."

Now the Buddha antelope was watching all of this from afar and said to the woodpecker, "You are my friends and you did what friends should do for one another. Because you have saved my life I must now save the life of the tortoise."

Running toward the hunter, the Buddha antelope caught the hunter's eye. Seeing that the antelope had escaped his trap, the hunter discarded the bag on the ground and began running toward the antelope to recapture it. But the Buddha leapt through the forest and soon outdistanced the hunter. Then, circling back to the discarded bag, it punctured the bag with its horns, releasing the tortoise, and then the three friends escaped. They returned to the deepest regions of the forest and lived there together happily.

★

There are many Buddhist parables of crisis and friendship, usually with the Buddha in animal form. Here a crisis is averted because of the great love and sacrifice of the Buddha, who teaches friendship through example. Friendship, indeed, can overcome many crises.

The Oak and the Sycamore (Dodsley)

An oak and a sycamore grew side by side. One year, at the first hint of spring, the sycamore put forth its leaves and began to make fun of the oak, which was still naked. "I am full of leaves," the sycamore boasted, "but you are still barren."

But the oak, confident of its superiority and heartiness, responded: "You have put forth the early leaves, this is true. But beware the frost, which may kill your glorious buds. I will wait for warmth to confirm my case, and then I will put forth leaves that will overtake your canopy.

Remember, the tree that exults first in the spring is always the one to drop its leaves at the first sign of winter."

★

Another Dodsley nature parable—this one insightful for its practicality. Those who are first in line, or who come first to the dance, are not always the ones who reach the highest levels of success. Being first doesn't necessarily equate to winning. In fact, as the parable points out, many who are swift out of the gate often fade at the close or when difficulties arise. Consistency over the long haul is far more important to success than speed. One could also think "quality" ahead of productivity. Perhaps this is the nature of spirit, too. The race is not usually to the swift, but to the wise.

Mixed Bag (Buddhist)

Learn the lesson of the passions. Suppose you caught a snake, a crocodile, a bird, a dog, a fox and a monkey—and you tied them together with a rope so that they could not get away. You know what will happen. Each will attempt to get away and return to its natural habitat. The snake will seek a covering in the grass, the crocodile will seek the swamp, the bird will want to fly away, the dog will seek to return to its home in the village, the fox will seek its den and the monkey will seek to return to the trees in the forest. All will attempt to flee, but at any one time the strongest will drag the others along.

★

Centuries ago the church set upon the idea of the seven deadly sins—those lusts and weaknesses that often vie for our hearts and souls. But anyone—regardless of religious background, culture, or tradition—can understand that there are many ideas that are alluring, but do not ultimately satisfy.

Here the Buddha offers a practical, and yet spiritually adept insight: We are that which dominates our thoughts and actions. The question for every person is then: What are the passions and practices that will dominate my life?

The Way (Jewish)

Abraham, the father of the faithful, lived in the land of Haran along with his father, Terah, and all of his cattle. After his father died at a ripe old age, Abraham buried him and was preparing to inherit all of his father's goods when the Word of the Lord came to Abraham and said, "Go! Leave your native land, your kindred and your father's house and go to a land that I will show you."

Abraham obeyed and did as the Lord commanded him. He went out of Haran not knowing the way to the land that God would show him.

After he had gone many days' journey he met with some traveling merchants who were returning from Egypt and Arabia. They had camels and many precious wares. When they spoke with Abraham they asked him where he was going.

Abraham replied, "I am going to a far land."

When the merchants pressed him further for information, "But what is the name of this country and what is the road that leads to it?"

Abraham answered, "I don't know the name of the country, and neither do I know the way."

Upon hearing this, the merchants laughed at Abraham and ridiculed him. They asked, "But who will guide you through the desert, or see that you do not perish, or give you food, or see that you arrive at your destination safely?"

And Abraham answered, "The One who has called me to go will see me safely to my destination."

After this the merchants went on their way, making fun of Abraham. And Abraham journeyed on his way as well and reached the land of Promise.

★

The faith of Abraham is recalled and celebrated by all three monotheistic faiths (Judaism, Christianity, and Islam). All regard Abraham as the father of faith. This traditional legend offers more for the journey from Haran to the Promised Land—in this instance another kind of resistance. Faith is courage lived out. Courage is hope with feet. And in the journey of life, we are always moved by our convictions and our ultimate concerns. The faith that moved Abraham still moves people today.

The Legend of Multnomah Falls (Native American)

Centuries ago there was a chief who had a beautiful young daughter. She was especially dear to the chief because all of his sons had been killed in battle. He wanted to please her and to insure her happiness, and so the chief arranged for his daughter to marry a young chief from a neighboring tribe.

The chief made the arrangements and prepared a wedding celebration that would last for a week. The festivities were to include horse races, bow and arrow competitions, foot races, and feats of strength. There would be food and drink. But just as the wedding celebration was getting underway, a terrible sickness swept through the village. Children died first, and then the young braves. And eventually the illness killed the old and the feeble. Finally, as the illness began to plague even the strongest in the village, the elders gathered together.

"The Great Spirit is angry with us," one of the elders said.

"Yes, but what can we do?" asked another.

"We are doomed," answered a third elder. "If the Great Spirit wants to kill us all, then we must face our deaths as brave men. We have always been brave in the face of death and this is no different than any battle."

At last the oldest member of the council spoke out. He was a medicine man of advanced age, an elder who had seen many battles and had survived many close calls with death. He said, "My brothers, indeed the Great Spirit is angry with us. But I have held my tongue until now. Many years ago my father—who was great medicine man of the Multnomah—told me a story. He revealed to me that this day would come, that our village would encounter a great sickness and that many would die. But he also revealed to me that we could appease the wrath of the Great Spirit if there was a young maiden of the village, a daughter of a chief, who would willingly give her life to save the people."

The elders immediately balked at this idea, regarding it as sheer folly and foolishness. But the chief gathered the young maidens around the council and said, "I think the medicine man speaks truth. But there shall be no sacrifice. We will face death bravely." The meeting had ended.

A few days later the sickness settled upon the young warriors. The chief's daughter noticed the sickness would soon take her lover and secretly she decided that she would give her life to save the people.

That night she crept out of the camp and hiked up into the mountains. She travelled all day and that night, as the moon was full in the sky, she looked out over a high cliff and prayed to the Great Spirit. "I know you are angry with my people," she said, "But I willingly give myself to save the people. All that I ask is that you not let my death be in vain. Please send a sign to my people so that they may know that the illness will pass over them."

After this prayer, she jumped from the face of the cliff.

The next morning, all of the people in the village miraculously rose from the beds, completely well. Someone asked, "What made the illness pass away?"

The elders began to take a head count of the young maidens and it was soon discovered that the chief's daughter was missing. The chief gathered an entourage and set out in search of his daughter. A few hours later, they discovered her body at the foot of the cliff, and buried her there.

Heartbroken, the chief prayed, "O Great Spirit, show us a sign that my daughter is well and that she has been welcomed into the tribe of the spirits."

Immediately there was a sound high above, and when they looked up, there was a silvery band of water spilling over the edge of the rock. The water continued to fall and formed a pool at their feet.

All of this happened many years ago, but the falls continue to flow. And it is said that on certain nights the spirit of the young maiden returns to stand on the edge of the pool and, gazing up in the moonlight, beholds the place where she offered herself to save her people.

★

The legend of Multnomah Falls is about personal sacrifice for the redemption of a people. This concept, indeed, is found in many Native American legends and is closely aligned with other stories of sacrifice (or near sacrifice) and salvation. Consider, for example, the story of Abraham's near sacrifice of his son, Isaac (Genesis 22), and the sacrifice of Jesus (New Testament Gospels).

This Native American tale has a remarkable emotional weight to it and also assigns the beauty and force of nature to the signs and wonders of the divine. There has always been a respect for personal sacrifice, and the ways that personal responsibility impacts the whole of the social order. Great leaders are those who make the greatest sacrifices and power and respect are earned, not bestowed by title or privilege. People do not follow titles, but will follow leaders who are willing to walk through the fire with others. And as the legend of Multnomah Falls reveals, personal sacrifice is often required for greater healing and wholeness.

The Elder Stick (Krummacher)

A huntsman went out hunting with his son, and they became separated by a deep stream. At length the boy wished to cross over to his father, but was not able, for the stream was wide. He immediately cut a stick out of the bushes, set one end in the brook, supported himself fearlessly and nimbly upon it, and gave himself a powerful swing. But lo! The stick was of an elder-bush, and while the boy hung over the stream, the pole broke in two, the boy fell deep into the water, and the waves rushed in and overwhelmed him. A shepherd saw it at a distance, ran to assist, and raised a tremendous shriek. But the boy, breathing heavily, parted the water from him, and swam laughing to the shore.

Then said the shepherd to the hunter: You seem to have taught your son many things well, but one thing you have forgotten. Why have you not also taught him to examine well what is within, before he opens his heart to confidence? Had he proved the tender pith within, he would not have trusted to the deceptive bark!

★

Built around the image of the parted waters of the Red Sea (the Moses saga of Exodus), this parable demonstrates the importance of looking deeper. As the prophet Samuel reminded the leaders of Israel when considering young David as king: "People look upon the outward appearance, but the Lord looks at the heart." Indeed, outward appearances can be deceiving. Courage is, in part, being able to find the hope in a hopeless situation—and this often involves seeing the possibilities within.

The Story of Ali (Rumi)

Ali, who was known as "the Lion of God," was once engaged in an argument with a Magian priest. In the middle of the argument the Magian priest spit in Ali's face. But to the Magian priest's astonishment, Ali did not retaliate. Instead, he dropped his sword on the ground.

When the Magian priest asked Ali to explain his attitude, Ali said, "I never take a life for the cause of vengeance, as this belongs to God alone. I am here to carry out God's will, and even in battle, I will usually spare

•178•

the life of my foe, as this is the nature of forbearance and the mercy of Allah. Besides, the Prophet revealed to me years ago that I would die at the hand of a close and trusted friend, and this friend has frequently asked me to kill him so that he will not suffer the pain of carrying out such an action. But I will not kill the one who shall, someday, take my life—for to me, death is as sweet as life, and I feel no animosity toward one who is merely carrying out the will of Allah."

When the Magian priest heard Ali's testimony, he was so moved by his faith that he accepted Islam, along with his family, even unto the generations.

★

Rumi's wonderful parables often reveal the heart of Sufism, which is forbearance and love. And here, in the case of Ali and his foe, Rumi paints a wonderful picture of long suffering, even patience, as one awaits the final will of God to be fulfilled. In the hands of Sufi expression, faith is not to be used as an excuse for the taking of life, but as a means of advancing the gift of life. Patience is a virtue. And forgiveness is the path the leads to friendship and cooperation.

The Incarnation of the Deer (Buddhist)

Once, the Buddha was born as a deer. He became a great leader and gathered around him a herd. The Deer led the herd wisely, and eventually took them deep into a secluded forest where they could live in peace and harmony.

In time, however, a new king began to rule the land. This king loved to hunt, and he would frequently make forays into the forest. Often he would bring back wagons filled with trophies: deer, antelope, rabbit, pheasant, leopards, tigers, bears and lions. The king was very happy with his hunt.

But the people were growing weary of the king's hunting expeditions. In his pursuit of game he would often trample over their crops, cut down their trees, and even destroy their farms. They were unhappy about this and the people came together to find a solution. Eventually the decided that it would be best to give the king his own herd of deer, so they built a large stockade, lured many herd of deer into it, and then transported these herds onto the king's palace grounds so that he could hunt as much as he liked without ruining their land.

As it happened, one of the herds that the people gathered up was the herd led by the Buddha Deer. This herd was troubled by their captivity, and they turned to the leader for answers. "Don't worry," the Buddha told them, "we are still alive, and wherever there is life there is hope. There is a path."

But there was much suffering.

Day after day the king and his nobles would stand on the top of the palace walls with their bows strung. They would shoot arrows into the milling herds of deer. Some deer were killed outright. Others were injured. And there was no way to tell where the arrows were coming from or where they would strike. All of the deer were in a panic.

At last there were but two herds left. The Buddha leader came to the leader of the other herd and said, "Let our two herds make a pact that we will no longer suffer and die in this way. Each day we will choose one deer from our respective herds to sacrifice its life so the others may live. Each day, one deer from our respective herds will stand at the gate of the stockade in full view of the king so that he may shoot it and spare the others."

This plan seemed like the only solution to the other deer leader, so it agreed.

The next morning, when the king mounted the wall for his hunt, he noticed a solitary deer standing near the gate, trembling in fear. "Look," the king said, "it is as if this deer is sacrificing itself for the others. Perhaps there are noble deer after all."

And the king killed the deer with a single arrow and was satisfied.

But that night the king was troubled. He tossed and turned in his bed, dreaming of a large radiant deer with antlers, a noble beast that was beautiful to behold.

The next day, when it came time for the deer lottery, the short straw fell upon a pregnant doe. But she was disturbed and went to the leader and said, "I am pregnant. If I am the one to sacrifice my life for the herd, my fawn will also die. I am willing to sacrifice my life, but please allow me to wait until my fawn is born. And then I will go."

But the deer leader said, "No. You must go now. The law is the law."

But the doe went to the Buddha Deer and explained her plight. The Buddha deer said, "You are right. The intent is that only one life will be sacrificed. If you are the one to go to the gate, then there will be two lives sacrificed. This is not right. And I will make a way."

After the doe left, the Buddha leader knew what he must do. There was no other way. He had decided that he would give his life for the herd. With great dignity he walked through the herd that day, head and antlers held high, his face radiant. The herd was comforted by his leadership and sacrifice.

That morning, when the Buddha deer approached the gate, the nobles were standing at the wall with their bows drawn. But when they saw the majestic deer, they could not shoot. This deer was unlike any of the others they had seen They summoned the king to come and see.

When the king arrived he asked, "Why have you summoned me?"

They said, "Look, your majesty. Have you ever seen such as deer as this?"

When the king looked at the deer standing at the gate he recognized it. He said, "I have see you in my dreams. You are the majestic deer that has troubled my sleep. Why are you here?"

The Buddha deer spoke. He said, "It is like this . . . a doe was selected to die for the herd today, but she was pregnant. It is unfair to take two lives, and so I offer myself as sacrifice. This is what a king does if he is truly a king. So now, draw you bow and shoot."

But the king could not draw his bow. He said, "You are right. A king must be concerned about the least in his kingdom. You have taught me something today. And because of this lesson, I release you and your herd from the stockade. You are free to go in peace."

The Buddha deer answered, "This is indeed a great gift. But I wish to speak further."

The king listened.

"O King, you have released my herd to roam the forests and live in peace. But that means that the other herd will still be in the stockade and that, as they are hunted, they will suffer all the more. And so, while I long to accept the King's kindness by granting this freedom, I cannot accept it knowing that others will suffer because of it. Do you understand what I am saying?"

The king was flabbergasted. "You mean, you would risk your own freedom for the sake of others?"

"This is, indeed, the case. And so I am asking the King to consider the sufferings of others . . . and I request that the other herd be set free as well."

The king pondered this last request for some time. At last he spoke: "Never have I heard of such nobility and such a concern for others. How can I refuse you? And so I grant your request. The other herd shall be given their freedom also. You and the other herd are now free to go and live in peace."

But the Buddha deer continued: "But King, I cannot live in peace yet. For I know that there are many other four-footed creatures in the woods that still suffer greatly. They are hunted and they are surrounded by terrors and hardships every day. Please, great King, grant your protection and freedom for these creatures also."

Again the king was astonished. He had never seen such compassion. He considered the Buddha deer's request for some time, and then came to conclusion that there would be no peace in the kingdom until this freedom and protection extended to all. "You are right," the king said. "And so I grant my freedom and protection to all four-footed creatures. Never again shall they be hunted. The bear, the boar, the lion, the fox, the leopard, the tiger, and even the rabbits—these are now free. Is this enough to make you accept your freedom and be at peace?"

The Buddha deer continued, "No, great King. There are others. Think of the birds of the air. These are always fleeing the arrow and the stone. Once the four-footed creatures are protected, the birds of the air shall suffer even more and they will be hunted day and night as well as being ensnared and captured. Please release them also."

Again the king was stunned. He answered, "You drive a hard bargain. But I understand what you are saying. Therefore, I extend this freedom and peace to the birds of the air also. They neither shall be hunted or ensnared. All of the birds may now build their nests in peace. Is this enough?"

But the Buddha deer continued, "But now think of the fish that swim. If I do not speak for them, who will. The fish of the rivers, the streams, the ponds, and the oceans—these are netted or brought up on hooks and flayed alive. How can I be at peace while they suffer so much? And so I beg you to spare them, too."

By now there were tears trickling down the king's cheeks. He was so moved by the Buddha deer's compassion. "How can I refuse you?" he said. "I grant my protection and free the fish as well. They shall swim in peace and no one shall kill them in my kingdom."

At this word the king called all of his courtiers and his lawyers and made a proclamation. "Make it plain," he said, "and let it be known that all are protected in my kingdom. All beings shall be treasured in my realm: the beasts of four-feet, the birds, the fish. Are you at peace now, O Noble deer?"

When the king said this, birds flew overhead and perched on nearby branches. The deer grazed calmly on the grass.

The Buddha deer answered, "I am indeed at peace!" He leaped for joy—feeling as young as a fawn. He had saved all of the creatures of the kingdom.

After the Buddha deer thanked the king again, he gathered his herd and returned to the forest, where he and the others lived in peace.

The king erected a stone pillar with his proclamation and the words of the Buddha deer. He also wrote: "Let all pay homage to the Noble Deer, the Compassionate Teacher of the Great King."

And from that time on, the king cared wisely for all living things.

★

It is often very easy for westerners to take traditional Buddhist tales such as this and create a system of belief from it. But, like many parables told to a first generation audience, the original meaning may be lost.

However, this is certainly a story that reveals the heart of the Buddha and the teachings that center on a compassion for all living things as well as the ways that make for peace. The metaphors of this story are rich in detail and intent, and the tale is certainly moving.

Those who would create peace must also be willing to participate in it, even by their own suffering. Likewise, freedom is not complete until all are free, and there are many great leaders over the centuries who have expressed these sentiments in various ways.

The Question of "Why?" (Jewish)

Following the destruction of the first Jerusalem Temple, there were many who began to ask deeper theological questions. Some questioned God's justice. Others questioned the reasons given. And still others simply wanted to know: "Why?"

These are questions that people have always asked when bad things happen to good people.

One of the oldest traditions regarding the destruction of the temple holds that God allowed the temple to be destroyed because there were three great evils in it: idolatry, sexual immorality, and bloodshed (murder/warfare). Others asked of this tradition—"If these were the reasons . . . then why was the temple destroyed? During the time that the temple stood people occupied themselves with Torah, they observed the statutes of the law, and they were generous."

Others answered: "The temple was destroyed because during the time it stood, people hated others without any cause. Therefore, this should demonstrate that hating others without cause is deemed to be an even greater sin than idolatry, sexual immorality and bloodshed combined."

★

The most common question people ask in the aftermath of a crisis is: "Why?" This is, of course, an age-old question—and a deeply theological one. Here the Mishnah addresses the question through the back door by doing the difficult work of introspection, the work of self-analysis. Motives are examined. And attitudes.

The outcome of this tradition points to hatred as the root of all evil. And in our time, it takes courage to note these same attitudes in ourselves.

The Power of the Tongue (Jewish)

There is an ancient story about the king of Persia who became so thin that he was on the verge of death. The king called together his physicians and asked them, "How can I be cured?" One of the physicians said to him, "You must drink the milk of a lioness." But the king asked, "How can I obtain this milk?"

At this one physician said, "I can obtain the milk for you if you give me ten goats."

The king obliged, and the following day the physician began feeding a lioness. He gave the lioness the first goat at a distance and then, each day subsequent, would draw closer to the lioness when he brought the goat. Eventually, after the tenth day, the physician was able to draw milk from the lioness.

On this way to the palace with the milk, however, the physician fell asleep along the road and dreamed that parts of his body were arguing among themselves. The feet were saying, "We are most important. If it had not been for us you would not have arrived at this point and would not have been able to obtain the lioness milk."

But the hands responded, "No, we are most important. We were responsible for carrying the milk to the king."

The eyes said, "What? But if not for us the rest of the body would have remained in darkness and would not have been able to see to obtain the milk."

Then the heart said, "But wait! I am responsible for giving the wise counsel in the first place."

At last the tongue spoke up and said, "None of this would have mattered had I not spoken to the king and offered the cure for his illness."

Upon hearing the tongue's argument, all of the other parts of the body joined in unison, "In fact, you are the most unimportant part of all. You dwell in the back of the mouth, sit in darkness, and have very little influence over the whole body."

But the tongue said, "Before the day is over, you will acknowledge that I am, in fact, the most important part of the body!"

When the physician awoke from this dream he continued on his journey and took the lioness milk to the king. He handed it over and said, "Here is the healing milk I obtained for you from a bitch. Drink it and live."

The king immediately became angry and ordered the physician to be hanged. As the physician was being led away to the gallows he heard all of the parts of the body saying to the tongue, "Didn't we say you were worthless? Look at what has become of us now."

But the tongue said, "Take me back to the king, for he misunderstands."

They led the physician back to the king's chambers and the physician asked, "Why did you order me to be hanged?"

The king replied, "Because you brought me the milk of a bitch."

But the physician replied, "Yes, but a lioness is also a bitch, your majesty. The milk of the lioness will heal you."

The king listened to the physician, drank the milk, and lived. After this, all of the parts of the body then joined in praising the power of the tongue. They said, "The proverb is true: Life and Death are to be found in the persuasion of the tongue" (Proverbs 18:21).

★

This parable from the Talmud is reminiscent of the apostle Paul's analogy of the church (1 Corinthians 12) where he compares the cooperation and inner workings of the church to the human body. In the Talmudic lesson it is the power of speech (and of wisdom born of speech) that takes primacy over the other gifts. Much of the wisdom literature of the Bible—including Ecclesiastes and the book of Proverbs—portrays speech in this light.

Indeed, the ability to speak truth with humility and persuasion is one of the greatest gifts—and there are many sages and saints who possessed it. In this age when speech has become acquainted with opinion—and more often with shouting or winning an argument—it is refreshing to find the truth that many crises in life can be averted through solid communication and depth of feeling. Learning how to speak well—and to express complex thoughts in a simple and precise manner—is something of a lost art.

Jesus also expressed these sentiments when he said, "Don't swear by heaven and earth, but let your 'yes' mean 'yes' and your 'no' mean 'no.' Anything beyond this is evil." When it comes to speaking plainly, one can't go wrong with simplicity. Truth is always best.

Saint Francis and the Wolf (Christian)

Francis was a lover of animals. He preached to the birds of the air, picked up worms along the road, and fed the mice in his cell where he slept.

Near the town of Gubbio, however, lived a wolf that was terrorizing the people. Each night the wolf entered the village and devoured animals and human beings alike.

When Francis visited the town the people warned him, "Don't go outside at night, Brother Francis. The wolf will eat you alive."

That night, however, Francis set out by himself to meet this wolf. The villagers followed him at a distance, each carrying a club, a spear, or a sword. Some climbed trees or trembled upon the rooftops.

Eventually the wolf appeared at the edge of the forest. When it saw Francis standing in the open, unarmed and vulnerable, it ran toward him with its teeth barred and snarling. But as the wolf drew near, Francis stood his ground, made the sign of the cross and said, "Brother wolf, in the name of Jesus Christ I order you not to harm another living thing."

Immediately the wolf stopped, bowed its head, and sauntered humbly toward the saint. "Brother wolf," Francis said, "You have harmed the people of the village. You have destroyed their livestock and killed those who are created in the image of God. But although you deserve to be treated like a murderer and put to death, I would like to establish peace between you and the people of Gubbio."

The wolf showed by its movements that it understood what Francis was saying. The saint continued, "I know that you have eaten and destroyed because you are very hungry. Such is the way of many people as well. But, Brother wolf, if the people of the village will feed you, can you promise not to harm another living thing?"

Gently, the wolf placed its paw into Francis's outstretched hand. When the people of the village saw this, they too agreed to keep the peace and offered to care for the wolf as one of their own.

★

Peacemaking is a difficult and dangerous venture. There are no guarantees that an enemy will turn away from violence. The many legends of Saint Francis, however, call people to a life of reconciliation and faithfulness to God—a way of life that requires far more courage, devotion, and self-control than a life built upon revenge and destruction.

We can forget that the world has always been a violent place. There have always been hatreds and animosities.

True peace, however, can only be achieved through courageous acts of reconciliation—through faith in God and faith in others. Risk is involved, and trust. But the final rewards far outweigh a life of perpetual fear and destruction. Courage is the first step needed when one is trying to reach out to an enemy in friendship.

Pride Before the Fall (India)

All of the beasts of the jungle feared the lion and they were being killed night and day. Fearing for their lives, the animals met in an assembly one day and determined that the best plan would be for one of them to sacrifice its life each day. In this manner the lion would be satisfied and would leave the rest of the creatures alone.

This daily sacrifice continued among the animals for some time until one day the lot fell upon an old stag who said to himself, "What do I have to lose if I attempt to play a trick on the lion?"

Meandering through the jungle to the lion's lair, the old stag arrived very late and the lion was not only hungry, but angry. "Where have you been?" the lion demanded.

The stag said, "I beg your pardon, but on my way here I was attacked by another lion. I barely escaped with my life to tell you about this intruder."

The lion said, "Show me this intruder and I shall tear it to bits."

The old stag led the lion to an abandoned well and said, "Look inside. The other lion, who is encroaching on your territory, resides inside."

When the lion peered into the well it saw its own reflection, drew itself into a powerful roar, and then attacked. The lion fell into the well and perished, leaving the animals to live in peace.

★

This traditional story of India points out the defects of pride. Indeed, pride always comes before a fall . . . and sometimes these falls are disastrous. Intellect and common sense are far more persuasive than power.

The Jungle Bell (India)

Once, a man who had stolen a bell fled into the jungle where he was killed by lions. Some monkeys, attracted to the bell, began to ring it. And soon afterward a story began circulating in a nearby village that the bell was being rang by demons. Everyone was afraid, and from that time forward no one left the village.

However, a old wise woman had figured out that the thief had died and that the bell was being rang by monkeys. She went to the king and said, "If you give me a large sum of money I will go into the jungle, find the bell, and appease the demons."

The king agreed to this plan and advanced her a large sum of money. The woman went immediately to the market, purchased some ripe fruit, and walked into the jungle. Sure enough, she found the monkeys ringing the bell.

She took the fruit out of her basket, led the monkeys to another part of the jungle, and then brought the bell back to the king. She never revealed her ploy and all of the people revered her from that day on.

★

Fear is one of the greatest obstacles we face in life. Fear produces many worries that never materialize into reality (most worries don't). And there is certainly no need to worry about what we cannot control.

This beautiful fable from India notes the latter and offers a way forward through fear: namely that of taking action and using one's intellect to reduce the fear into bite-sized portions. The bell can represent our senses, which often deceive us. But just because we hear a fearful sound (a rumor, a report, or even the drums of war) does not mean that this is necessarily the truth, or an accurate picture of the whole.

Some drums can signal the entrance to a new path.

Chapter Seven

Glimpses of Generosity

Do not neglect to show hospitality to strangers,
for in such ways many have entertained angels without knowing it.
—Hebrews 13:2 (Christian New Testament)

You never know what is enough unless you know what is more
than enough.
—William Blake

Generosity is the natural response to gratitude. When one is truly thankful, then a generous spirit follows.

This generosity can be poured out in a variety of ways: through works of kindness and volunteering, offering one's time and attention, small acts of helpfulness. Generosity could also be poured out in self-sacrifice and by offering attention to the needs of others. Money may also enter into the picture. But without the spirit of generosity, even the best of our actions can fall flat or fail to rise to the high notes of inspiration or thrill to the heartbeat of noble causes.

One doesn't always have to feel blessed in order to be generous, however. Sometimes, recognition can be enough.

There is an African proverb that explains this well: *a man with one eye is only grateful after he has seen a blind man.*

How we see generosity in ourselves and in others is not always an act of the pocketbook. We often think of people as generous who are always willing to help, who give to great causes, who are *there.* Generosity, then, isn't so much an attitude as an action. Generosity is a verb—not a noun.

One might also consider that each day offers its own opportunities for thanksgiving. Sometimes a kind word can open a pathway that might lift someone from depression or anxiety. A handshake of welcome and a smile can create new friendships. An extravagant gift can save an organization from bankruptcy or breathe new life into an otherwise hopeless cause.

What we choose to do with our twenty-four hours each day is exactly how we choose to live our lives. These daily decisions (and attitudes) begin to define our lives—and they also outline how others see us. In the end, everyone has had defining moments—choices made in every stage of life that paint our portraits. Each day is a brush stroke, another color. What will we look like?

In Jewish tradition, generosity is made possible by the greater generosity of God. (The idea is: we cannot out-give the Creator.) In the Christian tradition, generosity is aligned with gratitude for what God has accomplished and given. And in Native American teaching, one should live with a grateful heart, for all of creation (nature) is imbued with beauty, balance, and purpose. To live in the creation is to be thankful.

Poems can express this gratitude, as can prayers and thoughts. This beautiful Psalm is an expression of gratitude.

Praise the Lord, all you nations;
extol him, all you peoples.
For great is his love toward us,

and the faithfulness of the Lord endures forever.

Praise the Lord. (Psalm 177:1-2)

What one will discover in this chapter is a plethora of wonderful stories and teachings—all touching upon this great theme of generosity.

In the Inuit tradition there is a beautiful song that expresses the human condition and this longing for gratitude. In part it sings:

I drifted out in my kayak
And thought that I was in danger
Overtaken by my fears:
Small ones and big ones
Reaching for all I thought
I had to have . . .

And yet there is but one great thing
Which is the only thing that matters:
To live to see one's home
At the end of the journey,
The great day dawning,
And the light that fills the world.

There is enough beauty to make every heart glad. One doesn't have to live in splendor or possess treasures. If one is willing to give, then one is wealthy enough. The heart can sing with these stories and we may even discover that thanksgiving can be a daily ritual and not an event. Wonderful things can happen through the open hand.

Generosity is its own joy.

The Baskets (Desert Fathers)

There is one tale about a brother who made his living weaving baskets with handles. One day he heard another monk next door talking to himself saying, "What will I do? A trader is coming tomorrow and I don't have any handles to put on my baskets." The first brother promptly removed the handles from the baskets he had completed and took the handles to the other monk saying, "Here, my brother, I have extras. Use these to complete your baskets." And in this fashion he made his brother's work complete while leaving his own unfinished.

★

There are many facets to generosity and one of these dimensions is sacrifice. In this tale, the brother is also generous of spirit, as he saves the other monk from feelings of indebtedness. He allows the other monk to save face while also finding the joy of completed work—all to the detriment of his own. Such gifts are not always appreciated in our contemporary world—but if we look closely we can surely find this generosity among father and son, mother and daughter. Generosity is more than giving money. As the Biblical adage goes: "God loves a cheerful giver." Indeed, one can give a gift and still not find the joy of giving. This joy comes from full release. And release comes when one does not regard the gift as his own, but as a blessing he has simply borrowed from Almighty God.

Treasures (Jesus)

And what woman having ten pieces of silver, if she loses one piece, doth not light a candle, and sweep the house, and seek diligently until she find it? And when she has found it she calls her friends and says, "Rejoice with me for I have found the piece which was lost." (Luke 15:8-9)

The kingdom of heaven is like a treasure hidden in a field that, when a person finds it, sells everything and purchases that field. Again, the kingdom of heaven is like a merchant who seeks the finest pearls.

When the merchant finds the one pearl of extraordinary value, he sells everything he has and purchases that one pearl. (Matthew 13:44-46)

★

Many of the parables of Jesus, especially the parables of the kingdom, are difficult to interpret in the contemporary mindset. The meaning of these parables—initially spoken to a first-century Jewish audience—may well be lost on us today. But Jesus was a master storyteller, and many of his parables of the kingdom of God involve themes of being lost . . . and then found. Indeed, the way to God is fraught with pitfalls and detours, but most of the barriers we encounter may be more closely tied to our concepts of God.

In the kingdom parables, Jesus offers an image of a gracious God—the one who is most generous and kind and whose will is ever-directed toward the good of humanity. The Creator's generosity makes all things possible.

Pocket Change (Buddhist)

There is a story about a man who fell into a drunken sleep. Now a good friend stayed by his side for many hours, watching over him, but when he could wait no longer, he hid a coin in the drunken man's pocket so that, when his friend awakened, he might be able to buy what he needed. But the drunk man, when he awoke, began to wander aimlessly in poverty and hunger. He did not realize that, all along, he had a coin in his pocket. Many months later the friend advised the drunk man to look for the coin saying, "You already possess the answer and you need not be hungry any more."

★

There is a traditional saying, "If you give a man a fish you will feed him for a day. But if you teach a man to fish you will feed him for a lifetime."

Often, generosity is best defined as giving another person the means and provision to meet their own needs. A hand up, instead of a handout, is a beautiful expression of care.

The Cobbler and the Banker (La Fontaine)

There was a poor cobbler who was quite content with his family and his work. He sung throughout the day as he mended the shoes and he slept peacefully and soundly at night. His neighbor, however, was a banker. The banker worked long hours, slept little, never sang, and slept in fits and starts as he was always worried about his profits.

One day the banker entered the cobbler's shop and asked, "How much do you make each year?"

The cobbler said he had never given this any thought, as he simply worked each day to provide for the family and he enjoyed his work. "I eat every day," he said, "and this is enough."

"Well then," the banker continued, "how much do you make in a day?"

The cobbler answered, "Sometimes I make more, sometimes less. And not every day is the same. Some days, in order to keep the feasts of the saints or to honor a holy day, I do not work at all. And other days I work longer."

The banker said, "I thought as much. What a fool you are. But since you are my neighbor I wish to ease your suffering. Here are a hundred gold coins. Invest them wisely and you will have security for the rest of your life."

When the cobbler received the gold coins he was astounded and reasoned that he had then enough money to last him a lifetime. He immediately went and buried the treasure in the ground and set out to guard it day and night. The cobbler stopped working and singing, and when he heard the faintest sound in the night, he would spring out of bed and run to check on the security of his treasure. His every waking moment was dedicated to thinking about the treasure.

One day, however, the cobbler came to his senses. He dug up the gold coins and returned them to the banker. From that moment on he began to sing again and his sleep was filled with peace.

★

Money can be a source of enormous blessing, or it can be a curse. In the case of this beautifully told parable we see how money can often deprive people of happiness or, at least, be the source of so much worry and consternation. Treasures are nice, but when the treasures grip us with anxiety and transform our hearts, then it is best to look for other sources of happiness. Not all treasures are worth keeping. And often happiness is gained by giving instead of receiving.

The Scorpion and the Tortoise (Pilpay)

A Tortoise and a Scorpion were the best of friends. They spent each day together but were at last pressed to find new home. So they set out on a journey but soon found themselves on the banks of a deep river. The Scorpion pointed out that he could not cross the river without drowning, and the Tortoise, trusting his new friend, invited him hop aboard his shell for the ride across.

When the Tortoise was deep in the water, suddenly he heard a clicking sound and asked, "What are you doing back there on my shell?"

The Scorpion replied, "I am wetting my stinger, anticipating that I will soon sink it deep into your exposed flesh."

The Tortoise answered, "You ungrateful thing. Would you really betray my friendship at such a time as this, when my flesh is exposed because I am saving your life—in order to take my life from me?" At this word the Tortoise sunk into the water, leaving the Scorpion helpless and, eventually, drowned.

★

Generosity and gratitude go hand-in-hand, for there cannot be one without the other. Ingratitude always leads to self-preservation, while generosity both preserves one's life and grants a fuller life to others.

The Stone Test (Traditional Tale)

A king who wanted to test the hearts of his subjects once traveled to a distant region where he placed a large stone in the middle of a caravan intersection. One stretch of this road led to the sea port, another to a marketplace, and yet another led to the city. The king hid himself behind a hedgerow and waited.

Shortly a caravan of merchants came upon the stone in the middle of the road. They stopped, exited their wagons, and began to complain bitterly against the king. "Here is the evidence," they said, "that the king cannot make the roads passable. What a travesty this is." After going on like this for some time, the merchants eventually moved their caravan around the stone, leaving it for the next person to remove.

Soon after this a group of sailors came walking down another road on their way to the port. "Look at this," they said to each other, "this stone is in the way of progress and might even prohibit supplies from getting to the port." Again, they moved around the stone and left it behind in the road.

Minutes later a group of farmers were making their way to the city with their produce. They were angered by the presence of the stone in the middle of the road. Like the others, they stopped to complain. "This rock is blocking the way to town," they said. "This goes to show that the government workers are not doing their jobs." And like the other groups, the farmers walked around the stone, leaving for others to remove.

Eventually a solitary beggar came up the road in the other direction. When he came to the stone in the middle of the road he stopped to sit upon it, and then, after refreshing himself, set about moving it under

great duress. After finding a large branch nearby, the beggar began pry-
ing the stone up and moving it, inch by inch, until it was out of the
road.

Famished and thirsty, the beggar was about to set out for the city
when the king approached him from behind the hedgerow. After offering
the beggar food and water, the king then handed the beggar a large purse
filled with gold. "Of all my kingdom subjects," the king said, "you are the
only one willing to remove the stone. Here is your reward. Go in peace."

★

There is an African tale about a monkey that had reached inside of a
trap for a banana. It became ensnared. As hard as the monkey tried to
pull the banana from the trap, it could never break free. But as soon as
the monkey realized it could gain its freedom by opening its hand, it
was released.

This is a parable of the open hand. It is a parable of helpfulness. The
closed hand neither allows us to receive or to give. The open hand is
the only way to be generous, and to receive the generosity of others.
Sometimes, the open hand is the only way for us to break free from the
snare of greed or self-preservation.

The Poor Man and the King (Hebrew Bible)

Again I examined the facts and noted that the race doesn't always go
to the swift, battles are not always won by the strongest, rewards are not
always given to the wisest, wealth isn't always given to the most intel-
ligent, nor is favor bestowed on the most skilled. Rather, there are no
rules for life, and these things can happen to anyone at any time. After
all, can anyone really keep a disaster from occurring? We are all like fish
caught in a drag net, and we are like birds caught in a snare. A catastro-
phe can happen at any time, and any one of us can fall prey to a disaster
that is no fault of our own.

I have seen examples of this many times, and this reality is undeniable. But let me illustrate it.

There was once a little city that had few people in it. But a powerful king decided he would overthrow it. He marched his armies in, built siege ramps against the walls, and had every intention of starving the people inside.

As it happened, there was a poor man inside the city who was also very wise. Due to this one man's wisdom he actually told the people how they could survive—and they did! And yet, after the poor man died, no one remembered him. Can you believe it? That's why I always say, "Wisdom is better than military and political power, but is also the reason why people despise the wisdom of the poor, why people don't heed what the poor have to say. We are so blind to power!"

But listen: "The quiet words of the wise should be heeded far more than the speeches of our political leaders who merely shout among the other political fools. And humble wisdom is superior to any weapons of war." (Ecclesiastes 9:11-18)

★

Generosity involves far more than financial gifts. As the apostle Paul once wrote, "God loves a cheerful giver."

There is also wisdom to consider. Gifts of guidance, advice, and insight should be more deeply admired and cherished. There is much that the rich can learn from the poor. And there is much that the powerful need to learn from the weak. Those who are wisest are not always found in the courts of honor and among the trappings of luxury, but in fact wisdom is often born from daily struggles and the honest observations about how the world truly works.

The Sisters (Buddhist)

Once there was a beautiful woman who visited a house. The owner of the house welcomed her inside and asked her name. The woman said,

"My name is wealth." The owner of the house bid her to stay as long as she liked.

Soon afterwards, another woman came knocking on the door of this same house. This woman was ugly and shabbily dressed. The owner of the house welcomed her and then asked her name. She replied, "My name is poverty." When the owner of the house heard this he became frightened and attempted to drive the ugly woman out of the house. But she said to him, "The beautiful woman of wealth is my sister. If I leave, she will leave with me."

Sure enough, as soon as the ugly woman departed, so did the other.

★

A disciple asked Confucius, "Is it possible for a person to be generous and also help the masses?"

Confucius answered, "Such a person would be both a humanitarian and a sage. While being successful, this person would also help others to succeed."

As with many aspects of life, the extremes of poverty and wealth are not that far removed from one another. Success can be defined, in fact, in many ways. One does not achieve wealth without an understanding of poverty, and poverty becomes obvious only when wealth exists in proximity. There are still people who rise from rags to-riches, and these have a much different perspective on wealth than those who have inherited wealth or live on "old money."

The ancient Buddhist parable points out the widely accepted faces of these extremes—with wealth appearing more as the more beautiful option and poverty the ugly sister. But as with most, wealth is always welcomed and poverty is often just a tragedy away. Life is often lived on the tightrope, just a disaster away from financial ruin . . . or windfall. Hospitality, and being no respecter of persons, also makes life richer. The home is the heart, and true wealth proceeds from our attitude and posture toward others. Indeed, the truly wealthy are those who help others succeed.

The Greedy and the Frugal Cats (Pilpay)

Many years ago in a small, remote village, lived an old woman with her cat. The old woman could scarcely fend for herself, much less provide food for her cat, but the feline was, nevertheless, happy and industrious, for it was able to find an abundant supply of mice inside the woman's cottage. The cat did not regard itself as needy and, although it was thin, did not suffer from hunger or a lack of contentment.

One day, however, the cat decided to roam a bit further from the old woman's home and as it roamed the countryside in search of mice it came upon an enchanted castle. As the cat approached it noticed that there were other cats striding atop the walls of this opulent home. At first the country cat did not recognize the other felines, for they were so fat and corpulent. The country cat was astounded to see so many of them and drew near to the enchanted castle to inquire about the meaning of it all.

One of the fat cats sitting upon the wall spoke up: "This is our home and we enjoy it here very much."

The country cat then asked, "But how is it that you are so well-fed? I have never seen such size in any of my species before."

The palace cat continued, "We all live here in the King's home. All of us dine at the King's table. Every day, after every meal, the servants toss us such delicious morsels of food—venison, steak, chicken, and veal. We eat as we like and then, returning for our next meal, the servants again bring us the leftovers from the King's table." "But what about mice?" the country cat implored. "Do you not hunt for your sustenance?"

"Heaven's no!" the palace cat replied. "In fact, even the mice that live inside the castle walls have plenty to eat. We don't bother them at all—and they live among us in perfect peace and tranquility. Why bother with a few measly scraps of mice flesh when we receive all that we need from the King himself."

The country cat, of course, asked, "How can I gain entry to the castle? Is it possible that I can live among you?"

But the castle cat said, "Perhaps one day I will let you in, for I am a most charitable feline. But for now I am afraid you cannot enter. One day, when you return, I'll let you in on the secrets of our life so that you can live like us." And so the palace cat refused and sent the country cat on its way.

Hours later, when the cat returned to its meager cottage with the old woman, it was angry and confused. It spoke about its experience with the old woman. But the old woman, who was wise and industrious, replied, "You will never be admitted to the palace, for those in power never share their gifts with others—that is how they keep it. And be aware that those who do not lack for anything will never be satisfied, for no matter how much they have, they will always want more. Those who are not aware of their blessings, or who do not pause to give thanks for their blessings, cannot truly enjoy these gifts, for they believe they have created them. Those who have much, and who do not have to work for their sustenance, are never content with their fortune, but will come to believe that they are deserving of even the labors of others. Do not be deceived by the outward appearance of wealth—it is often a camouflage for those who have impoverished character and small moral fiber. The opulence of the rich allows them to grow fat upon their own arrogance. Stay true to yourself. Live frugally. And do not be afraid of work. These truths will form the foundation of a good life and will help you to be grateful for what you have."

★

This is one of those parables from the hand of Pilpay that speaks for itself, but just in case we miss the message he hammers it home at the end by offering his own commentary through the words of the old woman. There is something in the human spirit that makes us most

alive when we are seeking, growing, actively involved in our own salvation. Living is energy. And when we relinquish our energies to survive
upon our own fumes we begin to die. In fact, we stagnate. This has
nothing to do with appearances, but is an interior health that can only
be nurtured through forms of human struggle. Or, as this story would
remind us, we should be wary of seeking a sedentary life. We should
never pray for ease . . . but rather, pray to be a strong person.

The Leper's Test (Desert Fathers)

Father Agathon was travelling to town to sell his wares when he noticed
a leper sitting by the road. As [Father Agathon] approached the leper
asked, "Where are you going?" He replied, "Into town to sell my wares."

The leper said, "Carry me into town, and then put me down where
you will be selling your wares." After [Father Agathon] had sold his first
item the leper asked, "How much did you sell it for?" He told him how
much it was. The leper then said, "Buy me a gift with the money you
earned." He bought the leper a gift.

Each time, after Father Agathon had sold an item, the leper would
ask, "How much did you sell it for?" And he would tell him. At the end
of the day, after he had sold all of his wares, Father Agathon was about
the journey back. The leper said, "Take me back to the place where you
found me." So he carried him back to the place beside the road.

Father Agathon was about to leave when the leper said, "You are
blessed, Agathon, by Lord of heaven and earth."

But when Father Agathon turned to respond to the leper there was
nobody there. And then he realized that it was an angel of the Lord sent
to test him.

★

The writer of Hebrews (New Testament) mentions that we should
always show hospitality to strangers, for in so doing many have

entertained angels without knowing about it. Generosity is more than money—but it is an extension of our efforts and energies as well. Generosity can also be acceptance—offering someone, especially an outsider, the inclusion of the community. When we welcome, we entertain the divine pleasure.

The Desert Fathers have many such traditions and one is never far away from generosity whenever a hand is extended.

The Poor Artist (Buddhist)

A poor artist traveled abroad to perfect his art and seek his fortune. After three years he had saved three hundred pieces of gold. On his way back home, he happened to stop at a temple where a beautiful ceremony was in progress, and when the call came for the offering he said, "Up to this point in my life I have been seeking my fortune day-to-day, without giving any thought to my future happiness or the true nature of prosperity. I will plant seeds here so that I may have more in the future." And so he decided to give his three hundred pieces of silver to the monks.

When the artist returned home without any gold, his wife was furious. "How could you be so stupid?" she asked.

The artist replied, "I simply put the money in a safe place."

The wife took the matter to court and the judge asked the artist to explain his reasoning. "I earned the money from hard work," he said, "but it seemed wisest to me to plant seeds for my future good fortune by giving it to the temple. As soon as I gave the money I felt all desire and greed melt away and I realized that true wealth has nothing to do with gold, but is a state of mind."

When the judge heard the artist's explanation he praised him. And after returning to their home the artist and his wife lived out their days in harmony and good fortune.

★

In classic Christian doctrine, greed is one of the seven deadly sins. Judaism implores the faithful to care for the orphan, the widow and the stranger through the tithe (10 percent of income), and Jesus taught his followers to give without regard for fanfare or reward. The apostle Paul taught that one should give according to the abundance of one's blessings. And later, John Wesley, the father of the Methodist movement in England, would write: "Earn all you can, save all you can, give all you can, to as many as you can, for as long as you can."

In essence, there are many who are wealthy in purse but impoverished of heart, and likewise others who possess an enormity of spirit despite their outward poverty. As this classic Buddhist parable teaches: one's future is best expressed through faith and generosity, which leads to relationships and life.

A body of water that has only an inlet but no outlet soon becomes stagnant and useless. But a body of water that has an outlet is always fresh. In the same manner when we live only as consumers, believing that the purpose of life is found in obtaining, we soon become stagnant. A hand that can only clutch soon becomes useless and the fingers cannot open to give.

Generosity is the true gold of life, and those who discover this truth inherit and enormous fortune.

The Lesson of the Eight Monks (Buddhist)

Once there was a man who lived near a cemetery. One night he heard a voice calling from a grave, but he was too frightened to investigate. He did tell a brave friend about his experience the next day, however.

That afternoon, the brave man visited the cemetery to listen, and sure enough there was a voice calling from a grave. The brave man asked, "Who are you and what do you want?"

The voice answered, "I am a treasure and I have decided to give myself to someone. I tried to give myself to the timid man last night, but he was too frightened to accept it. Therefore, I will give myself to you if you prove that you are worthy of me."

"What do I need to do?" the brave man asked.

The voice answered, "Tomorrow morning I will come to your house with seven followers. Be ready for us."

"And how shall I prepare? What do I need to do?"

The voice said, "You will be visited by eight monks. Clean your house, prepare a room, and set out bowls of rice-porridge for a dinner."

The brave man went home and did as the voice had instructed him. Sure enough, the following morning he was visited by eight monks. The man welcomed them into his home. They ate together. And afterwards the monks retreated to the room he had prepared. When the man opened the door later, he discovered that the monks had been transformed into eight pots of gold.

Now there was also a greedy man in that same village. He heard about the brave man and how he had welcomed the eight monks who were transformed into pots of gold. He invited the eight monks into his house also; he fed them and gave them a room. But when the greedy man later opened the door the monks were enraged by the greedy man's motives and they reported him to the judge. Hours later the police came and arrested him.

But of course the timid man also heard about this. He came to the brave man's house, filled with greed and anger. He insisted that the pots of gold actually belonged to him saying, "I was the one who first heard the voice in the cemetery, so all of the gold rightfully belongs to me." He marched into the brave man's house and attempted to steal the gold pots, but he discovered that they were no longer filled with treasure, but with poisonous snakes.

When the king heard what had happened, he gave the pots of gold to the brave man and offered the following observation: "This is how it is in this world. Foolish people are greedy but they are too frightened to work for the results themselves. Their fear inhibits them, and that is why they are continually failing. Those who are fearful don't have the internal drive or the courage to face the internal struggles of the mind—which is the hardest work—from which true peace and harmony are obtained."

★

As this parable illustrates, fear is the most inhibiting force in life. Fear is what holds us back from taking risk, from growing, from giving. Jesus was always telling his followers: "Fear not." Or, in another Christian teaching, we are told that "a perfected love casts out fear."

As far as wealth is concerned, it is often the case that those who have little are often the ones who spend the most time thinking about money (because they have little of it). True wealth is a state of mind and heart, and money is never a primary consideration. Those who are courageous enough to face themselves (to battle their own demons, to look inwardly at their own sins and failures, to undertake the most difficult work of self-improvement and understanding) are the ones who obtain the true riches. Shortcuts are poisonous. Greed never leads to a fulfilled life, and fear is the most debilitating factor in creating the relationships that lead to harmony and peace.

The Talents (New Testament)

Jesus said: "The kingdom of heaven is like a landowner who was going away on a long journey. He called his servants to manage his accounts while he was away. To one servant he gave ten talents, to another servant he gave five talents, and to another servant he gave one talent. The owner entrusted these accounts to each and then went away.

"Many years later the landowner returned and called his servants together to settle his account. He asked the first servant, 'Well, what have you accomplished with the ten talents?' The servant said, 'Look, master, your ten talents have doubled. I now have twenty.' 'Well done,' the master said. 'Enter into the joy of the master.'

"He called the second servant and asked, 'What have you accomplished with the five talents?' The servant said, 'See, I have made the five talents ten.' The master said, 'You, too, have done well. Enter into the joy of the master.'

"Then he called the third servant and asked, 'And what have you accomplished with the one talent?' The servant answered, 'My Master, I knew you were a hard man and I was afraid of losing what you gave me. So I buried the talent in the ground and have kept it safe all of these years. See, here it is . . . your one talent. I return it to you exactly as you gave it to me.'

"But the landowner said, 'What a wicked and lazy servant you are! So, you considered me a hard man, huh? Well then, the least you could have done is taken the talent to the bank instead of burying it. That way I would have earned interest on my investment. Here's what happens now. I am taking away even the one talent I gave you and I am giving it to the servant who doubled the ten talents. And you? You won't be enjoying my company any longer, but will find yourself in darkness, weeping and gnashing your teeth.'

"Remember: to the one who possesses much, even more shall be given. And to the one who lacks, even what he has shall be taken away."

★

This is one of the most intriguing parables that Jesus told. What is it about? Faithfulness? Commitment? Courage? Generosity?

It is a kingdom parable, but seems to contain an idea about life's meaning and focus. Intent, purpose, and orientation around the things of God seem to be at the heart of this teaching. Fear and negative attitude produce nothing. Confidence, risk, and generosity of spirit are the hallmarks of growth that produce joy and peace.

In life, we never achieve great results or great movements by living in fear. Love is a freedom from fear, as is faith. Fear is one of the most insidious of attitudes and holds us back from accomplishing great things for God and others.

Or, as this parable asks us to consider: *What, exactly, are we accomplishing for the creator?*

The Greatest Gift (Tolstoy)

Once there was a couple who lived on a farm. They were quite wealthy, but their days were filled with labor and anxiety, and they were constantly worrying about the hired hands, or the livestock, or the harvest. Although they were always busy, God had blessed them with two children—a son and a daughter—and with many friends who enjoyed their company and who often sought the wisdom of the father.

As the children came of age, the ageing father placed the son in charge of the farm and the daughter was married and moved away. In time, however, the son became an alcoholic and was unable to work. The farm began to fall into disrepair, equipment was stolen, and much of the livestock died. Eventually the father had to part ways with his son, who became angry and departed to a far land. The father was also forced to sell the farm, the house, and most of what he and his wife owned.

Fortunately, a neighboring farmer took note of the plight of the old couple and invited them to life on his farm. "I always have plenty of machinery that needs repaired," the farmer said. "And your wife would be very helpful to us by doing household chores." The old couple was grateful, and they agreed to become hired hands on this neighboring farm.

One day a guest arrived at the farm and took note of the old man and old woman working as hired hands. The guest asked the landowner about them. "That couple," the farmer said, "used to have the best farm in the region. They were successful and wealthy. But now they work as hired hands for me because they have lost everything, including their family."

The guest was quite intrigued by this statement and he wondered if he might have a conversation with the old couple to learn more about them. That evening, he found them working in the barn and he said, "I am a man who is always interested in other people and their histories. I am intrigued by your story and how you lost everything. And yet, you seem to be happy working here on the farm. Can you tell me why this is so?"

The old man said, "Perhaps my wife can explain."

The old woman said, "For fifty years we worked long hours, raised a family, and had all the money in the world. But we were unhappy. There was little time for conversation, no time to enjoy friendship and family, and all of our days were filled with anxiety and worry over the smallest of details. But now that we have nothing, we find that we are much happier. We enjoy working for others and at the end of the day we can enjoy small pastimes and relaxing conversation. We have time to reflect upon the things of God and, while we are now poor, we find that we are rich in spirit and joy. Every morning, when we wake, we greet the day with hope and we have time to cultivate happiness. Now we never argue. And we worry over nothing. We are now wealthier than we have ever been."

The guest pondered the old woman's words as he returned to the house that night, and it seemed to him that he had been privy to a deep wisdom.

★

Tolstoy was a master storyteller and loved the moralistic fable. Here is one that reflects the spirit of true wealth, as it is possible to be rich in things but poor in soul.

In classic Christian theology, the seven deadly sins are ever with us—and most of life's difficulties and brokenness can be traced to these misshapen attitudes of greed, lust, envy, pride, gluttony, wrath, or sloth. Greed has always been part of the human condition—and all religions and philosophies speak to the insidious nature of this particular lust for money.

As Tolstoy relates in this work, wealth is not the product of having things, but having peace. The pursuit of wealth is often the cause of much agony in life—both personal and social—but once we discover that life is about so much more than money, we discover our life's true purpose.

In short, this wonderful story may help us to ask one of life's deepest and most important questions: How much is enough?

Generosity

Just as rain falls on all vegetation, so the Buddha's compassion extends equally to all people. (Buddha)

God makes the rain to fall upon the just and the unjust alike. (Jesus)

★

Both Buddha and Jesus understood the world as reflecting the widest grace and mercy of the divine. One of the most common human tendencies is to believe that good things happen to good people (because they are good) and that God sends punishment upon the wicked (because they are wicked). Both Buddha and Jesus spoke of this misshapen theology, and countered by pointing out that all people—good and bad alike—receive blessings and mercies every day.

Faith may be defined as an "eye-opening" experience. When we become aware of the source of our blessings, and show gratitude for these gifts (gifts that we did not earn or create ourselves) then we are able to see all of life as a gift and live with the ability to see others in the divine image.

Our generosity is only made possible by the greater generosity of God. The source of all good gifts is an endowment of the Creator.

The Beggars (Nursery Rhyme)

Hark, hark, the dogs do bark.
The beggars are coming to town.
Some in rags, and some in tags,
And one in a velvet gown.

★

Nursery rhymes served a double purpose. Inasmuch as they entertained children and provided a bedtime story, they were also social commentary—and often cutting and insightful at that. Here, in the nursery rhyme "The Beggars," we see a fascinating commentary on the social order and the pride and prejudice of wealth.

On the one hand the rhyme quickly paints a scene found in any city—with beggars standing at the corners in tattered clothing. But the end of the rhyme makes plain that not all beggars—or those who take money from public handouts—are actually in want. Some beggars (and here the rhyme imagines politicians, aristocrats, and those born into privilege and wealth) take from the public by means of taxation, extortion, or through dishonest means.

Rhymes such as this one also have a spiritual element to them, as they comment on the order of the day, and of any age, particularly when the wealthy are exploiting the poor, or when the poor of the land are overlooked. The Jewish prophets railed against such excesses (the velvet gowns of royalty and aristocracy) as did Jesus and Buddha and Mohammad. In the Qur'an we find: "Woe . . . unto the one who hoards wealth in this world and keeps it or believes that his wealth will make him immortal." (CIV:2)

As in most cultures, one can find social commentary in children's stories—and it is from the early and most humble paths that we discover the way to heaven. Or, as Jesus said, "You must become as children to enter the kingdom of heaven."

The Poor Man's Wallet (Brothers Grimm)

Once there was a poor man who was always complaining about the condition of the world and the unfairness of life. When he saw others who were successful, he said, "They are successful only because they have been give privileges that the rest of us do not enjoy." When he encountered a wealthy person the poor man would mumble under his breath, "There goes someone who has inherited his money and has not had to work for it." And when he saw someone who was happy he would say, "Surely this person is happy because he has many possessions and can afford the finer things of life."

One day Fortune came to town and was on the lookout for someone to bless. As it happened, the poor man encountered Fortune in the town square and Fortune said to him, "I will give you money if you have a purse."

The poor man produced a purse from his pocket—one that was old and was falling apart. Fortune said to the poor man, "I will place as much gold in your purse as you like. The only condition of my generosity is this: not a single gold coin can fall to the ground. So be careful to ask for only as much as your purse can hold, and take great care that it does not fall apart from your greed."

The poor man agreed to these conditions and held out the old purse. Fortune began to fill it with gold coins. The purse grew heavy and Fortune asked, "Shall I stop here?"

But the poor man said, "No! Keep filling it!"

Fortune placed a few more gold coins into the purse and watched it sag. Fortune said, "Shall I stop here?"

The poor man said, "No! I want more! Fill it to the brim!"

Fortune continued to fill the purse as the poor man had requested until suddenly the old purse broke apart and all of the coins tumbled to the ground. Immediately all of the coins disappeared, Fortune walked away, and the poor man was left with nothing.

★

It is often the case that the impoverished spend the greatest amount of time thinking about money. Those who have wealth may actually spend little time thinking about it—but far more time enjoying the benefits of industry, relationships, and those pursuits that lead to success in commerce and in life.

As this Grimm's tale shows, greed appears in many guises, as does Fortune. Money, just as with many other pursuits in life, can often become corrupted by too much of a good thing. Knowing when to pause (or to stop) in any of life's pursuits and desires is a wisdom learned. We don't always have to have more of a good thing in order to enjoy the benefits of it—nor even to appreciate what we do have. A day's blessings are sufficient for the day.

Planting a Tree (Jewish)

There is an ancient story about the Emperor Hadrian who, as he was marching with his troops through a certain village, came upon an old man who was planting an orchard of fig saplings. When Hadrian noticed this he asked the man, "How old are you?"

The old man answered, "I am a hundred years old."

Hadrian responded, "At your age, what difference does it make to plant an orchard of fig saplings? It will be years before the trees will bear fruit, and by that time you will probably be dead."

The old man answered, "This is true. I am not likely to see figs from this orchard, but I am not thinking about myself. I am planting this orchard for my children and my grandchildren—even my grandchildren's children."

Hadrian was impressed by the old man's wisdom.

As it happened, three years later, Hadrian was marching with his troops through that same town and he came upon the fig orchard planted by the old man. Hadrian was much surprised when he spied the old man—now a hundred and three years old—still working in the orchard. The Emperor called to him and when the old man noted the king, he took a basket and filled it with his best figs. Taking them to Hadrian the old man said, "My Lord, please accept these figs as a gift from your servant."

Hadrian accepted the gift, but he said to his servants, "Now take the basket, empty it of the figs, and fill it with gold coins." He gave the basket back to the old man. The man took the basket and returned home, wealthier than he had ever been.

Later, as he told this story to his family and friends, a woman next door said to her husband, "You see, this is what we have learned about wealth. The Emperor Hadrian loves fruit. Go quickly, fill a basket with your finest fruit, and take it to the Emperor so that we may become rich, too."

The man followed his wife's advice and filled a basket with ripe figs. He made the journey to Hadrian's palace, requested to see the king, and once he was introduced he offered up the figs with the words, "My Lord, I hear that you love fruit. Please accept this gift from your servant."

Hadrian, wise to the man's ploy, told his servants, "Take the fruit from him, strip him naked, and pelt him in the face with his own figs." The man was subsequently pelted with the fruit he had brought and was utterly humiliated. When he returned home empty handed his wife asked him, "What happened? Where is the gold?"

He said to her, "I'll get even with you for leading me down this path. How could you dishonor me by suggesting such a thing?"

She said to him, "Just be glad you brought figs instead of melons, and be exceedingly glad your figs were ripe and were not green!"

★

There is an ancient Jewish proverb that says, "The greatest act of hope is in the planting of a tree." Indeed, a tree is an act of faith, and when one plants an orchard, one doesn't expect to reap all of the benefits from it. Trees can live from one generation to the next.

This beautiful legend from the Mishnah is an affirmation of generosity born of vision. Visionaries see beyond themselves, and their aim is to benefit those who will come after them.

In certain Native American circles decisions were discussed with an eye toward future generations. Native American elders did not ask, "What's best for us?" but rather, "How will our decisions today impact those who will be living seven generations from now?"

The truth is, we cannot orchestrate another person's generosity or make someone respond in a certain manner—and why would we? Rather, our goal should always be to demonstrate generosity ourselves, even toward those who have more authority or wealth than we possess. Giving from the heart produces its own rewards. Any other approach leads us into hypocrisy and coercion. Another word for this truth is "integrity."

Chapter Eight

Inroads to Enthusiasm

I prefer the folly of enthusiasm to the indifference of wisdom.
—Anatole France

One can never consent to creep when one feels an impulse to soar.
—Helen Keller

*I*t has been said that perception is reality. How we see the world is our experience of the world. For any single event we can react in any number of ways—with responses ranging from fear to faith, from cursing to blessing, from despair to elation.

Remaining enthusiastic about life—about our work, family, friendships, and futures—is sometimes difficult. Confidence can wane. Enjoyments can ebb. The inevitable changes of life can deplete us of purpose.

The ancient Greeks believed in the concept of pantα rei ("Everything changes"). But so often in our modern mindset we forget that changes are happening every day. Each of us ages a bit. The seasons turn. New choices bring new opportunities.

In many ways we are far more comfortable living in the afterglow of yesterday—holding on to the familiar, the traditional. But change is required to offer new opportunities, new challenges, even new joys. Without these inevitable changes, in fact, life would actually be rather dull. Perhaps boring. We would simply repeat the same day over and over again.

One can retain an enthusiasm for life when one sees things for what they really are. A Zen teaching goes like this: Before one takes up the practice of Zen one sees a river as a river, and a mountain as a mountain. Then, when one takes up the practice of Zen, a river is no longer a river, and a mountain is no longer a mountain. Eventually, however, one sees that even this is an illusion. A river is indeed a river and a mountain is a mountain.

Zen offers these truths in juxtaposition to elusive and obvious truths. One thing is not as it appears. On the other hand, it is exactly as it appears.

But the pursuit of life—the pursuit of truth—is exactly that which can inspire us. We need not look to high moments and beautiful experiences in order to find this enthusiasm either. Inspiration can come by sunset, a back porch conversation, a favorite pastime. We can be inspired by the tried-and-true as well as these inevitable changes.

In the Talmud there is a beautiful passage that points to these truths. It states: *Remember—it is forbidden to live in any town that has no gardens or green spaces.*

Why?

One needs to be in the presence of living things, surrounded by the energy of life itself, in order to remain a creative and energetic human being. Sterile offices, cubicles, bricks and mortar, exhaust fumes, and asphalt can only take us so far. Of course, there is nothing intrinsically wrong with these modern advantages, but we can quickly and easily lose our enthusiasm without the sun upon our faces, without the grass beneath our feet. There is, in fact, much evidence to support the chemical imbalance that can take place in the body when we are deprived of sunlight, of fresh air, of this ambient energy of the universe. We need the stuff of earth to be earth's children—and if we are to enjoy a heaven, we need to live with enthusiasm and persuasion. We need to remain inspired.

Inspiration, of course, literally means to be "in-spirited" or to have spirit inside of us. We are more than flesh and blood.

There is a classic Taoist tale about a man named Lieh-tzu who, when asked why he enjoyed travel so much, responded: "When I travel I see that what amuses us never remains the same. And while some people travel to see the sights, I travel in order to notice how things change. There is travel, and then there is *travel* . . . but I have yet to meet someone who can tell the difference."

One doesn't have to travel far or wide to note the truth of Lieh-tzu's observations. Nothing ultimately remains the same, and in our enthusiasm we can take hold of these inevitable changes and create life anew. These pose great challenges for humanity, of course—but if these challenges be faced with confidence and inspiration of thought and practice, there is no telling what problems can be solved, what difficulties overcome.

The tales and teachings here possess their own inspiration, from the teller to the told. Whether by satire or humor, or inspiration gleaned from sacred books—it is a joy to revel in these encouraging words. No matter one's circumstances or station in life, there is certain to be a bit of inspiration gleaned from these wonderful thoughts. We may even discover that these stories can change us—and our attitudes. We might discover a new spring in our step, or find that we are now equipped to face an old nemesis with new answers. It's a short journey from the page to practice. One story can change a life.

Marco Polo (legend)

Centuries ago, when Marco Polo was traveling through China in order to see the Khan, he grew weary while riding his horse and fell asleep in the saddle. His horse, sensing the inattentiveness of its rider, fell behind the caravan and was soon distanced from it. When Marco woke up her realized that he was alone in the desert. But he thought he heard the voices of his family calling out to him, "Marco! Marco!" Every time he heard a voice cry out, "Marco", he would respond, "Polo! Polo!"

★

There are many legends attributed the Marco Polo, including one's attached to his name. Our own names can be, in fact, a source of inspiration and encouragement. The name we create for ourselves is built day by day on the foundation of integrity, helpfulness, and friendship.

Cookies (Jewish)

A rabbi was invited to dinner one day and, after enjoying a remarkable Sabbath meal, the hostess served cookies for dessert. Everybody at the table ate their fill and eventually there were only two cookies left on the plate—a large one and a small one.

Without hesitation the rabbi reached over and took the largest cookie. He ate it and enjoyed it, but his host was annoyed. When he could hold his tongue no longer the host asked, "Rabbi, I don't understand how you can come into my home and, at the end of the meal, take the largest cookie without asking me if I would like to eat it?"

The rabbi thought for a moment and then asked, "Well, what would you have done if you were in my place?"

The host said, "I would have taken the smaller cookie."

The rabbi quickly responded, "But that's *exactly* what you received— the smaller cookie. So what's the big deal?"

★

Hospitality can take many forms. And among these the ability to laugh at oneself is a sign of friendship. Most guests have a joke to tell. And what does it hurt if we are the brunt of a joke now and then? Laughter keeps us motivated.

•224•

The Boy and the Butterfly (Dodsley)

One day a boy was roaming through a flower field and became smitten by a most beautiful butterfly. The colors of the insect were so delightful that he watched it as it flitted from flower to flower. In time the boy became so enthralled by the butterfly that he wanted to possess it.

Running after the butterfly, the boy attempted to capture it in his hands, but each time he was about to touch it, it would dart to another flower and elude him. Sensing the boy's pursuit, the butterfly flew more swiftly from stem to stem until, at last, it settled inside the cone of a tulip. So eager was the boy to capture the butterfly's beauty that, when he reached for it, he crushed the insect in his palm. As it was dying the butterfly said to the boy, "Perhaps I will not die in vain if you learn this lesson: that all pleasures, if pursued with too much enthusiasm and frequency, will perish if you cherish them too dearly."

★

Yes, it is one thing to be enthusiastic, but as the saying goes, "All things in moderation." Too much of a good thing can transform into a curse—and all enthusiasms should be bridled lest they become a force of habit. This parable also points out that beauty—and our highest aspiration—is often elusive. Much enthusiasm is embodied in the pursuit itself, especially as we consider our need for self-improvement. Love is releasing people, not smothering them. And when we have a grand vision for our lives, it is best to remember that the end does not arrive without a deft touch and persistence. Nothing worth having ever comes easy. And why would we want it to?

Mere Generosity (Jewish)

A rabbi asked a parishioner if he gave a lot of money to God's work. The man replied, "Well, rabbi—I give a little, but I'm a modest person and I don't talk much about what I give."

The rabbi said, "Well from now on, give *a lot*, and talk a great deal about it!"

★

The Apostle Paul once wrote, "God loves a cheerful giver." But of course, Paul realized that there are many attitudes that can drive charity. Some people are motivated by a sense of community, others by gratitude. Some give out of abundance, and others lack. And as this wonderful story illustrates, some are motivated by anonymity.

There may be times, however, when a gift deserves the bright lights of recognition—and some gifts can certainly inspire others to give as well.

The Archery Contest (Zen)

There is a Zen parable about a new archery student who wanted to impress his class. Arriving early, he shot three arrows at a great distance and then rushed out and drew circles around them. When the teacher arrived he knew what the new student had done—and he asked the student to repeat the performance. The student shot three more arrows and each landed inside the circles. The teacher asked, "How did you do it?"

The student replied, "It was easy, as the arrows already knew the way."

★

Zen is many things if not playful, and as this beautiful parable illustrates there is something to be said for practice and confidence. Discipline in life and in faith are hallmarks of students who seek to shoot straight while also going the distance.

This parable may also illustrate the importance of building upon the foundation of past successes, and especially the wisdom *of the past*. Nothing is impossible for those who follow tried and true disciplines and practices. If certain paths have led to success for others, then these same paths can work for new disciples as well. We don't always have to aim far, but we can live with a confidence that we are aiming straight and true.

The Blind Man (Buddhist Sutra)

A man who was blind from birth could not imagine shapes or colors. When people told him some things were ugly and others beautiful, he had no way to distinguish between the two. In fact, he had no comprehension of either ugliness or beauty.

Some years later a physician met this blind man and determined that his blindness was due to something that had happened to him in a former life, and the physician desired to make him well. But because there were no medicines that could cure the man's blindness, the physician knew that he would have to use some special herbs found only in the mountains. There were four such herbs—and each of them had a special property.

One herb contained the power of colors, smells and tastes. Another herb had the property of curing all diseases. Another was an antidote for poison. And the fourth herb provided happiness.

The physician climbed the mountain, searched for these four herbs until he found them, and then returned to administer them to the blind man through various potions, powders and raw forms.

After taking the herbs the blind man could see. For the first time in his life he saw the light of the sun and the moon, the stars and planets, and all of the various shapes of the world. He noted beautiful forms and ugly forms—and realized that he was a fool for not believing such things before. In time, the man formerly blind also became arrogant, for he believed that, since his vision had been restored, he was able to see everything.

But some wise men came to the man's house one day. These wise men possessed the five divine powers: to see at a distance, to hear at a distance, to be transformed, to know the thoughts of others, and to know the thoughts from their former lives. When they saw the arrogance of the former blind man they told him, "Can't you see that there is much more to be seen? Although you can see shapes and colors, you cannot yet see your own thoughts, you cannot yet see or hear the thoughts of others, and you are ignorant of your own origins. What makes you believe you are wise? Can't you see that you are still in darkness?"

The man formerly blind asked the wise men how he could obtain this special kind of sight. They told him, "To obtain the five powers you must live in the forest, or sit in a mountain cave in silence, and think only of the Dharma. You must rid yourself of all blindness and fault."

The man formerly blind then set off to live in the forest and pursue the Dharma. He rid himself of all desires and obtained the five holy powers. At last he thought to himself, "In my beginning I was blind and not wise, and then I could see and was arrogant. Now I am awake and I can go wherever I want."

★

This Buddhist sutra (or teaching tradition) is remarkable for its depth of insight. As with many parables in various religious traditions, this Sutra has layers of interpretation. Some would read the Sutra and see Buddha as the physician. Others would see Buddha as the wise man. And there are other sutras that liken Buddha to the herbs—those mystical varieties that are every present, yet hidden, and for which a person must search until he finds them.

The opening of the blind man's eyes is a universal theme in Buddhism also, just as it is in Christianity. The metaphors of light and wisdom, of growth and change, are also common. And in the realization that there are levels of sight, or both physical and spiritual forms of "seeing," the Dharma takes root.

As this parable suggests, the Buddha is ever present and can be found whenever and wherever one is willing to open the eyes and see how the Buddha gives life to all through the sun, moon, stars, and even the flowers of the fields. This parable is also suggestive of the Buddha in disguise—that one should be ever vigilant and alert because one never knows when the Buddha may appear, and in what form.

Only after one masters the true vision can one see the Buddha plainly and without pretense.

The Lighthouse (traditional Christian)

Many years ago, along a particularly treacherous stretch of coastline, a small group of people built a lighthouse. They said, "There are many ships that will perish on the rocks and become battered by the waves without this light. Let us build the lighthouse high and let the beacon be bright so that others will not perish."

And so the lighthouse was completed. For many years it operated in the storms, casting its light across the waves and warning ships of the dangers that were before them. Many lives were saved and the people continued to operate the lighthouse efficiently.

As time passed, however, some began to say, "There has never been a tragedy under our watch. The light continues to shine, but we should concentrate on shining the light only on the darkness of nights. After all, ships know that the lighthouse is here. They should be aware of the rocks by now."

And so the lighthouse did not shine all the time, but only on those darkest of nights. Ships were saved from perishing in severe storms.

As time passed, however, there were some who began to say, "It is very costly and time-consuming to shine the light so far. We should not worry about shining the light miles out to sea but we should concentrate on the rocks that are close to the shoreline. After all, this is the greatest danger, and these are the ships that we can see."

And so the light was reduced and an increasing number of people who once worked in the lighthouse were no longer needed. Some, in fact, left the lighthouse and a smaller number of people were left to tend to the light.

One night, when there was a great storm at sea, the people of the lighthouse said, "There have been other storms like this before. And besides, the lighthouse has fallen into disrepair. We should concentrate on making these improvements and it is very costly to shine the light so far. For tonight, let us concentrate on doing the work at hand, and we will return to shining the light after the storm has passed."

And so they did.

That night, a great ship lost its way in the storm. Searching for the light to guide it home, it found no light on the horizon and crashed and sank upon the rocks.

★

This story has been retold in various forms, but points out that individuals and communities need a purpose. When we lose our sense of purpose, or attempt to navigate our lives without a clear direction or end in mind, we often meet with disaster. Likewise, without goals and a light to lead us, we have no clear destination. Living with the end in mind informs the decisions we make each day.

The Wall (Jewish parable)

There was a powerful king who was determined to build a new city—its location to be determined by the sages. When the sages came back to the king with their answer, they also insisted that the city be dedicated through a voluntary offering of a child, who was to be sealed up alive inside the walls as a sacrifice offered by the mother.

The king approved of this plan, and eventually a mother stepped forward with her son to serve as the sacrifice. But before the king could seal the wall, the boy asked the king and the sages, "Can you tell me: what is the lightest, the sweetest, and the hardest thing in the world?"

The sages, certain that they had the answer to the riddle, said, "The lightest thing in the world is a feather. The sweetest thing in the world is honey. And the hardest thing in the world is stone."

The boy laughed at them. "What simple answers," he said, "but you are wrong. The lightest thing in the world is a child in a mother's arms. The sweetest thing in the world is a mother's love. And the hardest thing in the world is for a mother to watch her child die."

Indeed the king and the sages were confounded by the boy's wisdom and they admitted that no sacrifice was needed.

★

The wisdom literature of the Bible is a marvelous corpus of material (e.g. Proverbs, Ecclesiastes, Song of Songs) that attempts to offer a counter approach to the strict legalistic strands of Jewish thought. As such, wisdom is a more playful and creative approach to the questions and difficulties of life. Sometimes, trickery and puzzles are needed to reveal truth.

In the instance of this story, we are here shown the true nature of love. Love can be described, defined . . . even ignored. But love experienced is a great power and a remarkable teacher.

Love moves us. And there are many decisions we make in life that have much more to do with heart than with the head.

The Chinese and the Greek Artists (Rumi)

The Chinese and the Greeks came before the Sultan to settle a debate regarding the question: Who are the better painters—the Chinese or the Greeks?

In order to settle the dispute, the Sultan assigned each a house to paint. The Chinese went to work on their house, coloring it with bright colors or varied hues. In the end, their house was elaborate.

The Greeks, on the other hand, did not purchase any paint at all. Instead, they set about cleaning the house from top to bottom. They polished all of the walls until they glistened.

When the two houses were compared, the Sultan praised the Chinese, saying that their painting was much admired. But he gave the highest award to the Greeks, saying, "All of the colors of the Chinese house are reflected in the pristine walls of your house."

★

The Sufi poet, Rumi (thirteenth century), was a master illustrator. Here he offers a delightful parable, a metaphor, for life. For centuries sages, prophets, and teachers of all persuasions have used the image of a house to describe the human heart. A house is a home and the interior life (thoughts, emotions, dreams, intention) is where each person truly resides.

In this instance, Rumi is pointing out the differences between interior knowledge and schools of knowledge. Or, as the writer of Ecclesiastes (Hebrew Bible) would note: "Of the writing of many books there is no end."

Rumi in no way discounted book knowledge or education, but per the Sufi way, he believed that heart religion was superior to head religion; he believed that too much philosophy and speculation spoiled a person's devotion to God. What matters most is our reflection of the divine, whereby others can see the true nature of God and enjoy the beauty and mystery of the Eternal.

The Long and Winding Road (Buddhist Sutra)

Once there was a long and winding road that was in very poor condition. It was steep, treacherous, and dangerous—in no small part because it was so remote and because there were no places to rest along the way.

A group of people decided that they wanted to travel on this road because they had heard about a treasure hidden in the mountains. The group was led by a guide who knew this road well—a guide who had great wisdom and knowledge of all of the potholes, detours, and pitfalls.

After a day on this road, however, the group became discouraged and tired. They forgot all about the treasure they were seeking and they said to the guide, "We are weary. We can't go any further. We wish to turn back."

But the guide was very skillful and compassionate and he said, "It would be a shame if you turned back now . . . especially since you are in search of the most wonderful treasure."

Because the guide was compassionate he also conjured up a beautiful castle-city that gleamed in the near distance. The guide said to the group: "See what is ahead. It is but a short distance. Let us go to the castle, take our rest there, find refreshment, and then we can continue on our way to search for the great treasure."

When the people saw the castle gleaming in the distance, they took heart and were no longer afraid. They followed the guide to the castle and took their rest there. They were refreshed, reenergized, and soon were quite comfortable and at peace.

After a short while in the castle, the guide made the castle disappear. He said to the group: "You are now ready to proceed to the treasure. It is but a short distance now, and you will find it. I created to the castle for you to rest in for a brief while so that you would not lose hope."

★

Without hope, people can wither and die. Hope, indeed, keeps us alive—especially in those dark nights of the soul. It can also be said that hope enables us to live with excitement and purpose. If there is more to come, or if we can anticipate a future, hope can get us there.

The War (Buddhist Sutra)

A powerful chariot king sought to make war with, and subdue, less powerful kings. First he asked them to surrender to him, but when they did not do this, he made war on them. In these various battles, there were many warriors in the king's service who distinguished themselves on the battlefield. The king rewarded them with many gifts, including houses, farms, cities, gold, jewels and servants. However, the king did not give his most valuable jewel—a precious stone that he kept pinned in the top of his hair. But one day the king noticed a soldier who had distinguished himself above all others in the field and the king gave this soldier his most precious jewel.

★

This Buddhist parable—akin to the kingdom parables of the lost and found, which Jesus told—are not principally about reward, but were meant to provoke the listener to paths of service and purpose. There are greater aims than individual pursuits. And often we discover life's greatest joys in unexpected places.

The Good Doctor (Buddhist Sutra)

Once there was a wise and good doctor who had many sons. One day the father left home to visit a patient and during his absence his sons drank some poison. They became deathly ill. When the father returned home he found his sons writhing in pain on the floor. Some were completely out of their minds, while a few were not so bad off.

Quickly the good doctor prepared a medicine in his laboratory. He showed the medicine to his sons and urged them to take it if they wanted to be freed of their pain and agony. The sons who were out of their minds refused to take the cure, believing that the father was trying to harm them. But the sons who were not so bad off took the medicine right away and were cured.

But the father, wanting to save all of his sons, decided that he would use a ploy to help them. He told them that he was going away because he was ill and would soon die. He left the medicines behind, and went to another place. After a day he sent word through a servant and told the servant to return to his sick sons with the word that he had died.

When the sick sons heard that their father as dead, they grew despondent. They felt lonely and afraid. They said among themselves, "If our father were here he would not have wanted to poison us. He would surely have wanted to help us. We should take the medicines he had prepared for us."

The sick sons did take the medicines and were cured. Soon after this the father returned, having used this ploy to save his children.

★

Again, we discover that this parable has many layers to it. The physician, of course represents Buddha, who desires to see all of his children well. Although the Buddha reached Nirvana (death) the universal Buddha is ever-present and helpful to his children and desires for them to be healed of all suffering. As with many great spiritual teachers, they are unable to reach some people due to the depth of their weakness or inability to hear the message of compassion.

Many of the Buddhist Sutras such as this one possess layers of meaning and offer a rich source of interpretation. One could make a study of the sutras on many levels, but their primary intent is to lead one into the Dharma, into the compassion of Buddha, who can free the disciple of all worldly desires and suffering.

The Sparrow and the Ostrich (Gotthold Lessing)

A sparrow and an ostrich met one day in the field. The ostrich, in its pride, pointed out the disparity in their sizes. "I am the largest of birds," said the ostrich, "and your size indicates that you can't fly very fast or far."

"This is true," replied the sparrow. "But although I am small and cannot fly fast or far, as you say, I can at least fly. And this is something you cannot do at all."

★

Being confident of and thankful for one's respective gifts is important. Instead of focusing upon what one does not have, one should embrace the strengths at hand. This is true enthusiasm—to see the possibilities based on blessings. Focusing on the positive is vital to maintaining a winning outlook. Lessing, a German writer of the eighteenth century, created many insightful parables filled with humorous characters and philosophical optimism.

The Lessons of the Ant (Lessing)

An industrious farmer—well past his prime—was working in the field in the heat of the day when an apparition appeared to him under the shade of an oak tree. "Who are you?" asked the old man.

"I am Solomon," said the ghost. "And I have come to ask why an old man like you is still working."

"If you really are Solomon," said the old men, "then you would not have to ask that question. You would have learned from the ant how to be industrious and accumulate wealth. I have learned this lesson from the ant and that is why I still labor."

"Ah," said the ghost, "but you have only learned half the lesson of the ant. If you were truly perceptive you would have also learned how to rest in the winter of existence. Does not the ant teach this also?"

★

A tale based on the book of Proverbs, here Lessing weaves an alternative ending to the lesson of the ant. True, industry is important—or making one's way in the world. But the smallest of creatures also teach valuable lessons about enjoyment and rest. For everything a season—as Solomon might say.

Aiming to rest well is equally important to one's focus upon work.

The Elephant (Traditional)

Four friends who had never seen an elephant traveled to India to catch a glimpse of the famous beast. At last they found a guide who took them deep into the jungle. One night the guide returned and said, "I have found an elephant up ahead inside a cave." But when the friends approached the beast, it was so dark inside the cave that none of them could actually see the elephant. Instead, they began to feel the elephant from where they were each standing.

Afterwards, back at camp, the four men began to argue about what the elephant looked like. The first man—who had felt the elephant's leg said, "It was like a pillar." The second man—who had felt the elephant's ear, insisted, "No! It was like a giant fan." The third man—who had felt the elephant's trunk, said, "It was like a snake." And the fourth man—who felt the elephant's hide said, "It was like a furry wall."

None of the men were wrong, of course, but neither did any of them contain the whole truth.

★

This wonderful parable, perhaps originating with the Sufi poet Rumi, articulates a common truth about the divine: as human beings we only perceive a small portion of the whole truth, or the whole of God. Rumi taught this principle as a Sufi—that enlightenment involves the inner being rather than just the intellect, and participation is the road to becoming rather than through arguments or proofs. Rumi also described faith as a drop in the ocean of becoming, and yet one should intend to drink the entire ocean if one is willing to receive the absolute Truth. Words themselves, likewise, do not describe Truth or the

Absolute nature of God—and yet words are used to convey what we learn.

Because of this dichotomy, Sufism is shot through with a wondrous wordplay, with parables and stories that are at once logical and illogical, transparent and yet mysterious. There is a humility that is required to begin the journey, an openness to learning. Even if one experiences only a fraction of the divine, it is enough to know the divine and to celebrate the very presence of God.

Blowing the Shofar (Traditional Jewish)

Long ago Rabbi Berdichever came searching for someone to blow the shofar. To each man who came forward to volunteer, the rabbi would ask the question: "What thoughts enter your mind when you blow the shofar?"

No one gave a satisfactory answer.

Eventually, however, a man came forward who admitted that, not only was he unlearned, but also unconcerned about religious matters. "Tell me then," the Rabbi asked, "what do you think about when you blow the shofar?"

"Rabbi," the man answered, "I have four unmarried daughters who are looking for husbands. When I blow the shofar I tell God, 'I am doing my duty by blowing this horn. Now you do your duty and provide some husbands.'"

The Rabbi immediately assigned this fellow to blow the shofar that year.

★

Motivation comes in many forms. Often we are motivated by desire for money, fame, recognition, or sex. But enthusiasm can also lead us to more nobler ends—being a part of a community, a desire to be helpful or productive, a need to be of service to others.

Without enthusiasm it is impossible to stay committed to a task, or to find the energy to continue in some virtuous work. Knowing our aim and our purpose is most important before setting out on any endeavor.

The Dragon Boy (Chinese legend)

Hundreds of years ago a mother and her son lived on the banks of the Min river. They were very poor, and the boy had to take care of his mother—for she was ill. Every day the boy went down to the banks of the river and cut grass. He sold the grass as hay for the cattle—but he barely made enough to feed himself and his mother.

One summer, in the midst of a drought, the boy was forced to travel a much great distance from home in order to find green grass. Miles from home, he eventually discovered a very strange patch of grass along the river that was full and leafy. In fact, after he cut the grass and carried it back to the village to sell, he was rewarded handsomely, and he and his mother were able to live on the money for more than a week.

The next week, the boy set out again. He had to travel a great distance from home but eventually came across the same patch of grass growing along the river. Surprisingly, the grass had grown tall again in just a week, and once again the boy cut it and sold it for a nice sum in the village. This pattern continued for many weeks—and the boy was amazed at how quickly the grass grew in that one spot. He guarded his secret, but also reasoned that me might be able to transplant the grass closer to home so that he would not have to walk so far to earn his living.

One day the boy set out to dig up this patch of grass, roots and all. But as he was digging up the deep roots he came upon a splendid pearl—large, white, and shimmering. He thought, "This must be the secret of the grass and what makes it magic."

The boy brought the pearl back to his ageing mother and she agreed that it was worth a great sum of money. She hid in the bottom of a rice jar to keep it safe.

The next day, when the boy returned to harvest the transplanted grass, he discovered that it had withered and died. He wept over his folly and returned home dejected and depressed.

However, when he entered the home, his mother was standing over the rice bowl. Magically it had filled to the brim and they ate of the rice for many days, and it did not run out of food.

In time, the boy and his mother became quite wealthy. They were able to repay all of their debts and help many of their neighbors—and others in the village, of course, became curious as to the new-found wealth of the mother and her son. Eventually word got around that they possessed a magic pearl, and one day many of the villages came to the home demanding to see it.

Now, in their greed, many in the village began to covet the pearl and some were making plans to steal it. While trying to protect the pearl, the boy accidently swallowed it. Immediately he felt a fire in his belly and he became parched. He drank gallons of water. A storm soon gathered overhead, lightening flashed, thunder cracked, and the boy began to change. He sprouted horns and began to grow scales. He became immense and eventually turned into a dragon.

And it is said that this is the source of the Min river—which is the dragon boy who guards the water and the most treasured pearl.

★

All cultures have legends associated with place and time—and there are also many stories that tell of abundance from poverty. The Biblical story of Elijah, the widow, and the oil jar is reminiscent of this tale, as are several of the Buddha legends. In this Chinese legend, the pearl explains the blessings of the river—the source of life, which is guarded by the dragon of the waters.

In life, we don't often have an explanation for our blessings—we can only point to some greater source or higher power. And as this legend also demonstrates, a blessing found is best expressed by sharing, for as the blessings are reaped, they also multiply if we use them appropriately. There is an abundance in the universe that we scarcely tap into. But when we find the pearl, we do need to treasure it. The one thing we know—the highest truth—will often be the source of all good things that flow into our lives.

Chapter Nine

The Importance of Integrity

Know thyself.

—Buddha

*In all relationships the highest person always considers
the beginning.*
—*I Ching* (Classical Chinese Text)

There are many ways that people—of all religions—view the life
of faith. Some regard faith as those actions and attitudes that posture the
individual toward others—the idea being that faith is not principally
about the self. Others regard faith as being comprised of certain rituals
or movements—those practices that may best be described as worship.
Others hold to a faith that unites people together—with the ideas of
community and tradition forming the crux of belief. And there are others
who see the life of faith as being principally about self improvement—
the notion that human beings need heart change, mind change, personal
growth, without which one cannot embrace a better life.

All religions hold to various forms of these ideas, even as there
has always been debate among those who practice their respective

faiths regarding the importance or significance of these tendencies. In short, some regard vital faith as being centered on "the other," while some regard faith as primarily interior. The Hebrew prophets and the Talmudic rabbis debated these questions, as did Jesus, and Buddha, and Muhammad and Confucius. And a person doesn't have to delve too deeply into any religion that is being practiced today to glean the disparate tendencies at play. Some will guard their traditions and teachings without regard to how these impact the world—while others will focus on the practice of faith *in the world* and *to the world*.

But even if there are disagreements within all faiths regarding these matters, most would agree that a person's actions should match a person's profession of faith. This may better be described as integrity—matching faith with action. Or, in modern-day language, we might say that one should "walk the walk" and not just "talk the talk."

The Buddha once said to his followers, "Know yourself." And Jesus described people in terms of salt and light—qualities that could be described as integrity.

Likewise, there are many wonderful stories in all faith traditions that were meant to call people back to these inner qualities—tales that could reform the heart and mind. These stories are at once challenging and comforting—and in them we may find a bridge between the ancient the contemporary, between history and the needs of our own time.

Your Light (Buddha)

The Buddha said, "Make yourself a light. Rely upon yourself and do not depend upon others. Make my teachings your light. Consider your 'self'. Remember how fleeting your life is. If you do, you will not fall into delusion and become proud or selfish. Do this and you will be my disciples. My teachings are not only to be treasured, but practiced. If you follow these teachings you will indeed be happy."

You are the light of the world. A city that is set on a hill cannot be hid. Neither do men light and candle and put it under a bushel, but on a candlestick, and it gives light to all who are in the house. Let your light shine before others that they may see your good works and give glory to your Father in heaven. (Jesus)

(A teaching of Jesus) KJV (Matthew 5:14-16)

★

As these two teachings reveal—one from Buddha, one from Jesus—we are meant to be a light in the world. As many have expressed through the years, the similarity between the teachings of Buddha and Jesus are startling—so much so, in fact, that we might say that Jesus and Buddha would recognize each other in their teaching.

Both Jesus and Buddha taught that life is fleeting. But if we follow the light, we won't walk in darkness.

The Quality of Mercy (Buddhist)

Just as rain falls and waters all of the plants of the earth, so Buddha's compassion extends to all the people of earth. In the same way, just as different plants receive particular benefits from the same rain, so people of different natures and circumstances are blessed in different ways.

Though parents love all of their children equally, nevertheless, their compassion is extended to a sick child because the situation dictates this special care. In this way Buddha's compassion is extended to all people equally, but is expressed with special care toward those who are burdened by evil or who are suffering.

The sun rises in the east and clears away all of the darkness—and all receive it favorably. So Buddha's compassion encompasses all people. He clears away the darkness of ignorance and leads people toward Enlightenment.

(A teaching of Buddha)

But I say to you, Love your enemies, bless them that curse you, do good to them that hate you, and pray for them that despitefully use you, and persecute you, that you may be the children of the Father who is in heaven; for he makes his sun to rise upon the evil and the good, and sends rain to the just and to the unjust. For if you love them that love you, what reward to you have? (A teaching of Jesus) Matthew 5:44-46

★

Another pair of teachings, from Buddha and Jesus, that are mirror reflections of each other. The life of compassion is the life worth living, and when we recognize that there is a greater power that rules the world in love, our compassion takes on cosmic significance. There is a greater heart than our own. And no matter how it is described, this love can be at the center of our life's decisions and relationships—including how we treat those who are on the margins.

The Miser (Aesop)

Once there was a man so miserly that he sold all of his possessions for a huge nugget of gold. In order to keep the gold safe, he buried it in the ground. Each day, however, he would dig up the gold nugget, admire it, and then bury it again.

One day a farmer observed the miser digging in the field. Later that night, the farmer returned to the spot and dug up the gold nugget.

The next morning, when the miser returned to his treasure, it was gone. In his anguish, the miser told his story to a friend. "What will I do, now that my gold nugget is gone?" asked the miser.

The friend replied, "Why don't you find a rock in the field, paint it gold and bury it again, since all you were doing with the gold was admiring it."

★

It is true that possessions can often possess us. Or, in our attempt to be in charge of our money, we discover that money is actually calling the shots. It is difficult to give wealth its proper place: as necessary for the basics of life and enjoyment of creature comforts.

Rather, wealth can become the most sought after ingredient in life—and can even become paramount to life itself. Still, not all desires can be fulfilled by wealth, and security through wealth is an illusion.

As this parable of Aesop's demonstrates, so often our admiration of money (and those who have it) can far surpass the proper use of it. What we end up worshipping isn't even the money itself, but the thought of having it.

Integrity (being true to one's values) is vital to the enjoyment of life.

The Miser and the Magpie (Dodsley)

A miser was sitting at his desk counting his money when a magpie flew from its cage, grabbed a penny, and hopped away with it. A few minutes later, when the miser counted his money a second time, he realized that he was a penny short. He discovered the penny on the bottom of the magpie's cage. "What is this?" the miser cried. "You have robbed me of a penny when you don't even know the proper use of money?"

"And what of you?" the magpie answered. "Surely I am only using the money in the same way you use it. You miss a penny, but how many have you taken from others? And if I am guilty for taking a penny, how much more guilty are you for taking thousands?"

★

Another of the Dodsley parables detailing the nature of greed and avarice. But the parable is also about integrity—our ability to judge others under the same scrutiny by which we judge ourselves. Perhaps this is what Jesus meant when he said, "Judge not, lest you be judged . . . for by the same measures you use to judge others, you yourself will be judged." Tough stuff . . . but integrity is the lens through which others see us. Be true to yourself, yes—but also be true to others.

Unlearning Latin (Desert Fathers)

Father Arsenius met an old Egyptian peasant in the desert and began asking him for advice on several problems. There was a brother who was standing nearby and overheard this conversation. He later asked Father Arsenius, "Why would someone as learned as you—who knows Greek and Latin—ask an Egyptian peasant for advice?" Father replied, "Yes, it is true that I know Greek and Latin, but I don't even know as much as this peasant's alphabet."

★

Head knowledge is not everything, as we continue to learn. Rather, there is also such a thing as emotional intelligence, relational intelligence, and even intuitive intelligence. Dare we say there is also a spiritual intelligence? One's true journey to God begins on the inside. Or, in the Zen articles: "The journey of a thousand miles begins with a single step."

One can never disregard another person as a potential source of learning or wisdom, for there is much to learn from others—especially those who are very different from us. This is one of the gifts of travel. In being exposed to other cultures, other tongues, other ideas, we are challenged to redefine our own, to grow in our own understanding, even our appreciation, of what we have and who we are. And beyond this, there is much more potential for learning from those unlikely sources.

The Human Equation (Hindu)

There is a famous quote from Ghandi: "I have only three enemies. My favorite enemy, the one most easily influenced for the better, is the

British Empire. My second enemy, the Indian people, is far more difficult. But my most formidable opponent is a man named Mohandas K. Ghandi. With him I seem to have very little influence."

★

There are many remarkable, even prophetic, teachings from Ghandi. But chief among them is the importance of humility and integrity for success. As Ghandi suggests here, one doesn't have to look far to find an opponent. Our greatest challenges always lie within. And we can never assume to change the world or offer solutions until we have changed ourselves.

Two Parables (Pilpay)

The following stories were told my two travelling companions to urge each other on in wisdom and insight. They would see who could tell the better story.

The first companion's tale went this way:

Once there were two friends who were travelling on horseback. One could see and the other was blind. As they rode along, the man who was blind happened to misplace his whip and he could not find it among the items in his saddlebag. When they agreed to stop for the night they made camp in a grassy meadow, slept soundly under the stars, and awoke refreshed in the morning to begin their journey again.

Now it happened that the blind man, as he was packing his possessions onto his horse in the morning, picked up a snake by accident. Based on touch, the snake was stiff with the cold of the morning dew, and the blind man happened to think it was a stick. However, as they rode along and the sun began to shine and the snake warmed, it became limber in the blind man's hand, leading him to believe that he was once again in possession of his whip. He began to use the whip on his horse, unable to see that it was, indeed, a venomous snake.

A few minutes later the blind man's friend realized what had happened and he cried out, "You are holding a serpent! Drop it at once or you will be bitten!"

But the blind man thought that this was a joke and he laughed: "Ahhh, why would you deny me the good fortune of finding my whip again? Would you make a fool of me just because I am blind? Don't you think I know a serpent from a whip?"

And the blind man continued to beat his horse with it.

The friend continued, "I would never try to trick you. I am telling you the truth—you are holding a snake in your hand. Throw it away at once!"

But the blind man continued to use the snake as a whip and even became exasperated by his friend's advice. "I know what you are trying to do. As soon as I throw the whip away, you will circle back and pick it up and keep it as your own. It is a fine whip and I have no intentions of throwing it away."

The friend continued to admonish the blind man to toss away the snake. He pleaded with him. But eventually the snake crawled up the blind man's arm and bit him on the neck, killing him.

After this story, the other traveler told this tale:

There were two doctors who lived in a remote part of the East. One of these doctors was completely incompetent, but he believed that he was the greatest doctor in the world. This doctor was so terrible, he could not distinguish the difference between colic and cholera. He loved to make house calls on his patients, but he never visited his patients twice, for all of his patients died after his first visit, as he usually killed them.

Now, there was also a very competent doctor who lived in this same region. This doctor was an expert, and he had a one hundred percent cure rate. Every patient under his care recovered, and yet he was a humble man and kind, and he did not wish to take any credit for his skills. But eventually this doctor became blind, and since he was no longer able to see the patients he was treating, he withdrew to the desert to live out his final days.

It came to pass that when the ignorant doctor heard about the competent doctor's retirement, he became even more brazen in talking up his skills, leading an increasing number of people to fall under his care. This also included the King's daughter, who had become ill with a disease.

When the King realized that he needed the good doctor, who had once served in his palace, he sent word to him in the desert, asking for his help. The good doctor sent back the word that he knew what was wrong with the princess and that she could be cured through a simple prescription of medications that were kept inside the palace. The medications, he told the King, were kept in boxes in a cabinet, all carefully labeled, and that if he followed his prescription, she would be cured.

When the King received this word he went immediately to the other doctor—the one who was incompetent and arrogant—and he told him where to find the medications and how to follow the prescription. But the ignorant doctor, instead of admitting his limitations, decided that he would prescribe his own medications. He could not bring himself to admit that the other doctor knew more, but instead, he put on airs and pretended to know the remedy. He gave the princess his own concoction and, straightway, the princess died.

★

These two tales—both from the hand of the sage, Pilpay—offer insights that strike at the heart of the adage: "Know thyself."

In the first tale, the companion closes with the words: "This story teaches the truth—it is best not to trust our senses, or our own judgment, when we have fallen under the spell of something we love." How true. That is why many have warned of making decisions when we are "in love" or why wisdom is so often born from our mistakes. Our senses—particularly our emotions—can be deceiving and can often lead us to make snap or hasty or illogical decisions.

The second tale is equally impressive, pointing out the foibles of pride and arrogance. But at its heart we also learn the lesson meant by the teller: "We should never speak about, or pretend that we know about, what we do not understand."

Although this sounds very philosophical, it is more common sense. Why pretend to be something one is not? Why open the mouth when one should be silent and learn? Or why are the most ignorant of people often the most vocal?

These tales echo a familiar Biblical proverb: Pride always comes before a fall.

Joseph and the Mirror (Rumi)

A friend came to visit Joseph (in Egypt) and after making some derogatory comments about Joseph's brothers, the host asked his friend if he had brought any gift to pay his respects. The friend replied that he had been considering his gift for a long time, and subsequently produced a small mirror from his pocket. He gave the mirror to Joseph, while at the same time asking his host to admire his own reflection.

★

What is this parable about? Self-absorption? Narcissism? Vanity? Perhaps. But as Rumi would point out in his poetic commentary, the goal of life is to be free of self conceit and admiration, to be able to see true Beauty as reflected in the faces of others, and particularly in human need.

Centuries before, Jesus had spoken of this truth in a parable, too: "In as much as you have done it (fed the hungry, satisfied the thirsty, healed the sick, visited the imprisoned) to the least of these, you have done it to me." Our true selves are discovered in acts of charity, in work that moves us beyond our own self-interests and self-absorption. When we look in a mirror we can see ourselves, true. Or we can look past ourselves and see what lies behind—which is the Beauty that Rumi describes as being a reflection of our true soul, which is the wonder of God and the needs of others.

The Lion, the Wolf and the Fox (Rumi)

A lion went out on the hunt with a wolf and a fox. The lion in short order killed an ox, an ibex, and a rabbit. Then the lion said to the wolf, "Why don't you decide how to divide the kill?" The wolf studied the situation and then said, "Well, why don't you take the ox? I'll take the ibex. And we can give the rabbit to the fox." But the lion was enraged, for the wolf had presumed to use "I," "You," and "We" when describing a situation that was entirely the domain of the lion. With one fell swoop the lion struck the wolf and killed it.

The lion then turned to the fox and said, "Now it is your turn to decide."

The fox, seeing what had happened to the wolf said, "Everything belongs to you."

At this word the lion grew calm and gave everything to the fox saying, "You are no longer a fox, but are now a lion."

★

Nearly all religions speak of devotion as a way of life—one's true passion for God. In the Buddhist religion, for example, the goal is to free oneself from desire, thus abdicating the throne of the self for enlightenment. The Christian faith speaks of abandoning one's heart (home) so that Christ may enter and set up residence: "Behold, I stand at the door and knock, if anyone open the door I will come in and feast with him, and he with me." (Jesus) And here, in the case of Sufism, we see how self-elation and delusion leads to destruction, whereas a recognition of God's power leads to life.

Rumi would illustrate this animal parable with a human one—both meant to demonstrate the importance of self-emptying and one's devotion to God, by saying:

A man knocked on a friend's door late one night. Inside, he heard the friend ask,"Who are you?" "It is I," said the man.

But the friend said, "There is no room in this house for both raw and cooked meat. Leave at once and be cooked in the fiery flames until there is no more self, no more 'I' inside of you."

The poor man left immediately, wondering what his friend meant by this. He roamed the earth for a full year, missing his friend greatly, yearning to be in his home again. He wandered abroad for so long, and yearned for his friends so greatly, that his heart burned inside his chest until it cooked.

Later, when he returned to his friend's house, he knocked on the door with fear and trepidation. This time when the friend asked, "Who is there?" he answered, "It is you who is at the door, My Beloved."

The friend replied, "Well, since it is me, then come in. There is no room for two 'I's' in this house."

The Fox and the Eagle (Phaedrus)

An eagle snatched a fox's cubs
And placed them in her nest for food.
The mother fox pursued her brood
And begged the eagle with her sobs
To spare her children and her loss.
But in the safety of her nest
The eagle just ignored the rest.
The fox then said, "I'll be the boss."
And set the forest floor on fire.
She let the flames climb up the tree

Hoping that this fatality
Would melt the eagle's heart from ire.
Then seeing that her chicks were next,
The eagle reversed course and flew
The cubs back to their den like new
Knowing she could not out-fox the fox.

★

Phaedrus, a Roman fabulist of the first century who adapted many of Aesop's fables to verse form, had a knack for recreating the Aesop moralities into more expressive stories, including works that served as social commentary among his contemporaries. He was, in many ways, a satirist in light verse.

In classic Aesop form, Phaedrus uses animals and domestic inter-play to weave his morality plays. While usually pessimistic in tone, Phaedrus did have a knack for the clever invention and a dignified air of certainty in his protestations. And, in order to drive his point home, he often included an explanation at the end of each story (also in verse form).

Here, in this Phaedrus story of the fox and eagle, I have translated his verse loosely into a rhyme scheme for the modern reader (Phaedrus wrote, usually, in six metered iambic, unrhymed lines). Others have attempted to do the same with Phaedrus, including Christopher Smart, who published his own rhymed translations of the moralist's verse in 1764, including this one about the fox and the grapes.

A hungry fox with fierce attack
Sprang on a vine, but tumbled back,
Nor could attain the point of view,
So near the sky the bunches grew.
As he went off, "They're scurvy stuff,"
Says he, "and not half ripe enough—

And I've more reference for my tripes
Than to torment them with gripes."
For those this tale is very pat
Who lessen what they can't come at.

What Phaedrus offers in the manner of Aesop is an enthusiasm for truth—and especially the truth the lies beneath the obvious.

Here is another, which may lead us speedily to laughter—or perhaps to the nature of integrity and being true to one's self . . . in the lesson of the boar. Or, as Phaedrus himself might opine, those who are asses are hardly worthy of response. They are best ignored. Fools are best left to their own devices and opinions, and the wise can walk away knowing that they have far better pursuits. As this next parable implies, insults are rarely worth a reply, and the best response is silence.

The Ass Insults the Boar (Phaedrus)

When the ass met the boar it brayed out, "Brother,
Good morning!" But the boar was quite bothered
And asked the ass to explain his meaning.
The ass then produced his penis into the greeting
And said, "Hey, look, as everyone knows
This here resembles the shape of your nose!"
The boar was about to mount a charge
But then remembered his heart, which was large,
And it managed to gain control to opine:
"Revenge would be sweet, but you're not worth my time."

Alcibiades and Socrates (Classical)

Alcibiades was joking one day, as he sometimes did, with his beloved teacher Socrates, and said: "You are indeed the most wonderful of all men. All Athens, except the sophists and your enemies among the avaricious and unrighteous demagogues, call you the wisest. And even these secretly believe you to be so, although unwilling to confess it. Now I have long thought of learning of you the art, by which you so operate on men, that they all honor you, even those who hate and shun you. But all my efforts so far have been fruitless, for you always slip out of my hands when I think I have caught you."

Socrates replied, smiling: "Lately you compared me to the satyr-formed cases of statues; now probably you intend to honor me by comparing me with the reptile that guides Sculapius, or the winds around his staff. I might be pleased with it, if the subject of discourse were merely the healing art, and the name of the animal did not at the same time remind one of the venomous fang."

"Here you are again pronouncing your own sentence," interrupted Alcibiades. "You are proud, Socrates!"

"Now," replied Socrates, "I guess you have at last apprehended me."

"Yes," said the pupil of the sage, "you are proud. Therefore you talk of a divine spirit, who animates you, and reveals to you the truth. And in what mystery you envelope yourself and your discourse, when any one approaches you who is not agreeable to you. But, — and that is the mischief and incomprehensibility — you are also as modest as a child, and will not once attribute your wisdom to yourself. In short, you are unintelligible and full of contradiction in yourself, you strange man!"

"No, surely not" replied Socrates. "Look at the sun! Is he not the brightest luminary? Yet he draws up the vapors around him and forms them into a frightful thunder-cloud, in which he hides his face. But the little dew-drop also, after he has reflected his image in it, and given to it the brilliancy of the diamond, he causes to ascend, and forms out of it the bow of heaven."

Alcibiades answered, "In the future then must I compare you with the sun or his fore-runner, Phoebus Apollo? At the first entertainment I will correct my mistake."

"If I should concede this to you, my dear Alcibiades," replied Socrates, "you would certainly be right when you call me proud, and would contradict yourself when you ascribe to me a childlike modesty."

Alcibiades answered: "Then I must take the middle course and compare you to Eos (Aurora)."

"How would you proceed in that?" asked Socrates.

And Alcibiades said: "Peaceful and luminous, she announces the approach of the beaming sun-god as soon as he appears; she bows herself before him as the superior. At the end of his glorious career, she again opens to him the gates of heaven: and when

the damp night comes, she retires in the brightness of her beauty into her quiet tent."

Socrates smiled, and said: "Here now you have certainly found the way to gain the respect of the good and the secret regard of the wicked. Pride, in the feeling of your human dignity and destiny —and modesty in view of the loftier One."

★

Few people engage in philosophical debate any longer—especially in a pure form devoid of any political or religious implications. In classical Greek philosophy, one's integrity was situated within the ability to reason through classical problems, and all the more by an ability to express both the pros and cons of a position, or an ability to argue from both sides. These practices are all but lost on us today, but they hold out the offer, nevertheless, of respect. There is, as Socrates knew, a quiet dignity in the ability to reason well.

As a figurehead, Socrates plays into many parables. Here is one from Krummacher that bears the weight of humility and patience. Integrity is not what we manufacture, but the essence of who we are. It is vital to stay humble.

Just Passing Through (*Traditional Jewish*)

In the last century there was a famed Polish rabbi named Hofetz Chaim. A tourist once visited the rabbi's house. As the tourist sat in the rabbi's living room, he noted that the man lived a simple life—for the room contained only a table, chair, and desk, along with a clutter of books.

"Rabbi," the tourist asked, "where is all your furniture?"

"Where is yours?" asked the rabbi.

"What? My furniture? I'm only a guest in this house. I'm just passing through."

"And so am I," answered the rabbi.

★

There are many voices and messages that seek to entice us away from our true selves. We are constantly bombarded with images of bigger and better things, newer and finer objects, the latest gizmos and gadgets that we must purchase. Likewise, there are moments when we are tempted to believe that we are nothing unless we look a certain way, dress in a certain style, or keep up with the latest developments.

Integrity, however, is the voice that moors us from within—the resolve that keeps us sane and focused on what truly matters. Integrity is the virtue that keeps us from being taken in and tossed about by every whim that comes along. Integrity is the foundation of our lives that allows others to know that they can trust us, and that our word and bond are secure, because we know our own motivations and desires.

One aspect of integrity is simplicity. The ability to live within our means.

Watering a Tree (Desert Fathers)

It is said that Little John travelled to see an aged Theban who lived in the desert. Before taking his leave, Little John found a piece of dry wood, planted it in the ground, and told the old man to water the stick every day until it bore fruit. This proved difficult, however, as the water source was very far from where the old man lived. Nevertheless, he followed Little John's instructions and watered the stick every day. Three years later the tree sprouted and bore fruit. The old man took some of this fruit, brought it to church with him and said, "Brothers, come see the fruit of my obedience."

★

Integrity is not simply an interior characteristic, but is very much an outward expression of our hopes and dreams. We tend to work toward what we desire the most—and everything from our pocketbooks to our bank accounts to how we spend our free time reveals what is most important to us. Indeed, no one would dare say that walking for charity was an important element in one's life unless one was actually walking for charity. We are what we practice. We do what we love. And these interior motives are revealed through our actions—which is integrity.

Persistence and consistency of practice is also vital. In fact, the fruit of obedience is the fruit itself.

The Tadpole (Stevenson)

"Be ashamed of yourself," said the Frog. "When I was a tadpole, I had no tail."

"Just what I thought," said the tadpole, "you never were a tadpole."

★

There is much to remember from our beginnings, including how far we have come. Our history is, in fact, a most important ingredient in our future. It is not wise to allow another to suggest that we should forfeit our history in order to embrace our future—or to deny what we have learned from the past in order to create a future for ourselves.

In this brief parable from Stevenson we have a wise insight about integrity: namely, the importance of knowing who we and being proud of our heritage. If we know where we have come from, we are much more likely to get to where we are going.

Chapter Ten

Leaning Toward Laughter

A wise man always chooses the path of joy.
The fool chooses the path of pleasure.
> —Katha Upanishad (Hindu Sacred Text)

There is nothing better for people under the sun than to eat,
and drink, and enjoy themselves for this will go with them
in their toil through the days of life that God gives them.
> —Ecclesiastes 8:15 (Hebrew Bible)

Some of the best teaching stories are also humorous. Many of the parables of Jesus—though lost on us in our modern idiom and seriousness—were no doubt humorous to the original audience. When Jesus asked, "And which of you, if your child asked for a fish, would give him a scorpion instead?" he no doubt said the words with a wry smile upon his lips. Some of the Buddha's teachings were also humorous, as are the words of the Tao. Sufism is rife with humor, and so is Judaism.

This is not to say that serious—even life-and-death matters—are not addressed by these works. Rather, quite the opposite is true. Humor often breeds introspection and can be a much more effective means of capturing an audience's attention and their hearts than a serious speech or debate. Comedians, of course, have always known this truth, and speakers like Mark Twain utilized humor and satire to perfect their points and observations about human foibles and weaknesses.

The ancient Greeks were also masters of humor—and much of their laughter has stood the test of time. We can still get a chuckle and an insight from humorists like Aristophanes. And Aesop, perhaps the most familiar of all Greek satirists and moralists, retains a high place in the pantheon of highly-effective teachers.

Consider, for example, this lesser known fable from the master Aesop:

Heracles was walking along a narrow road when he spied an object ahead of him that looked like an apple. Thinking he would squash it, Heracles stepped on it—but it doubled in size. He proceeded to jump on it, then beat it with his club—but the object then became so large that it blocked the road entirely. Heracles grew weary, threw down his club, and stood amazed before the insurmountable object. Suddenly, the goddess Athena appeared to him and said, "Leave that thing alone, my dear brother. You have inadvertently stumbled upon the spirit of an argument. If you don't touch it—it will do you no harm. But the more you try to fight it—the larger it becomes."

This is classic Aesop. And classic humor. But what one discovers through the laughter is a marvelous truth. One is not likely to forget it.

For many decades *Reader's Digest* has run a short column entitled "Laughter Is the Best Medicine." This page, filled with pithy jokes and personal insights about life, is often the first place that readers turn. Laughter, indeed, can become a panacea for many of life's difficulties, and there have been sages and mystics from all faiths and all walks of life who have ensconced themselves in laughter to make a point.

What one will discover in these marvelous stories is a lightness that might be just what the doctor ordered. Tough times can become more manageable. Heaviness can lift into joy. A scowl can turn into a smile. Humor can do this for us—and to us!

Although many of the stories here are old, or come from seemingly outdated or outmoded times, there is something about humor that can bridge that gap. Yes, much humor simply does not translate well through time or divergent cultures, but the best humor somehow retains a universal understanding. We can still hear echoes of laughter in these tales and teachings . . . and we can learn much about ourselves and about life from them.

A wonderful Zen parable goes like this:

A student once painted a portrait of his master and presented it to him. The master took one look at the portrait and responded, "If this is an accurate representation of me, you may kill me now. If it is not accurate, please burn it."

Can we miss the insights without a chuckle?

The truth is, laughter does change things. We dare not live a dour existence. We need to find a source of laughter, however we can find it. We need to be able to laugh at ourselves—our weaknesses, fears, failures, and faint attempts. Too much focus on the head leaves us with too little in the heart.

When the apostle Paul wrote "The foolishness of God is wiser than men" (1 Corinthians) he was being light-hearted, perhaps even telling a joke to point out the human capacity to make more of ourselves and our knowledge than is actual. Those first readers may have laughed at Paul's point, said "yes" to his humor.

We are blessed when we laugh. And many of the richest people on earth are those who have the capacity to find humor regardless of their circumstances. Love is humorous. So is marriage. So is faith. Even death can be a howler. And for those who have never experienced these episodes, well . . . read on.

But be prepared to laugh. Learn from it. Keep it going.

The laugh shall be first.

The Boy Man (Sioux)

In the beginning the One-Who-Was-Created-First was utterly alone. He had all of the earth and the forests and his disposal and pleasure and lived among the animals as his friends. All living things spoke one language.

One day, after he had returned to his teepee, he felt a pain in his left foot. He reached down and removed a splinter from his big toe and he tossed the splinter out of the teepee through the smoke hole at the top. Outside, he could hear the splinter roll down the side of the teepee and as soon as it hit the ground, there was the cry of a newborn infant.

The One-Who-Was-Created-First took the infant into this arms—the Boy Man—who was the father of the human race.

The Boy Man grew and enjoyed his life in the forest and the fields. He had all of the animals as his friends and every day they would play games. The One-Who-Was-Created-First taught the Boy Man how to use his superior mind to outwit the animals in their games, although sometimes the animals prevailed because of their superior strength or speed. This was a happy time, for there was peace between the Boy Man and the animals.

One morning, however, the Boy Man wandered away and The One-Who-Was-First-Created searched for him. When he could not find the Boy Man, he questioned all of the animals. But they could not help, and when he returned to his teepee, he wept for days.

At last The One-Who-Was-Created-First decided to go on a long journey. He followed all of the rivers, he walked the shores of the Great Lakes, and at last heard the singing of an old Beaver-Woman who informed him that the Boy Man had wondered into the water and had been swallowed up by the monsters of the deep.

The One-Who-Was-First-Created turned himself into a tall pine tree. When the monsters of the deep came along, they tried to pull the pine tree up by the roots, but they did not prevail. At last, worn out from the struggle, the monsters fell asleep on the waves. The One-Who-Was-First-Created assumed his own shape and killed the monsters with his spear.

★

Every culture and people has their own creation myths. But no matter the origin, there are central ideas that make up the primordial soup. Mystery of beginning, power from beyond, and development of life are common features in these stories. And, as with the Bible and the more ancient Sumerian and Babylonian myths, there are also sea monsters and giants that contend for the right to exist.

In the end, there is always a celebration of human triumph— brains beating out brawn, ingenuity triumphing over sheer force of size.

What remains is life. And history always disappears into the fog of mystery. Beyond the mystery is where faith lies—and our common relation as children of the earth.

The Honey Wasp (Jonathan Swift)

A man noticed a wasp creeping into a jar of honey that had been hung on an apple tree. The man said, "You fool, why would you go into a jar of honey, knowing full well that it is a sweetened trap, as you have seen hundreds of your own kind perish in this way?"

The wasp responded, "You speak the truth, but not out of your own experience, as you human beings never learn from the destructive habits of others but, rather, continue to perpetuate the same mistakes. But believe me, if I fell into this jar and did manage to escape, I would not return to the same predicament. In this way I am far superior to you people, as you return time and again to your own follies."

★

This quaint parable from Jonathan Swift dishes some sweet truth. One can often find the deepest and most profound humor by simply examining the foolishness of human behavior.

The Guru Nanak (Traditional Sikh story)

There was a great prophet in India, Guru Nanak, born four hundred years ago. Some of you have heard of the Sikhs, the fighting people. He was a follower of the Sikh religion.

One day he went to the Mohammedans' Mosque. These Mohammedans are feared in their own country, just as in a Christian country no one dare say anything against their religion. They think they have liberty to kill and criticize everybody who does not agree with them. So this man went in, and there was a big Mosque, and the Mohammedans were standing in prayer. They stand in lines; they kneel down, stand up, and repeat certain words at the same times, and one fellow leads. So Guru Nana went there, and when the mullah was saying "In the name of the most merciful and kind God, Teacher of all teachers", he began to smile. He says "Look at that hypocrite". The mullah got into a passion.

"Why do you smile?"

"Because you are not praying, my friend, that is why I am smiling".

"Not praying?"

"Certainly not; there is no prayer in you".

The mullah was very angry, and he went and laid a complaint before a magistrate, and said, "This heathen rascal dares to come to our mosque and smiles at us when we are praying; the only punishment is instant death, kill him".

The man was brought before. the magistrate, and asked why he smiled.

"Because he was not praying".

"What was he doing?" the magistrate asked.

"I will tell you what he was doing, if you will bring him before me".

The magistrate ordered the mullah to be brought, and when he came he said "Here is the mullah, explain why you laughed when he was praying".

He said, "Give the mullah a piece of the Koran [to swear on]. When he was saying Allah, Allah, he was thinking of some chicken he had left at home".

The poor mullah was confounded. He was a little more sincere than the others, and he confessed he was thinking of the chicken, and so they let the Sikh go.

★

Although nearly every faith claims to be the exclusive way to God, all universally agree that prayer is joining our hearts and wills to God. Jesus taught as much, as did Buddha, and regardless of one's form of prayer, it is helpful to be reminded that we need to pause and occasionally laugh at the inexactitude of our religious pursuits.

Introspection is always more difficult than inspection. Being mindful of one's own faults is never easy. That is why some of us never get around to examining our own motives and hearts. We are too chicken.

The Donkey (Sufi)

A neighbor gave a bit of advice to Nasrudin. "If you want your donkey to move faster, rub some ammonia on his buttocks."

Nasrudin tried this procedure on his stubborn donkey and found that it worked.

One day, when Nasrudin himself was feeling a bit listless and low on energy, he rubbed some ammonia on his own buttocks. He was immediately burning and began running around the room in a state of frenzy.

His wife shouted at him, "What's wrong?"

Nasrudin shouted back, "If you want to understand me, use the contents of that bottle over there!"

★

Nasrudin, the Sufi trickster and comic, is full of wisdom. Sufism—the mystical and artistic expression of Islam—offers many traditional stories that both delight and enlighten. Here, the parable illustrates the nature of "understanding." Or, as one Native American expression so aptly puts it: "If you want to understand another person, walk a mile in his moccasins."

This is a parable about empathy—the ability to feel with another, to come alongside and experience hurt, anguish, joy, or even celebration. Not all people embrace empathy, or even know how to understand another person. And so the ability has to be learned, or is a spiritual discipline.

Laugher is one of the highest expressions of empathy. It has been said that we never really know another person until we can laugh with him or her. We may be able to feel loss or anguish, but the comfort of laughter is a far more intimate empathy, as it makes us vulnerable. Friendship is born of laughter. Likewise, those who desire to form true community don't find it until they learn how to laugh in the presence of others . . . and relax. Vulnerability is honesty, is integrity. And laughter often leads the way.

The Boar and the Lion (Buddhist)

A boar was drinking at the waterhole one day. Not far from the waterhole, a lion had killed both a giraffe and an antelope and, because it was thirsty, approached to drink. When the lion saw the boar at the waterhole it thought to itself: I am already full and so I won't kill the boar today. I will save this kill for another day."

Now the boar noticed the lion from afar and, because it did not attack, the boar thought to itself, "The lion must be afraid of me." The boar grew very conceited and full of itself and as it passed by the lion it heard the lion say, "You are safe for now, boar—but seven days from now you will be my meal."

But when the boar heard this it said to itself: "This only serves to confirm that the lion is afraid of me." When the boar returned to its kin it said, "I just met a lion and seven days from now we shall do battle and I shall prevail."

When the other boars heard this they said, "What are you thinking? You will ruin us all."

★

Whether a teaching about the folly of warfare, the pride of power, or the insanity of nations and ideologies of superiority, this parable makes a strong but humorous statement (perhaps satirical) about our human predicament. Whether we be a lion or a boar, it is best to know the nature of our situation before we make assumptions.

More to the point, another Buddhist parable relates a similar tale:

A lowly dung beetle, while crawling upon the ground in search of dung, stumbled across a puddle of wine that someone had poured out on the ground. Walking through the puddle and drinking of it, the dung beetle became drunk and, upon finding his first pile of dung began to eat. Moments later an elephant approached, and smelling the dung, retreated. The dung beetle, seeing the elephant flee, thought to itself: "I shall do battle with this fellow and prevail."

Soon after the elephant returned for its business and, in one fell swoop, buried the dung beetle beneath a great pile and killed it outright.

The Playful Servant (based on a Grimm's tale)

A master with many servants wanted to send one of his brightest and best to search for a lost cow. When the servant did not return in a timely manner the master thought, "I know my servant and surely he is looking for the lost cow. He would not disobey my orders."

But after some more hours passed the master went into the fields to look for his servant. He was surprised when he found the servant running around, chasing after the wind. The master asked, "Have you found my lost cow?"

The servant answered, "No! But I have found something better!"

"And what is that?" asked the master.

"I have found three blackbirds."

"But where are they?" asked the master.

"I see one. I hear one. And I am chasing the third," cried the servant as he ran off.

★

An old tale that may have many meanings—including an insight about being one's own person and note taking orders too seriously. This story could also be about creativity and looking outside of the box. Or it could just be about chasing after butterflies in the head.

In most instances, we dare not chase too long. And some opinions are best kept to ourselves. We don't, after all, want to be the one who ends up in the butterfly net.

Little John (Desert Fathers)

There is a story about Little John who, one day, said to his brother: "I don't want to work any longer, but desire to be totally free so that I can worship God without interruption." He removed his monk's robes immediately and departed into the desert.

He was gone only a week when he returned to his brother's home and knocked on the door. "Who is there?" the brother asked from inside.

"It is Little John," he replied.

But the brother inside said, "You cannot be Little John, for he has become like the angels and no longer lives among us."

Little John said, "But it is me! Please open the door."

The brother inside refused and thus made Little John sleep outside until morning. When the sun rose the brother opened the door again and said, "If you are human being than you must work in order to live."

Little John repented and said, "Yes, I was wrong. Please forgive me, my brother."

★

There are many decisions that we regret in life (and should). This is the nature of repentance—which is a word that means "to turn around and move in the other direction." But repentance is only possible when there is acceptance—by God, by ourselves, and by a community that cares. In Buddhism we also find many stories of turning and returning, a joy born of hope and relationship.

This humorous story points out the foibles of our decisions (especially those that are, in essence, self-centered or littered with spiritual arrogance). It is sometimes helpful to be able to laugh at ourselves and the folly of our ways. This laughter can be transformative, especially, when we return to love.

The Wolf and the Tortoise (Bierce)

A wolf meeting a tortoise said, "My friend, you are the slowest thing out of doors. I do not see how you manage to escape your enemies."

"As I lack the power to run away," replied the Tortoise, "Providence has thoughtfully supplied me with an impenetrable shell."

The Wolf reflected for a long time, then he said: "It seems to be that it would have been just as easy to give you long legs."

★

Often, we prefer one solution over another—but we must be content with what we have been given. If one cannot use the best, then use the second best. Also, it makes no sense to lament what we do not have. Rather, it is best to concentrate on what we already have in our pockets.

Two Tales of Woe (Pilpay)

Once there was a man who had neither wife nor children. He planted a garden and because he had no other interests, tended it until it became a paradise. He would spend day and night in the garden, grooming it to luxurious beauty and splendor and it became a garden of delicious fruits.

One day, however, the man became rather lonely, having no person with which to share the garden. He set out on a journey into the mountains and as he was ascending, happened to meet a bear that was coming down out of the mountains to seek companionship. Their eyes me, and that day the man and the bear became great friends.

The man brought the bear back to his garden, introduced the animal to the luscious fruits, and the bear would spend hours enjoying these delicious repasts. Likewise, the man slept close the bear at night and found its fur to be a warmth against the cold nights.

One day, while the man was sleeping in the heat of the afternoon, a fly began buzzing around the man's head. It landed on his lips and the bear tried various ways to shoo the fly away, but the insect would always return to the man's lips. Eventually, exasperated, the bear picked up a large rock and heaved it at the fly, killing it . . . but in the process also knocking out the man's teeth.

Once there was a very rich merchant who was extremely ugly. He had married, however, a very beautiful woman who loved him only for his money. The man loved his wife passionately, but the wife merely endured her husband for the sake of the riches. The man, in fact, craved intimacy with his wife but never received it—as she would scarcely look at him, much less touch him.

One evening a thief broke into the home and stumbled into the bed chamber. The husband was asleep, but when his wife woke up and saw the thief standing at the foot of the bed, she was so terrified that she rolled over, embraced her husband, and held him tightly as she trembled. When the husband woke up and realized that he was being embraced by his wife he was thrilled. He said, "I am truly blessed! I don't know what precipitated these delights, but I would give thanks to anyone who would tell me!"

At the moment he uttered these words he also noticed the thief, realized why his wife was embracing him, and said aloud to intruder: "You don't realize how much you have done for me! Take whatever you wish!"

★

These two humorous tales from the legendary material by Pilpay remind us of two truths. The first, that it is better to have a natural enemy than a stupid friend. And the second, that sometimes blessings arrive from unlikely sources.

Likewise, life's humorous episodes are not always discovered in manufactured frivolities, but frequently arrive when we are least expecting it. Sometimes the greatest laughter is of the spontaneous variety. And laughter, as they say, is often the best medicine.

The Miser and His Crow (Jonathan Swift)

A miser owned a crow which he had domesticated. The crow would steal gold coins and stick them into a hole in the floor. When the house cat noted this, it said to the crow, "Why would you hoard so much money when you can't make any use of it?"

At which point the crow responded, "I am only mimicking my master. He has closets filled with them and makes no more use of them than I."

★

Swift's point cuts deep: people don't like to admit their own follies. And we especially do not like to admit the uselessness of greed.

The Philosopher at the Gate (Sufi)

Once a philosopher made an appointment to debate with Nasrudin, but when he arrived at the house, he discovered that Nasrudin was not at home. Infuriated by this lack of manners, the philosopher wrote, "Stupid Idiot" on the front gate.

As soon as Nasrudin returned home and saw this message on his gate, he rushed to the philosopher's house and said, "I had forgotten our appointment. I am sorry that I was not at home. But I remembered the appointment as soon as I saw the words 'Stupid Idiot' on the gate and realized that you had left your name."

★

This Sufi parable, again featuring Mulla Nasrudin—practical joker, philosopher, and Sufi persona—offers some of the most humorous touches found in Islamic teaching. As Mulla usually teaches, not all things in life are as they appear, and frequently the tables can be turned to dig at a deeper lesson in human nature. In the former parable, we see how it is imperative to walk in a person's shoes before we pass judgment or assume we understand what they are experiencing. This is one of the most difficult lessons in life, as our first inclination is always to reach a judgment about another's situation or life experience. Unless we've been there, we may not know all that's involved. We may not have all the facts.

And here, in this latter parable, Mulla teaches that harsh words and epithets may not always have the desired results. Sometimes name-calling merely serves to reveal those very character traits within ourselves. Sometimes the fool is the one residing inside our own skins.

The Voice in the Temple (Zen)

A humorous Zen parable tells the story of an old woman who visited a certain temple every night. She always prayed: "The Lord Buddha can take me whenever he likes—I am ready to go; I have lived a full life."

One evening two boys were hiding behind the statue of Buddha, and when the old woman prayed this prayer they yelled, "Tonight is the night!"

The old woman dropped dead when she heard the voice.

★

Every faith and culture has its humor, and Buddhism is no exception. Zen, in particular, is a wonderful repository of laughter. Here, we see that not all prayers are meant to be answered and, as the old adage often stands, we should be careful what we pray for.

The Bear Man (Native American)

Once a man left his camp to go hunting. He journeyed deep into the mountains looking for bears, and when he encountered one, he shot it with an arrow. But he did not kill it. In fact, he had shot a medicine bear—a bear which could heal itself and which could read the mind of human beings. The bear pulled the arrow out of its hide and the man thought, "I am going to die." But the bear, reading the man's thoughts, told him, "No, I am not going to kill you. Come with me and you will live."

The man, supposing that it was a trap, followed the bear back to a cave where the bear council was gathering. Inside the cave there were bears of every description: black bears large and small, brown bears, and a great white bear who was the council leader. The white bear said, "What stinks?"

The medicine bear said, "It is only this hunter. I have brought him here to live among us. Let us welcome him."

The bears were reluctant, but they did welcome him and soon afterwards the medicine bear took the hunter back to its own cave. The hunter thought that he was going to starve to death, but the medicine bear raked its claws through its hide and produced chestnuts.

He gave these to the hunter. The bear also produced acorns and black-berries in the same manner and provided for the man while he lived in the cave.

Now the hunter lived with the bear a long time. He did not shave his beard or his head, and in time he began to look like a bear himself. In fact, he began to act like a bear, too, and he took on the bear nature.

Years later the medicine bear had a dream and told the man, "Soon there will be other warriors who will come looking for you. They will kill me, but after they have cut me to pieces and taken away my fur, you must promise to bury what is left of me and cover me with leaves. If you do this, I will reveal a secret to you."

The man agreed, and the next day a small group of warriors appeared at the cave entrance. At first they did not recognize the man—they believed that he was a bear, too—for he looked like a bear and had taken on the bear nature. But after they realized he was man, they shot the medicine bear, cut it into pieces, and divided the fur among them. But before he returned to the camp, the man kept his promise and buried what was left of the bear, covering it with leaves.

As the man was leaving with the other warriors, he looked back and noticed that the medicine bear was rising from the leaves and returning to its cave.

Now, when the man returned to his camp the people did not rec-ognize him. He looked like a bear and acted like a bear. The man said to them, "You must place me in a lodge by myself and give me no food or drink for seven days until the bear nature leaves me." And so they did it.

But the man's wife could not stay away. She brought him food and fed him like an animal. And so he died. But had they left him alone, he would have been able to throw off the bear nature and return to a man.

★

Many Native American stories deal with the tensions between human and animal—experiences that were no doubt part of daily existence.

But these stories also provide some wonderful psychological and social fodder—especially when dealing with the question of what it means to be fully human. Different cultures and times have answered this question in various ways, and in our modern era many of these insights about human and animalistic nature are derived from examining environments such as prisons and the growing tendencies of living through technology rather than social interaction. Can we realize our full potential as human beings in isolation? Can we become more fully alive and cognizant through machines, or is social interaction and conversation essential?

Many Native American stories can add to this discussion—and as is often the case, sometimes the ancient ways provide the answers needed in modern times.

The Crow and the Pitcher (Aesop)

A crow, ready to die of thirst, flew into a house and attempted to drink from a deep pitcher of water. But the water inside the pitcher was so low that the crow could not reach it. The crow first tried to break the pitcher. But when this was unsuccessful, the crow tried to overturn it. When this proved fruitless, the crow noticed some small rocks nearby. Placing the rocks inside the pitcher, one at a time, the crow was eventually able to raise the level of the water and quench its thirst.

★

The old adage: There is more than one way to skin a cat. This may be true, but there are also proven methods—and wise choices—that can produce results much faster than some others. As this Aesop story reveals, it is also the case that small choices made over time can have a lasting and more profound effect upon a later outcome. Often, it is not the last-minute decision, nor even the most obvious one, that produces the desired outcome. Rather, slow and steady wins the race, and consistency is one of the most important ingredients to success. One day at a time lived under a disciplined approach and practice will always produce a great reward.

On the other hand, it is often the case that many believe that great results can be enjoyed without any commitment or practice. To be a great pianist, one must practice daily—and the same would hold true for any sport or any art. Adding the daily ingredient of practice will eventually produce an expert in any field. Those who lack this discipline, or who refuse to endure the tedium of the daily step, will most always fail to achieve the result.

If one desires the greatest reward, one must also endure the pain and sacrifice of the daily grind. Practice makes perfect. And the greatest blessings in life are born from long-term commitments.

The Crabs (Aesop)

A baby crab was walking along the shoreline with its mother. The mother crab exclaimed, "Why are you walking so crooked? Try harder and walk straight." To which the baby crab said, "If you show me how to walk straight, mother, I'm sure I will learn how."

★

It is far more difficult to be an example than a critic. And, as Jesus once explained, "Only after we first remove the beam from our own eye can we then see to take a splinter from another's." It is often the case that the weaknesses we see in others are the same weaknesses we also possess. It is a rare gift when one can invoke an honest judgment of another while also building up the individual. The purpose of criticism is not to destroy, but to inspire and improve.

The Mule (Aesop)

A mule that had grown quite fat from eating too much corn was one day galloping around the pasture like a stallion. "Look at me," the mule said, "I'm as fast as any that ever raced!" All at once, however, the mule became winded and then realized that she was nothing but an Ass.

★

Putting on airs can be humiliating—especially if we don't have the capacity to laugh at ourselves when we fail. Aesop was a master at pointing out these human foibles, and he wrote centuries ago. Perhaps not much has changed in the human condition—especially when it comes to pride and arrogance.

Jesus and the Fool (Rumi/Sufi)

Jesus was seen one day running for the hills. It was as if he were being chased by a lion. A friend, who encountered him on the way, asked, "What are you running from? You are running as if you are being chased by a hungry beast."

Jesus didn't slow at all, but ran all the faster. The friend followed behind Jesus, losing breath with every step as the climbed higher and higher into the hills. At last the friend cried out, "For God's sake, slow down! There's nothing behind you. There is no reason to be afraid. What in the world are you running from?"

"Don't try to stop me," Jesus said, "I'm running away from a fool."

"But aren't you the Messiah?" the friend asked. "Aren't you the Christ who healed the blind and the lame?"

"Indeed I am," Jesus answered.

"And aren't you the sovereign one—the one who understands the mysteries of God?"

"This also is true," Jesus replied.

"And aren't you the same one who prayed over a corpse and watched it spring to life again?"

"I am."

"And aren't you the same Jesus who fashioned birds out of clay, and clapped your hands, and watched them fly away?"

"This I have done also," Jesus said.

"But then, O Pure Spirit, if all of these things are true, why do you fear? Who would refuse to be your disciple when presented with such irrefutable proofs?"

Jesus grew somber and answered, "By God I tell you, I have prayed to the One who created body and soul before creation, who is hidden by impenetrable light, the very heavens swirling about Him and rapturous praise. I have uttered His name over the mountains and whispered the Name in the cleft of the rock, and I have even raised the dead in His name. But I tell you when I recite the Name and pray to God a thousand times over, I have never been able to penetrate the heart of a fool!"

★

In Sufi tradition, Jesus occupies the high honor of being the prophet of love, the Messiah, the Christ, and the giver of life. Jesus also captures the essence of holy humor, and in this wonderful story we see that even Jesus himself is afraid of a fool.

As with other traditions, especially wisdom lore, fools are a wild card. Better to steer clear of the fool than attempt to reason with one.

The Dog's Curly Tail (Traditional Sikh)

Once there was a poor man who had heard a rumor that, if one captured a ghost, the spirit would be forced to give him money. Naturally, since he was destitute and needed cash, this man began his search for a ghost. But he had no idea how to about capturing a spirit.

In time he found a sage who had great powers and the man told the sage his plan. "What would you do with this ghost once you captured him?" the sage asked.

"I would force the spirit to work for me," the poor man replied. "But I need you to tell me how to obtain one. This is my deepest desire in life."

"Forget this foolishness," the sage told him. "Go home."

But the man returned the following day, weeping and wailing at the feet of the sage, saying, "Please give me a ghost. I must have one!"

Weary from the man's pleading, the sage relented at last and said, "Here, take this charm, repeat the magic words and the ghost will appear to you and do whatever you ask. But beware—ghosts are horrible things. If you don't keep a ghost busy with other chores he will surely take your life when you are not expecting it."

The man replied, "I can keep this ghost busy day in and day out. I am not afraid."

And so the poor man took the charm and journeyed into the woods where he incanted the magic words and *poof*—suddenly a ghost appeared before him and said, "I am your servant. I will do whatever you ask me to do. But the moment you stop giving me chores, I'm going to kill you."

The poor man was not frightened when he heard this, but blurted out, "Give me lots of money."

The ghost immediately placed piles of money at the man's feet.

Undeterred, the poor man then said, "Okay, cut down every tree in this forest and build me a beautiful city right here."

The ghost went to work and in short order the forest was felled and a gorgeous palace stood in its place. The ghost then asked, "Is there anything else?"

At this word the poor man became frightened. Suddenly he realized that he had most everything he wanted and he had obtained it all so quickly. What more could the ghost do for him?

The ghost became agitated at the man's hesitancy and said, "Give me something to do, quickly, or I'll kill you on the spot."

Upon hearing this, the poor man ran back to the sage and cried out, "You were right, this ghost wants to kill me! Please protect me from it."

"Whatever is the matter?" asked the sage.

"I have my ghost," the poor man answered, "and he has done all of the work I asked him to do. But he does it all so quickly that I cannot think of other work for him to accomplish and now he is trying to kill me."

Just then the ghost appeared and said again, "I'm going to kill you on the spot."

"I will think of something," the sage said. Spying a dog with a curly tail, the sage told the poor man, "Quick, cut off that dog's tail and give it to the ghost. Ask him to straighten it out."

Following the sage's instruction, the poor man cut off the curly tail and handed it to the ghost. "Straighten this dog's tail," he commanded.

The ghost took the tail and sneered. He slowly bent the tail until it was straight, but as soon as he released it, the tail went crooked again. The man went home with his ghost, which was occupied with the dog's tail for days.

After some weeks, the exasperated ghost appeared to the poor man and said, "I've never had so much difficulty in my life. But I'm an old ghost and just want to rest. Perhaps we can reach a compromise. If you pledge to release me from your bond I will allow you to keep all that I have given you thus far. I will not kill you and you will allow me to return to the earth."

When the poor man heard this he was elated and accepted the offer.

★

This bit of Sikh humor holds many startling truths. Among them: greed is a fascination that often leads us to take drastic measures, but in the end can destroy us. And even when people obtain things, they quickly learn that these things do not satisfy and they must then have more.

The cycle of addiction continues, but in the meantime life erodes and fears worsen.

On another level the parable offers some wider observations about the human condition and about life itself. The world, in fact, is like the curly tail of the dog. As the parable demonstrates, people have been trying to straighten out the world for thousands of years—but to no avail.

Finally, on the spiritual level, this parable is about fanaticism. Those who spend all of their work and effort on trying to straighten the world can easily become fanatics, thinking that they can do it, that they alone have the answers that the world needs. Fanaticism is no answer—it is not what the world needs. Rather, fanaticism merely breeds hatred and contempt, a desire to kill and destroy.

Letting go of one's anger and frustration is a first step toward understanding and compromise. The world eludes change. We are not able to fix everything. It is best to accept what one holds in one's hands, find contentment in life, and be at peace with the world and with others. Nothing good comes from greed—and contentment comes when we realize that life is precious.

Who Am I? (*Sufi*)

Mullah Nasrudin grew up in a small village, so when he went to Baghdad and found himself amid the huge crowds, he was confused. "I wonder," he said to himself, "how people in a town this size remember who they are and where they are going? I must be careful, or I could easily lose myself."

With that thought, Mullah decided to take a break after his journey and get some sleep. As he lay down on the ground, however, he wondered, "How will I find myself again when I wake up?" Mullah asked another gentleman for help, not knowing that his fellow was a prankster.

"Here's what you do," the fellow said. "Take this ribbon and tie it around your leg. When you wake up and see the ribbon, you will know that you are *you*!"

Nasrudin thanked the man and went to sleep. While Mullah was dreaming, however, the prankster removed the ribbon from Mullah's leg and tied it around his own.

A few hours later, when Mullah woke up, he immediately looked for the ribbon. Suddenly he spied it. "That must be me!" he concluded.

Thrown into a panic, Mullah beat on the man, crying, "Wake up! Wake up! There is something terribly wrong!"

The prankster opened his eyes and said, "What ever is the matter my friend?"

Mullah pointed to the ribbon. "Look, there's the ribbon. You must be me! But if you are me . . . then who in the world am I?"

★

We've all had the experience of trying to find ourselves—figuratively, at least. Perhaps we are still trying to discover what we want to do with our lives, or what we want to be, or what is most important to us. No, it is not only the thirty-five-year-old college student or the forty-year-old snowboarder who are searching for meaning today.

Over the years I've met plenty of men and women who have awakened at mid-life to ask the question: Who am I? I've known an eighty-year-old college freshman (still looking for a good time) and a fourteen-year-old astrophysicist (who has always had his head in the stars). I've known many people who have given up on themselves and their dreams, and others who embrace each new day with the question: What can I do next?

Perhaps the old practice of tying reminder ribbons around our fingers is not so bad after all. It's so easy to forget what life is all about.

Jesus and the Dead Lion (Rumi/Sufi)

A fool approached Jesus and asked him about a pile of bones that he had seen on the roadside. The fool said to Jesus, "Teach me how to utter the Divine Name so that I may bring those bones back to life. I would like to work some good dead."

Jesus answered, "You should hold your tongue. In fact, you should not be concerned about such things. In order to raise the dead you must have a pure breath, a pure heart, and it is not in the prayer that this power comes. If you were to hold Moses's staff in your hands, would that mean that you have the arm of Moses?"

The fool answered, "Well, then, if I can't do it, why don't you go over there and make those bones come to life?"

Jesus prayed for the fool, wondering how it was that a man could be so concerned for a pile of dead bones and yet so oblivious to, and unconcerned for, his own sick and lifeless soul. "Be aware," Jesus said, "that if you sow thistles in this world, you will not be seen walking in the rose garden in the world to come."

But the fool persisted, wanting to engage Jesus in an argument. The fool, in fact, was so aggravating to Jesus that eventually the Messiah grew weary of the fool's annoying conversation and relented. "Very well then," Jesus said in his exasperation. "I shall revive the dead."

The fool was standing next to Jesus when the Messiah prayed. Instantly the bones became a fierce lion. As soon as the lion saw Jesus and the fool, the lion swiped at the fool with his razor claws and killed him instantly.

Jesus asked the lion, "Why did you kill that man?"

The lion answered, "I could see that he was annoying you."

Jesus then asked, "But why didn't you devour your prey?"

The lion answered, "This was not my portion. For even I pray that I may be given my daily bread."

★

Another Sufi masterpiece, this one from the poet and sage, Rumi, demonstrates the nature of foolishness. First, that fools are more concerned about situations and circumstances that do not matter rather than their own conduct and integrity. And secondly, fools are unable to envision the outcome of their actions.

In this humorous tale, Jesus plays the straight man to the fool's foil, but the lesson is deadly serious. It is also the habit of fools to argue their point incessantly, and the fool is one who must always be in the right (or, it is equally important to the fool that others be proven wrong). Wisdom is silent and humble. Foolishness is gregarious and proud.

Only the meek shall inherit the earth.

The Musicians (Kriloff)

A certain man had a group of friends who loved to sing, though none of them could sing well. One evening the man invited a guest to his house to listen to his choir. This guest accepted the invitation but soon felt trapped in the house, as none of the people in the choir could sing. In fact, their voices were so discordant that the guest's teeth were set on edge and he began to develop a headache.

At last, unable to withstand the wailing any longer, the guest told his host, "Please! Enough! I don't see how anyone can stand this. None of these people in the choir can sing."

The host then answered, "Oh, I know that's true. They would give anyone a headache. But I'll have you know that all of these choir member are above reproach, none of have ever been arrested, and none of them ever drink a drop on an intoxicating beverage."

★

This humorous parable from Kriloff possesses many insights, among them: We rarely like to have our faults exposed and when they are we usually like to point out our merits. There is something in the human spirit that needs to be recognized. The parable may also delight in showing how we have a tendency to perpetuate bad habits, often to the demise of our better attributes. Looking for the best in ourselves and in others takes practice, even focus. If we look deeply enough we can find the good in others.

The Kitchen Whisk (Kriloff)

Once, a kitchen whisk was dropped on the floor, but was later picked up by a lazy chef and placed back on the counter. When the other chefs began working on their master recipes they also used the whisk to mix their bowls of flour, sauces and icings. But the more they mixed with the whisk the dirtier and more disgusting their recipes became. No matter how much they tried to add ingredients over the top of the dirt, their recipes were ruined and they eventually had to throw away all of the food.

★

This Kriloff parable points out the folly of attempting to incorporate bad practices or bad ideas into an otherwise good mix. Long-standing spiritual practices, for example, have often been honed through centuries of trial and error, through the crucibles of human experience and failures. There are reasons why some practices have remained intact for thousands of years. As they have worked for one generation, so they work for future generations.

Jesus once said that a little leaven will eventually leaven the entire loaf. This is true of good practices as well as bad ones. But the point of the parable is that care must be taken to guard those treasures that have been passed along to us. Once compromise is introduced, it is often difficult to determine the source of the problem, but it is especially difficult to fix the problem by adding more elements to it.

The Frog and the Ox (Aesop)

An ox was grazing in the pasture one day and nearly trampled an entire brood of young frogs to death. Only one small frog escaped. The little frog hopped back to its mother and said, "Oh, mother, all of the others are dead because a giant creature trampled them to death."

The mother frog said, "But how big was this creature? Was it this big?" And the mother frog puffed herself up to a considerable size.

"Oh, but it was much bigger than that, mother," said the baby frog.

"Was it this big?" asked the mother frog, puffing herself to an even greater size.

"Mother," the baby frog said, "It was so large, no matter how big you can get, it would still be a hundred times larger."

At this point the mother frog tried to puff herself up so much, she actually exploded.

★

Some experiences in life cannot be explained. In fact, to speak of them may actually harm the gravity and scope of the experience itself. This is often the case with tragedy.

Because we live in a culture that has an insatiable need to dissect tragedy and find an explanation for it, we are especially susceptible to the foolishness of pride. It is always best to provide comfort and assistance through disaster rather than interrogation and explanation.

Burning Down the House (Tolstoy)

Once there was a man who lived in a big house. Inside the house was a big oven. The man used the oven to heat his house and to cook, and since it was just he and his wife who lived there, they had plenty of room.

One winter the man burned up all of his firewood in the oven trying to heat his house. He had no other fuel, and so he decided to tear out the rafters in his home to heat his house. His neighbors noticed what he was doing and tried to dissuade him. "Look at the futility of your efforts," they pointed out. "You are tearing off the roof of your house to stoke your oven, but in the meantime you are letting in cold air."

But the man pointed out that he owned the largest house and the largest oven in town. "I know what I'm doing," he said.

The neighbors pointed out that the man would eventually have to tear off his roof and even tear down the walls of his house in order to stoke the oven. "You might as well build a smaller house and get a smaller oven," they told him. "You would save yourself a great deal of trouble."

But the man would not relent. He said to his neighbors. "I know what you are trying to get me to do. You are jealous because I own the largest house and the largest oven. You are asking me to go smaller." Eventually the man consumed the roof of his house, tore down the walls, and even pulled up the foundation in order to feed the oven. In the end, he was forced to live off of the charity of others.

★

This Tolstoy parable is classic irony. It is also deeply observant of the human conditions of pride, avarice, greed, and envy. As the old adage says, "As we get older, we don't stop playing with toys. We just buy bigger ones."

Here Tolstoy makes a brilliant commentary on the human desire for bigger and better things—but often with disastrous results, and not at all the results we intended. More often than not, our unbridled consumptions simply lead to disaster and despair, if not a final poverty. In an age where most people live beyond their means and consume far more than they create, it's no wonder that the ovens supersede the life we are trying to create.

One cannot build on what one is constantly consuming.

The Argument (Tolstoy)

Two peasants happened to meet each other in the road as they were travelling in opposite directions. One peasant said, "Move over so I may pass. I'm in a hurry." The other peasant said, "No! You move over so I may pass. I'm in a bigger hurry." This argument went on for quite some time, with neither peasant budging.

Eventually a third peasant came upon the argument and said, "If each of you is in such a big hurry, then why don't you each budge a little?"

★

This is a classic Tolstoy parable about the nature of disagreement. What makes it all the more humorous is that Tolstoy has introduced the element of haste into an otherwise innocuous impasse. Neither man, apparently, was actually in a hurry. The force of the meeting was actually the need to argue.

We've all been there. Most arguments, at their core, rarely achieve their intended purpose: is to persuade the other person to relent or to come around to our way of thinking. Few arguments, of course, produce this result. But there are people who enjoy arguments for argument's sake. And moreover, most people who enjoy an argument don't really want to relent or learn anything from the other person, but argue solely for the sake of being right. Being right, or having the upper hand, *is the purpose*.

Those long Russian winters were good for something . . . and in this case, making an observation about human nature.

The Hungry Dogs (Phaedrus)

Some dogs spied a carcass in the river's flow
And said to themselves, "Let's bring it ashore."
But first they devised a scheme to drink
The water from the river so it would sink.
And so they drank until they died,
Their greed the cause of their demise.

★

Another masterful fable from Phaedrus, this time exploring the very nature of greed, which at its heart is trying to consume too much of a good thing. Greed can get the best of anyone, and in our time greed is most commonly expressed in the excesses of good gifts such as money, or sex, or entertainment, or wine. As Buddha would have it: it is best to find the Middle Way—neither too far to the left or the right. Or, as others have expressed it, "All good things in moderation."

Laughter certainly has the capacity to back us off of many excesses, and to cause us to appreciate the smaller blessings of life instead of constantly striving after the large and stressful ones. We may not laugh all the way to the bank, but we can laugh with good friends and even find humor in our own foibles and idiosyncrasies. Being able to laugh at oneself keeps a person in the center of humility. Most matters are not of the life or death variety, and many problems in life are made tolerable through humor.

The Fly (John Aikin)

A fly was complaining about her life. She said to the swallow: "I can't live out in the open, exposed to your whims, for no sooner would I fly about the yard than you would swoop down and consume me."

And with that word she flew into a nearby stable and immediately announced, "This is where I need to be. Here I have shelter, security, and a great future." But as soon as she examined more closely she discovered that the stable was filled with cobwebs and spiders. Realizing this situation was neither perfect, she flew into a house and quickly announced, "This is where I need to be. Life is dandy now." But again, as she examined more closely she realized that there were fly traps hanging in the windows. "I'll have none of this, either," she announced.

And with that word she eventually flew into a courtroom where she announced, "This is where I need to be. Great situation, and because of the many candles in this room, I will have light both day and night."

She had no sooner said those words than, disregarding the heat from the flame, she flew too close to one candle and was consumed.

★

Aiken's fables have a universal appeal and speak most eloquently to the verisimilitudes of life. The search for happiness is common among all people, and so is the penchant for complaining about one's situation. In fact, there are no perfect situations in life and no matter where or how we look for this happiness, it will always elude us. Unless, of course, we search for the key within.

The Thorn Bush (Lessing)

The willow tree was speaking to the thorn bush one day and asked this question: "Why is it that you are so anxious to seize people's clothing? You can't use the clothing, so why do you want it?"

"Oh, I don't want the clothing," said the thorn bush. "I only want to tear it."

★

How often we have met those who enjoy tearing into other people. They may not want another person's position, title, or responsibilities— but they cannot live without criticizing. A little humor can go a long way at deflecting some of the ire. Often, those who are most critical of others are also the most insecure about themselves. One doesn't have to tear others down in order to be elevated. Rather, supporting other people and encouraging them in their endeavors is a sign of security and happiness inside one's own skin.

Acting the Fool (Jewish)

There is the story about a man who had it inscribed in his will that his son would not be allowed to inherit any of his worldly goods until he should act like a fool. Two expert rabbis were consulted on this provision in the man's will—and many wondered whether it should be valid. The rabbis went to the man's house one day to talk to him about this odd proviso, but they were shocked to find the father outside the house, crawling on his hands and knees, a piece of straw sticking out of his mouth, and his child pulling him in a wagon. The rabbis asked him, "What do you mean by this?"

The father answered, "Let me tell you plainly—this business you ask me about—I started acting the fool a long time ago. After all, you have heard the saying, 'When a man looks upon his children, his joy makes him act like a fool.'"

★

The book of Proverbs states that a father's joy is his children. Indeed, everyone has seen how adults act foolish whenever children are near, for there is a joy and wonder in their presence. Perhaps this is what Jesus meant when he said we could only inherit the kingdom of God by becoming his children. We dare not lose the wonder and the delight—even the mystery—of looking at the world through these youthful eyes.

It has been said that as soon as we lose our childhood wonder, we begin to die. Keeping that wonder alive is one of the most difficult aspects of life, but it is essential to our well-being of body, mind, and spirit. When we learn how to play well we learn how to live well. There should be no dried up disposition for those who are drinking deeply from the well of the spirit, who are being renewed each day in the day's delights.

When we become depressed, anxious, stressed, or confused about life, it always helps to be in the presence of children again. This sandbox is large enough to hold adults, too. And once we lose ourselves in creating and seeing all things new, we can't help but feel energized and refreshed. That's just the way children work. And laughter, too.

Acknowledgments

I owe a debt of gratitude to many people who have helped me during the years of research and writing devoted to this book. I wish to thank Cynthia Zigmund, my agent, for first seeing the promise in this book and conveying it into the capable hands of the Skyhorse team. My thanks is conveyed to the Skyhorse staff in every page, and I am especially grateful to Marianna Dworak and Leah Zarra for their editing work.

In addition, I must thank those teachers, students, and friends who have kept me pointed in the right direction and who have provided not only ample support but helpful suggestions.

I also thank my children and my wife, Becky, for providing the needed space and time for the task and for also keeping me entertained. I hope this one may prove to be another labor of love.

~T. O.

Notes

*T*he author wishes to thank the various publishers, authors, and editors cited below. In most instances, the author created his own adaptations from works (English translations) in the public domain and, in some instances, translations. Certain other stories were written based on oral sources, including some Chinese and African, in particular. Among those works frequently used in this book, the author has employed initials to indicate these book titles or collections. All diligence has been made to cite copyright holders of any material or translations used in this collection and if oversights have occurred the author apologizes for these mistakes, but would like to know about them so that corrections can be made in future editions of the work.

Frequently cited works include

Aesop	*Aesop's Fables* translation by Thomas James. Lippincott & Co., Philadelphia, 1873
B	*Teachings of the Buddha.* Bukkyo Dendo Kyokai: Society for the Promotion of Buddhism. Tokyo, Japan, 1966
BP	*Buddhist Parables*, translation by Eugene Watson Burlingame. Yale University Press, 1922
D	*Robert Dodsley: Poet, Publisher & Playwright* by Ralph Straus. John Lane Co., New York: 1910
FP	*Fables of Pilpay.* Hurd & Houghton, New York, 1871
GF	*The Great Fables*, ed. Manuel Komroff. Dial Press, NY, 1928

GR	*Gesta Romanorum*—an ancient collection of Christian tales and fables found in various public domain editions.
J	*The Jakata: Stories of the Buddha's Former Births.* Cambridge University Press, 1895
K	*Kriloff's Original Fables,* trans by L. Henry Harrison. Remington & Co., London: 1883
KJV	King James Version of the Bible
MT	Mishnah/Talmud—various Hebrew and public domain versions
P	Phaedrus (Greek text, Loeb Classical Library)
PG	Patrilogia Graeca—Greek versions (and my translations) of Desert Fathers
PK	*Parables of Krummacher.* Hooker & Agnew, Philadelphia, 1841
Rumi	Rumi translation by Reynold Alleyne Nicholson, Cambridge, 1925
T	*Master and Man and Other Parables and Tales* by Count Leo Tolstoy. J.M. Dent & Sons (London) and E.P. Dutton (New York), 1910
U	Upanishads. Project Gutenberg, Oxford, Mississippi, 2002
WD	*The Wisdom of the Desert*, by James O. Hannay. Methuen & Co., London, 1904.

Preface Fable	GF
Introduction fable	Aesop

Chapter One: Sage Wisdom

Feathers in the Wind	adapted from the Mishnah
The Miser and His Treasure	GF
The Distinguished Stranger	*Fables of Robert Louis Stevenson*, 1901

Lord Krishna's Request	Traditional Hindu
Progress	Taoist
The Two Matches	*Fables of Robert Louis Stevenson*, 1901
The Meaning of Work	PG
Flower Garden	adapted from *The Exploits of the Incomparable Nasrudin* by Idries Shah, Octagon Press, Ltd. London
Journey to the Beloved	traditional Islamic
Muhammed and the Cat	traditional Islamic
The Sick Kite	Aesop
Two Forms of Knowledge	Adapted from The Upanishads
Mercury and the Woodsman	Aesop
A Light for the Blind	Jewish, adapted from the Talmud
Tongues	Jewish, adapted from the Talmud
The Grateful Lion	GR
Rich Man, Poor Man	oral source adaptation
The Archer and the Nightingale	GR
The Pears	T
The Load	T
Awake	B
Soul Food	Greek
Breath	adaptation KJV
Spirit	adaptation KJV
The Wind	B
The Rabbis Debate	MT
True Goodness	adaptation KJV
The Rabbi's Dream	MT
Simple Prayer	MT
Where Wisdom Resides	MT
The Parable of the Linen and Coat	MT
The Merchant and the Parrot	Rumi

Chapter Two: The Heart of Helpfulness

Seeking and Finding	B
The Elm and the Tree	D
Just a Cup of Water	adapted from *Essential Sufism* by Fadiman, James and Robert Frager. Edison, N.J.: Castle Books, 1997
Why There is Evil in the World	T
The Comb	K
On Being Truly Dead	PG, my translation
The Wisdom of the Elders	B
The Mountain and the Squirrel	GF
For Everything a Time	adapted from KJV
A Swallow and a Spider	GF
Cultivation	*The Essential Confucius*, Thomas Cleary. HarperSanFranciso, 1992
The Birds Elect a King	adapted from FP
Competition	*Confucius: The Analects*, by Arthur Waley. Wordsworth Editions, 1996
Oh, Rats!	GF
Good Neighbors	adapted from *Yiddishe Legendes*, Eliezer Shindler. Ferlag, Vilna, 1936.
The Three Philosophers	GF
The Earthquake	Traditional Fable
The Ladder of Charity	MT
The Golden Rule	MT
Hillel's Piety	MT
The Prayer of the Pure Land	adapted from Tibetan Book of the Dead
The Little Parrot & Buddha Quote	B
The Legend of Babushka	Russian Traditional Christmas tale

Chapter Three: The Path of Humility

The Shared Sacrifice	adapted from the Upanishads
Folded Hands	*The Art of Happiness* by the Dalai Lama. Riverhead Books, New York, 2009
The Sower and the Seeds	adapted KJV
Rock, Sand and Water	B
The Pumpkin	GF
The Way of Humility	WD & PG
The Poodle and the Lion	GF
The Mouse and the Elephant	GF
The Eagle and the Bee	K
Desert Ways	PG
Appearances	adapted KJV
The Swan and the Stork	GF
Change of Mind	adapted KJV
The Snake	GF
The Wild Apple Tree	GF
The Promise	adapted KJV
The Crusader	traditional Chinese, oral source
The Eight Qualities	traditional Sufi
Reflections	adapted from Upanishads
Lightening Strikes	traditional Zen
Clarity	adapted KJV
Two Trees	adapted KJV
The Village	adapted MT
The Dervish, the Raven and Falcon	FP

Chapter Four: The Quality of Mercy

A Final Mercy	adapted KJV
Jesus and the Donkey	adapted from Jesus in the Eyes of the Sufis
God's Mercy	MT
A Final Compassion	B
The Fire of Mercy	B
Sheep and Goats	adapted KJV
Yama King	B
The Burning House	B
Jealousy	adapted KJV
The Captured Hawk	GF
Origins of Evil	traditional Mohawk tale
Overcoming Evil with Good	BP
The Prodigal Son	B
Lost and Found	adapted KJV
The Devil's House	MT
The Gates of Hell	*The Holy Longing: The Search for a Christian Spirituality* by Ronald Rohlheiser (quoting C.K. Chesterton). Doubleday: New York, 1999
The Pope's Visit	contemporary Christian
The Way Out of Hell	traditional Hindu
Getting Dirty	traditional Chassidic
The Measure of the Kingdom	adapted KJV
The Legend of the Pelican	traditional Christian tale

Chapter Five: Simplicity of the Saints

Riversides	B
The Harp	B

The Teaching River	GF
The Three Hermits	traditional Russian Christian tale
Praying the Mystery	traditional Sikh
Gold Diggers	MT
The Twelve Apostles	Christian legend
Two Horses	GF
The Good Samaritan	adapted KJV
Brother Anthony and the Bow	WD & PG
Polycarp and the Kingdom of Truth	PK
Simple Prayers	adapted KJV
Three Ways to Pray	MT
More Prayers	adapted KJV
Saint Francis and the Vineyard	adapted from *The Little Flowers of Saint Francis*, Raphael Brown. Doubleday: New York, 1958 Francis and the birds adapted from *Brother Francis: an Anthology of Writings by and about St. Francis of Assisi*. San Francisco: Harper & Row, 1972
Asking and Receiving	adapted KJV
Practice Makes Perfect	PG
The Seed	T

Chapter Six: Crisis and Courage

The Fugitive	B
The House Mouse	GF
The Hazel Branch	Christian legend
The Dream	B
The Great Adventure	based on a Greek legend
The Land Crisis	MT (commentary quotes from *Lao Tzu: Tao te Ching*, trans. By Arthur

	Waley Ware. U.K. Wordsworth, 1997 and Chief Seattle from United Nations Environmental Programme "Only One Earth". New York: United Nations, 1990
The Cat and the Sparrow	GF
The Trout and the Sucker	D
The Vision of Peace	adapted KJV
The Three Friends	adapted from BP
The Oak and the Sycamore	D
Mixed Bag	B
The Way	adapted from KP
The Legend of Multnomah Falls	oral source, traditional Native American tale
The Elder Stick	KP
The Story of Ali	Rumi
The Incarnation of the Deer	adapted from J
The Question of "Why"	MT
The Power of the Tongue	MT
Saint Francis and the Wolf	traditional Christian tale
Pride Before the Fall	traditional Native American tale
The Jungle Bell	adapted from J

Chapter Seven: Glimpses of Generosity

Treasures	adapted KJV
Pocket Change	B
The Cobbler and the Baker	GF
The Scorpion and the Tortoise	FP
The Baskets	WD
The Stone Test	traditional
The Poor Man and the King	adapted KJV

The Sisters	B (Confucius quote from *The Analects of Confucius*, William Edward Soothill, 1910)
The Greedy and the Frugal Cats	FP
The Leper's Test	PG
The Poor Artist	B
The Lesson of the Eight Monks	B
The Talents	adapted from KJV
The Greatest Gift	T
Generosity	B & KJV
The Beggars	traditional nursery rhyme
The Poor Man's Wallet	adapted from the Brothers Grimm
Planting a Tree	MT

Chapter Eight: Inroads to Enthusiasm

Marco Polo	legendary, adapted from Ask.com
Cookies	MT
The Boy and the Butterfly	D
Mere Generosity	MT
The Archery Contest	traditional Zen
The Blind Man	Buddhist Sutra adapted from *Samantabhadra: The Bodhisattva. Universal Worthy* (e-book)
The Lighthouse	traditional Christian
The Wall	adapted from *The Exempla of the Rabbis*, by Moses Gaster. Asia Publishing Co., London, 1924
The Chinese and the Greek Artists	Rumi
The Long and Winding Road	B
The War	B

The Good Doctor	adapted from *The Stories of the Lotus Sutra*, by Gene Reeves. Wisdom Publications, 2010
The Sparrow and the Ostrich	GF
The Lessons of the Art	GF
The Elephant	traditional tale
Blowing the Shofar	traditional Jewish
The Dragon Boy	Chinese, oral source

Chapter Nine: The Importance of Integrity

Your Light	B
The Quality of Mercy	B
The Miser	Aesop
The Miser and the Magpie	D
Unlearning Latin	WD
The Human Equation	FP
Joseph and the Mirror	Rumi
The Lion, the Wolf and the Fox	Rumi
The Fox and the Eagle	Phaedrus, my translation
The Ass Insults the Boar	Phaedrus, my translation
Alcibiades and Socrates	adapted from KP
Just Passing Through	MT
Watering a Tree	WD & PG
The Tadpole	*Fables of Robert Louis Stevenson*, 1901

Chapter Ten: Leaning Toward Laughter

Introduction Fable	Aesop
The Boy Man	adapted from *Wigwam Evenings: Sioux Folktales Retold*, by Charles

	and Elaine Eastman. Little Brown & Co., Boston, 1909
The Honey Wasp	GF
The Guru Nanak	adapted from Bhakti Yoga, 1896
The Donkey	adapted from *The Magic Monastery*. London: Octagon Press, 1981
The Boar and the Lion	adapted from BP
The Playful Servant	adapted from Grimm's
Little John	WD
The Wolf and the Tortoise	GF
Two Tales of Woe	FP
The Miser and the Crow	GF
The Philosopher at the Gate	adapted from *The Pleasantries of the Incredible Mulla Nasrudin* by Idries Shah. New York: Penguin Putnam, 1968.
The Voice in the Temple	traditional Zen
The Bear Man	adapted from *The Myths of the Cherokee*, James Mooney. Government Printing Office, 1900
The Crow and the Pitcher	Aesop
The Crabs	Aesop
The Mule	Aesop
Jesus and the Fool	Rumi
The Dog's Tail	traditional Sikh
Who Am I?	adapted from *Subtleties of the Inimitable Mulla Nasrudin* by Idries Shah. London: Octagon Press, 1989.
Jesus and the Dead Lion	Rumi
The Musicians	K

The Kitchen Whisk	K
The Frog and the Ox	Aesop
Burning Down the House	T
The Hungry Dogs	Phaedrus
The Fly	GF
The Thorn Bush	GF
Acting the Fool	MT

About the Author

*T*odd Outcalt is the author of thirty books including *The Other Jesus, Candles in the Dark, The Best Things in Life Are Free,* and *Where in the World We Meet* (poems). His work has been translated into six languages and he has written for such magazines as *American Fitness, The Christian Century, Cure,* and *Midwest Outdoors.* Todd lives with his wife of thirty years in Brownsburg, Indiana and enjoys hiking, kayaking and exploration—and he also speaks to groups large and small.

Bibliography

Among the dozens of books I read to gather information for this collection, the following were especially helpful. I am indebted to the various translators, authors, and publishers of these works. In addition to the list below, it is essential that I give credit to those works (their publishers and authors) that are also in the public domain (see list of frequently cited works in the Notes).

This list includes, especially, my own adaptations from these public domain works such as The King James Translation of the Bible, several English translations of the Qur'an, English translations of the Dhammapada, Talmud, the works of Confucius, and the excellent resources provided by Bukkyo Dendo Kayakai pertaining to the many legends, parables and teachings of Buddha. In addition, wherever possible, I completed my own translation or adaptation work from the Greek for the works of The Desert Fathers (from the Patrium Graeka) and Phaedrus (from the Loeb Classical Library Greek edition). The works of David Margoliouth also provided many of the Muslim traditions pertaining to Jesus.

I am also indebted to the many stories told and retold in oral form at student gatherings at the University of Indianapolis (i.e. African, Chinese) that I was able to adapt for this book.

Abdullah, Allama Sir and Al-Mamum Al-Suhrawardy, *The Sayings of Muhammad*. New York: Citadel Press, 1990.

Abrahams, Roger. *African Folktales*. New York: Pantheon Books, 1983.

Ausubel, Nathan. *A Treasury of Jewish Folklore*. New York: Crown, 1948.

Baha n'llah. *Gleanings from the Writings of the Baha u'llah*. Wilmette, Ill: The Baha'I Publishing Trust, 1978.

Bayet, Mojdeh and Mohammad Ali Jamnia. *Tales from the Land of the Sufis*. Boston: Shambhala Publications, 1994.

Breuilly, Elizabeth and Martin Palmer. *The Book of Chuang Tzu*. New York: Penguin Putnam, 1996.

Buber, Martin. *Tales of the Hasadim*. New York: Schocken Books, 1948.

Canonge, Elliott. *Comanche Texts. Vol. 1*. Linguistics Series, Norman, Okla.: Summer Institute of Linguistics of the University of Oklahoma, 1958.

Cleary, Thomas. *The Essential Confucius*. New York: HarperCollins, 1992.

—. The Essential Tao. San Francisco: Harper, 1991.

Confucius. *The Analects of Confucius*. Translated by James Legge. 1897.

Eberhard, Wolfram. *Folktales from China*. Chicago: University of Chicago Press, 1965.

Fadiman, James and Robert Frager. *Essential Sufism*. Edison, N.J.: Castle Books, 1997.

Frankel, Ellen. *The Classic Tales: 4000 years of Jewish Lore*. Northvale, N.J.: Jason Aronson, Inc., 1989.

Funk, Robert and Roy Hoover. *The Five Gospels*. New York: Polebridge Press, 1993.

Gaster, Moses. *The Exempla of the Rabbis*. London: Asia Publishing, 1924.

Giles, Herbert A., trans. *Chuang Tzu: Mystic, Moralist, and Social Reformer*. London: Bernard Quaritich, 1989.

Griffith, Tom, ed. Confucius: *The Analects.* Herfordshire, England: Wordsworth Editions, 1996.

Hahn, Thich Naht. *The Heart of Understanding*. Albany, Calif.: Parallax Press, 1988.

—. *Zen Keys*. New York: Image Books, 1995.

BIBLIOGRAPHY

Hamill, Sam and J.P. Seaton. *The Essential Chuang Tzu*. Boston: Shambhala Publications, 1999.

Hewitt, James. *Parables, Etc.* vol. 2, no. 11, 1984.

Kierkegaard, Soren. *The Parables of Kierkegaard*. Edited by Thomas C. Oden, Princeton, N.J.: Princeton University Press, 1978.

Knowles, J. Hinton. *Folk-tales of the Kashmir*, 2nd ed. London: Kegan Paul Tranch, Tribune and Company, 1893.

Kornfield, Jack and Christina Feldman. *Soul Food*. New York: HarperCollins, 1996.

Langer, J. *Nine Gates*. Northvale, N.J.: Jason Aronson, Inc., 1993.

Levin, Meyer. *Classic Hassidic Tales*. New York: Viking Press, 1975.

Mair, Victor H. *Wandering the Way: Early Taoist Tales and Parables of Chuang Tzu*. Honolulu University of Hawaii Press, 1998.

Komroff, Manuel. *The Great Fables of the Nations*. New York: Tudor Publishing Company, 1928.

Merton, Thomas. *The Wisdom of the Desert Fathers*. New York: W.W. Norton and Co., 1988.

Miller, John and Aaron Kenedi, eds. *God's Breath*. New York: Marlowe, 2000.

Miller, Robert J. *The Complete Gospels*. Sonoma, Calif.: Polcridge Press, 1994.

Nomura, Yushi. *Desert Wisdom*, rev. ed. Maryknoll, N.Y.: Orbis Books, 2001.

Novak, Miroslav. *Fairy Tales from Japan*. London: Hamlyn Press, 1976.

Novak, Philip. *The World's Wisdom*. New York: HarperCollins, 1995.

Radin, Paul. *African Folktales*. New York: Schocken Books, 1983.

Reps, Paul. *Zen Flesh, Zen Bones*. New York: Doubleday, 1981.

The Sayings of the Desert Fathers. Kalamazoo, Mich.: Cistercian Publications, 1972.

Schloegl, Irmgard. *The Wisdom of the Zen Masters*. New York: New Directions, 1975.

Shah, Idries. *The Exploits of the Incomparable Mulla Nasrudin.* London: Octagon Press, 1983.

—. *The Magic Monastery.* London: Octagon Press, 1981.

—. *The Pleasantries of the Incredible Mulla Nasrudin.* New York: Penguin Putnam, 1968.

—. *The Subtleties of the Inimitable Mulla Nasrudin.* London: Octagon Press, 1989.

Silverman, William. *Rabbinic Wisdom and Jewish Values.* New York: Union of American Hebrew Congregations Press, 1971.

The Teaching of Buddha. Tokyo: Bukkyo Dendo Kyokai, 1966.

Theophane the Monk. *Tales of a Magic Monastery.* New York: Crossroad/ Continuum, 1981.

Waddell, Helen. *The Desert Fathers.* New York: Vintage, 1998.

Warmington, E.H., ed. *Loeb Classical Library.* Cambridge, Mass.: Harvard University Press, 1995.

White, William R. *Stories for the Journey.* Minneapolis Augsburg Publishing House, 1988.

Zerah, Aaron. *The Soul's Almanac.* New York: Tarcher/Putnam, 1998.